THE POWER OF POSITIVE
THINKING

THE POWER OF
POSITIVE THINKING

by

NORMAN VINCENT PEALE

A Cedar Book
No. 100

WORLD'S WORK LTD
KINGSWOOD TADWORTH SURREY

FIRST PUBLISHED IN GREAT BRITAIN 1953
First published as a Cedar Book 1953
Reprinted 1964, 1965, 1967, 1968, 1970

To my brothers
Robert Clifford Peale, M.D.
and
The Reverend Leonard Delaney Peale
Effective Helpers of Mankind

*Printed in Great Britain by Richard Clay (The Chaucer Press), Ltd.,
Bungay, Suffolk*

PREFACE

on the occasion of the printing of the two millionth copy

AT THE TIME I wrote this book it never occurred to me that a two millionth copy anniversary would ever be observed. Frankly, however, my gratitude for this event is not from the viewpoint of books sold, but in terms of the many persons to whom I have been privileged to suggest a simple, workable philosophy of living.

The dynamic laws which the book teaches were learned the hard way by trial and error in my personal search for a way of life. But I found in them an answer to my own problems and, believe me, I am the most difficult person with whom I have worked. The book is my effort to share my spiritual experience, for if it helped me, I felt it might also be of help to others.

In formulating this simple philosophy of life I found my own answers in the teachings of Jesus Christ. I have merely tried to describe those truths in the language and thought forms understandable to present day people. The way of life to which this book is a witness is very wonderful. It is not easy. Indeed, it often is hard, but it is full of joy and hope and victory.

I well recall the day I sat down to begin writing the book. I knew that the best work required more ability than I possessed and therefore I needed help that only God could give. My wife and I have the policy of taking God into working partnership in all our problems and activities. So we had a very earnest session of prayer, asking for guidance, and we put the project into God's hands. When the manuscript was ready for the publisher Mrs. Peale and I again prayed, dedicating the manuscript. We asked only that it might help people to live more effective lives. When the first book of these two million copies came from the press to us it was again a spiritual moment. We thanked God for His help and dedicated the book once more.

The book was written for the plain people of this world, of whom certainly I am one. I was born and reared in humble Midwestern circumstances in a dedicated Christian home. The everyday people of this land are my own kind whom I know and love and believe in with great faith. When anyone of them lets God have charge of his life the power and glory are amazingly demonstrated.

The book is written with deep concern for the pain, difficulty and struggle of human existence. It teaches the cultivation of peace of mind, not as an escape from life into protected quiescence, but as a power centre out of which comes driving energy for constructive personal and social living. It teaches positive thinking, not as a means to fame, riches or power, but as the practical application of faith to overcome defeat and accomplish worthwhile creative values in life. It teaches a hard, disciplinary way of life, but one which offers great joy to the person who achieves victory over himself and the difficult circumstances of the world.

To all who have written me about the joyous victory they have had through practising the spiritual techniques of this book and to those who will yet have such experience may I say how happy I am for all that is happening to them as they live by dynamic spiritual formulas.

I wish finally to express deep appreciation to my publishers for their never-failing support, co-operation and friendship. May God continue to use this book in human helpfulness.

NORMAN VINCENT PEALE

INTRODUCTION

What this Book can do for You

THIS BOOK IS WRITTEN to suggest techniques and to give examples which demonstrate that you do not need to be defeated by anything, that you can have peace of mind, improved health, and a never-ceasing flow of energy. In short, that your life can be full of joy and satisfaction. Of this I have no doubt at all for I have watched countless persons learn and apply a system of simple procedures that has brought about the foregoing benefits in their lives. These assertions, which may appear extravagant, are based on bona fide demonstrations in actual human experience.

Altogether too many people are defeated by the everyday problems of life. They go struggling, perhaps even whining, through their days with a sense of dull resentment at what they consider the 'bad breaks' life has given them. In a sense there may be such a thing as 'the breaks' in this life, but there is also a spirit and method by which we can control and even determine those breaks. It is a pity that people should let themselves be defeated by the problems, cares, and difficulties of human existence, and it is also quite unnecessary.

In saying this I certainly do not ignore or minimise the hardships and tragedies of the world, but neither do I allow them to dominate. You can permit obstacles to control your mind to the point where they are uppermost and thus become the dominating factors in your thought pattern. By learning how to cast them from the mind, by refusing to become mentally subservient to them, and by channelling spiritual power through your thoughts, you can rise above obstacles which ordinarily might defeat you. By methods I shall outline, obstacles are simply not permitted to destroy your happiness and well-being. You need be defeated only if you are willing to be. This book teaches you how to 'will' not to be.

The purpose of this book is a very direct and simple one. It makes no pretence to literary excellence nor does it seek to demonstrate any unusual scholarship on my part. This is simply a practical, direct-action, personal-improvement manual. It is written with the sole objective of helping the reader achieve a happy, satisfying, and worthwhile life. I thoroughly and enthusiastically believe in certain demonstrated and effective principles which, when practised, produce a victorious life. My aim is to set them forth in this volume in a logical, simple, and understandable manner so that the reader, feeling a sense of need, may learn a practical method by which he can build for himself, with God's help, the kind of life he deeply desires.

If you read this book thoughtfully, carefully absorbing its teachings, and if you will sincerely and persistently practise the principles and formulas set forth herein, you can experience an amazing improvement within yourself. By using the techniques outlined herewith you can modify or change the circumstances in which you now live, assuming control over them rather than continuing to be directed by them. Your relations with other people will improve. You will become a more popular, esteemed, and well-liked individual. By mastering these principles, you will enjoy a delightful new sense of well-being. You can attain a degree of health not hitherto known by you and experience a new and keen pleasure in living. You will become a person of greater usefulness and will wield an expanded influence.

How can I be so certain that the practice of these principles will produce such results? The answer is simply that for many years in the Marble Collegiate Church of New York City we have taught a system of creative living based on spiritual techniques, carefully noting its operation in the lives of hundreds of people. It is no speculative series of extravagant assertions that I make, for these principles have worked so efficiently over so long a period of time that they are now firmly established as documented and demonstrable truth. The system outlined is a perfected and amazing method of successful living.

In my writings, including several books, in my regular weekly newspaper column in nearly one hundred dailies, in my national radio programme over seventeen years, in our magazine, *Guideposts*, and in lectures in scores of cities, I have taught these same scientific yet simple principles of achievement, health, and happiness. Hundreds have read, listened, and practised, and the results are invariably the same: new life, new power, increased efficiency, greater happiness.

Because so many have requested that these principles be put into book form, the better to be studied and practised, I am publishing this new volume under the title, *The Power of Positive Thinking*. I need not point out that the powerful principles contained herein are

not my invention, but are given to us by the greatest
Teacher who ever lived and who still lives. This book
teaches applied Christianity; a simple yet scientific
system of practical techniques of successful living that
works.

Norman Vincent Peale

Contents

1 | Believe in Yourself

BELIEVE IN YOURSELF! Have faith in your abilities! Without a humble but reasonable confidence in your own powers you cannot be successful or happy. But with sound self-confidence you can succeed. A sense of inferiority and inadequacy interferes with the attainment of your hopes, but self-confidence leads to self-realisation and successful achievement. Because of the importance of this mental attitude, this book will help you believe in yourself and release your inner powers.

It is appalling to realise the number of pathetic people who are hampered and made miserable by the malady popularly called the inferiority complex. But you need not suffer from this trouble. When proper steps are taken, it can be overcome. You can develop creative faith in yourself—faith that is justified.

After speaking to a convention of business men in a city auditorium, I was on the stage greeting people when a man approached me and with a peculiar intensity of manner asked: "May I talk with you about a matter of desperate importance to me?"

I asked him to remain until the others had gone, then we went back-stage and sat down.

"I'm in this town to handle the most important

business deal of my life," he explained. "If I succeed, it means everything to me. If I fail, I'm done for."

I suggested that he relax a little, that nothing was quite that final. If he succeeded, that was fine. If he didn't, well, tomorrow was another day.

"I have a terrible disbelief in myself," he said dejectedly. "I have no confidence. I just don't believe I can put it over. I am very discouraged and depressed. In fact," he lamented, "I'm just about sunk. Here I am, forty years old. Why is it that all my life I have been tormented by inferiority feelings, by lack of confidence, by self-doubt? I listened to your speech tonight in which you talked about the power of positive thinking, and I want to ask how I can get some faith in myself."

"There are two steps to take," I replied. "First, it is important to discover why you have these feelings of no power. That requires analysis and will take time. We must approach the maladies of our emotional life as a physician probes to find something wrong physically. This cannot be done immediately, certainly not in our brief interview tonight, and it may require treatment to reach a permanent solution. But to pull you through this immediate problem I shall give you a formula which will work if you use it.

"As you walk down the street tonight I suggest that you repeat certain words which I shall give you. Say them over several times after you get into bed. When you awaken tomorrow, repeat them three times before arising. On the way to your important appointment say them three additional times. Do this with an attitude of faith and you will receive sufficient strength and ability to deal with this problem. Later, if you wish, we can go into an analysis of your basic problem, but whatever we come up with following that study, the formula which I am now going to give you can be a large factor in the eventual cure."

Following is the affirmation which I gave him—"I can do all things through Christ which strengtheneth me." (Philippians iv. 13.) He was unfamiliar with these words, so I wrote them on a card and had him read them over three times aloud.

"Now, follow that prescription, and I am sure things will come out all right."

He pulled himself up, stood quietly for a moment, then said with considerable feeling: "O.K., Doctor. O.K."

I watched him square his shoulders and walk out into the night. He seemed a pathetic figure, and yet the way he carried himself as he disappeared showed that faith was already at work in his mind.

Subsequently he reported that this simple formula 'did wonders' for him, and added: "It seems incredible that a few words from the Bible could do so much for a person."

This man later had a study made of the reasons for his inferiority attitudes. They were cleared away by scientific counselling and by the application of religious faith. He was taught how to have faith; was given certain specific instructions to follow (these are given later in this chapter). Gradually he attained a strong, steady, reasonable confidence. He never ceases to express amazement at the way in which things now flow towards rather than away from him. His personality has taken on a positive, not negative, character so that he no longer repels success, but, on the contrary, draws it to him. He now has an authentic confidence in his own powers.

There are various causes of inferiority feelings, and not a few stem from childhood.

An executive consulted me about a young man whom he wished to advance in his company. "But," he explained, "he cannot be trusted with important secret information and I'm sorry, for otherwise I would make him my administrative assistant. He has all the other necessary qualifications, but he talks too much, and without meaning to do so divulges matters of a private and important nature."

Upon analysis I found that he 'talked too much' simply because of an inferiority feeling. To compensate for it he succumbed to the temptation of parading his knowledge.

He associated with men who were rather well to do, all of whom had attended college and belonged to a fraternity. But this boy was reared in poverty, had not been a college man or fraternity member. Thus he felt himself inferior to his associates in education and social background. To build himself up with his associates and to enhance his self-esteem, his subconscious mind, which always seeks to provide a compensatory mechanism, supplied him with a means for raising his ego.

He was on 'the inside' in the industry, and accompanied his superior to conferences where he met outstanding men and listened to important private conversations. He reported just enough of his 'inside information' to cause his associates to regard him with admiration and envy. This served to elevate his self-esteem and satisfy his desire for recognition.

When the employer became aware of the cause of this personality trait, being a kindly and understanding man, he pointed out to the young man the opportunities in business to which his abilities could lead him. He also described how his inferiority feelings caused his unreliability in confidential matters. This self-knowledge, together with a sincere practising of the techniques of faith and prayer, made him a valuable asset to his company. His real powers were released.

I can perhaps illustrate the manner in which many youngsters acquire an inferiority complex through the use of a personal reference. As a small boy I was painfully thin. I had lots of energy, was on a track team, was healthy and hard as nails, but thin. And that bothered me because I didn't want to be thin. I wanted to be fat. I was called 'skinny', but I didn't want to be called 'skinny'. I wanted to be called 'fat'. I longed to be hard-boiled and tough and fat. I did everything to get fat. I drank cod-liver oil, consumed vast numbers of milk shakes, ate thousands of chocolate sundaes with whipped cream and nuts, cakes and pies innumerable, but they did not affect me in the slightest. I stayed thin and lay awake at night thinking and agonising about it. I kept on trying to get heavy until I was about thirty, when all of a sudden did I get heavy! I bulged at the seams. Then I became self-conscious because I was so fat, and finally had to take off forty pounds with equal agony to get myself down to respectable size.

In the second place (to conclude this personal analysis which I give only because it may help others by showing how this malady works), I was a minister's son and was constantly reminded of that fact. Everybody else could do everything, but if I did even the slightest little thing —"Ah, you are a preacher's son." So I didn't want to be a preacher's son, for preachers' sons are supposed to be nice and namby-pamby. I wanted to be known as a hard-boiled fellow. Perhaps that is why preachers' sons get their reputation for being a little difficult, because they rebel against having to carry the banner of

5

the church all the time. I vowed there was one thing I would never do, and that was to become a preacher.

Also, I came of a family practically every member of which was a performer in public, a platform speaker, and that was the last thing I wanted to be. They used to make me get up in public to make speeches when it scared me to death, even filled me with terror. That was years ago, but the twinge of it comes to me every now and then when I walk on to a platform. I had to use every known device to develop confidence in what powers the good Lord gave me.

I found the solution of this problem in the simple techniques of faith taught in the Bible. These principles are scientific and sound and can heal any personality of the pain of inferiority feelings. Their use can enable the sufferer to find and release the powers which have been inhibited by a feeling of inadequacy.

Such are some of the sources of the inferiority complex which erect power barriers in our personalities. It is some emotional violence done to us in childhood, or the consequences of certain circumstances, or something we did to ourselves. This malady arises out of the misty past in the dim recesses of our personalities.

Perhaps you had an older brother who was a brilliant student. He got A's in school; you made only C's, and you never heard the last of it. So you believed that you could never succeed in life as he could. He got A's and you got C's, so you reasoned that you were consigned to getting C's all your life. Apparently you never realised that some of those who failed to get high grades in school have been the greatest successes outside of school. Just because somebody gets an A in college doesn't make him the greatest man in the United States, because maybe his A's will stop when he gets his diploma, and the fellow who got C's in school will go on later to get the real A's in life.

The greatest secret for eliminating the inferiority complex, which is another term for deep and profound self-doubt, is to fill your mind to overflowing with faith. Develop a tremendous faith in God and that will give you a humble yet soundly realistic faith in yourself.

The acquiring of dynamic faith is accomplished by prayer, lots of prayer, by reading and mentally absorbing the Bible and by practising its prayer techniques. In another chapter I deal with specific formulas of prayer, but I want to point out here that the type of prayer that produces the quality of faith required to eliminate inferiority is of a particular nature. Surface skimming, formalistic and perfunctory prayer is not sufficiently powerful.

A wonderful coloured woman, a cook in the home of friends of mine in Texas, was asked how she so completely mastered her troubles. She answered that ordinary problems could be met by ordinary prayers, but that 'when a big trouble comes along, you have to pray deep prayers'.

One of my most inspiring friends was the late Harlowe B. Andrews of Syracuse, New York, one of the best business men and competent spiritual experts I ever knew. He said the trouble with most prayers is that they aren't big enough. "To get anywhere with faith," said he, "learn to pray big prayers. God will rate you according to the size of your prayers." Doubtless he was right, for the Scriptures say: "According to your faith be it unto you." (Matthew ix. 29.) So the bigger your problem, the bigger your prayer should be.

Roland Hayes, the singer, quoted his grandfather to

7

me, a man whose education was not equal to that of his grandson, but whose native wisdom was obviously sound. He said: "The trouble with lots of prayers is they ain't got no suction." Drive your prayers deep into your doubts, fears, inferiorities. Pray deep, big prayers that have plenty of suction and you will come up with powerful and vital faith.

Go to a competent spiritual adviser and let him teach you how to have faith. The ability to possess and utilise faith and gain the release of powers it provides are skills and, like any skills, must be studied and practised to gain perfection.

At the conclusion of this chapter are listed ten suggestions for overcoming your inferiority pattern and for developing faith. Practise these rules diligently and they will aid you in developing confidence in yourself by dissipating your feelings of inferiority, however deeply embedded.

At this point, however, I wish to indicate that to build up feelings of self-confidence the practice of suggesting confidence concepts to your mind is very effective. If your mind is obsessed by thoughts of insecurity and inadequacy it is, of course, due to the fact that such ideas have dominated your thinking over a long period of time. Another and more positive pattern of ideas must be given the mind, and that is accomplished by repetitive suggestion of confidence ideas. In the busy activities of daily existence thought disciplining is required if you are to reeducate the mind and make of it a power-producing plant. It is possible, even in the midst of your daily work, to drive confident thoughts into consciousness. Let me tell you about one man who did so by the use of a unique method.

One icy winter morning he called for me at a hotel in a Mid-Western city to take me about thirty-five miles to another town to fill a lecture engagement. We got into his car and started off at a rather high rate of speed on the slippery road. He was going a little faster than I thought reasonable, and I reminded him that we had plenty of time and suggested that we take it easy.

"Don't let my driving worry you," he replied. "I used to be filled with all kinds of insecurities myself, but I got over them. I was afraid of everything. I feared an automobile trip or an aeroplane flight; and if any of my family went away I worried until they returned. I always went round with a feeling that something was going to happen, and it made my life miserable. I was saturated with inferiority and lacked confidence. This state of mind reflected itself in my business and I wasn't doing very well. But I hit upon a wonderful plan which knocked all these insecurity feelings out of my mind, and now I live with a feeling of confidence, not only in myself but in life generally."

This was the 'wonderful plan'. He pointed to two clips fastened on the instrument panel of the car just below the windscreen and, reaching into the glove compartment, took out a pack of small cards. He selected one and slipped it beneath the clip. It read: "If ye have faith . . . nothing shall be impossible unto you." (Matthew xvii. 20.) He removed that one, shuffled expertly through the cards with one hand as he drove, selected another, and placed it under the clip. This one read: "If God be for us, who can be against us?" (Romans viii. 31.)

"I'm a travelling salesman," he explained, "and I drive around all day calling on my customers. I have discovered that while a man drives he thinks all kinds of thoughts. If his pattern of thought is negative, he will think many negative thoughts during the day and that, of course, is bad for him; but that is the way I used to be. I used to drive around all day between calls thinking fear and defeat thoughts, and incidentally that is one reason my sales were down. But since I have been using these cards as I drive and committing the words to memory, I have learned to think differently. The old insecurities that used to haunt me are just about all gone, and instead of thinking fear thoughts of defeat and ineffectiveness, I think thoughts of faith and courage. It is really wonderful the way this method has changed me. It has helped in my business, too, for how can one expect to make a sale if he drives up to a customer's place of business thinking he is not going to make a sale?"

This plan used by my friend is a very wise one. By filling his mind with affirmations of the presence, support, and help of God, he had actually changed his thought processes. He put an end to the domination of his long-held sense of insecurity. His potential powers were set free.

We build up the feeling of insecurity or security by how we think. If in our thoughts we constantly fix attention upon sinister expectations of dire events that might happen, the result will be constantly to feel insecure. And what is even more serious is the tendency to create, by the power of thought, the very condition we fear. This salesman actually created positive results by vital thoughts of courage and confidence through the process of placing the cards before him in his car. His powers, curiously inhibited by a defeat psychology, now flowed out of a personality in which creative attitudes had been stimulated.

Lack of self-confidence apparently is one of the great problems besetting people today. In a university a survey was made of six hundred students in psychology courses. The students were asked to state their most difficult personal problem. Seventy-five per cent listed lack of confidence. It can safely be assumed that the same large proportion is true of the population generally. Everywhere you encounter people who are inwardly afraid, who shrink from life, who suffer from a deep sense of inadequacy and insecurity, who doubt their own powers. Deep within themselves they mistrust their ability to meet responsibilities or to grasp opportunities. Always they are beset by the vague and sinister fear that something is not going to be quite right. They do not believe that they have it in them to be what they want to be, and so they try to make themselves content with something less than that of which they are capable. Thousands upon thousands go crawling through life on their hands and knees, defeated and afraid. And in most cases such frustration of power is unnecessary.

The blows of life, the accumulation of difficulties, the multiplication of problems tend to sap energy and leave you spent and discouraged. In such a condition the true status of your power is often obscured, and a person yields to a discouragement that is not justified by the facts. It is vitally essential to re-appraise your personality assets. When done in an attitude of reasonableness, this evaluation will convince you that you are less defeated than you think you are.

For example, a man fifty-two years of age consulted me. He was in great despondency. He revealed utter despair. He said he 'was all through'. He informed me that everything he had built up over his lifetime had been swept away.

"Everything?" I asked.

"Everything," he repeated. He was through, he reiterated. "I have nothing left at all. Everything is gone. There is no hope, and I am too old to start all over again. I have lost all faith."

Naturally I felt sympathetic towards him, but it was evident that his chief trouble was the fact that dark shadows of hopelessness had entered his mind and discoloured his outlook, distorting it. Behind this twisted thinking his true powers had retreated, leaving him without force.

"So," I said, "suppose we take a piece of paper and write down the values you have left."

"There's no use," he sighed. "I haven't a single thing left. I thought I told you that."

I said: "Let's just see, anyway." Then asked: "Is your wife still with you?"

"Why, yes, of course, and she is wonderful. We have been married for thirty years. She would never leave me no matter how bad things are."

"All right, let us put that down—your wife is still with you and she will never leave you no matter what happens. How about your children? Got any children?"

"Yes," he replied. "I have three, and they are certainly wonderful. I have been touched by the way they have come to me and said: 'Dad, we love you, and we'll stand by you.'"

"Well, then," I said, "that is number two—three children who love you and who will stand by you. Got any friends?" I asked.

"Yes," he said, "I really have some fine friends. I must admit they have been pretty decent. They have come around and said they would like to help me, but what can they do? They can't do anything."

"That is number three—you have some friends who would like to help you and who hold you in esteem. How about your integrity? Have you done anything wrong?"

"My integrity is all right," he replied. "I have always tried to do the right thing and my conscience is clear."

"All right," I said, "we will put that down as number four—integrity. How about your health?"

"My health is all right," he answered. "I have had very few sick days, and I guess I am in pretty good shape physically."

"So let's put down as number five—good physical health. How about the United States? Do you think it's still doing business and is the land of opportunity?"

"Yes," he said. "It is the only country in the world I would want to live in."

"That is number six—you live in the United States, land of opportunity, and you are glad to be here." Then I asked: "How about your religious faith? Do you believe in God and that God will help you?"

"Yes," he said. "I do not think I could have got through this at all if I hadn't had some help from God."

"Now," I said, "let's list the assets we have figured out:

"1. A wonderful wife—married for thirty years.

"2. Three devoted children who will stand by you.

"3. Friends who will help you and who hold you in esteem.

"4. Integrity—nothing to be ashamed of.

"5. Good physical health.

"6. Live in the United States, the greatest country in the world.

"7. Have religious faith."

I shoved it across the table at him. "Take a look at that. I guess you have quite a total of assets. I thought you told me everything had been swept away."

He grinned ashamedly. "I guess I didn't think of those things. I never thought of it that way. Perhaps things aren't so bad at that," he said pensively. "Maybe I can start all over again if I can just get some confidence, if I can get the feel of some power within me."

Well, he got it, and he did start all over again. But he did so only when he changed his viewpoint, his mental attitude. Faith swept away his doubts, and more than enough power to overcome all his difficulties emerged from within him.

This incident illustrates a profound truth which is expressed in a very important statement made by the famous psychiatrist, Dr. Karl Menninger. He said: "Attitudes are more important than facts." That is worth repeating until its truth grips you. Any fact facing us, however difficult, even seemingly hopeless, is not so important as our attitude towards that fact. How you think about a fact may defeat you before you ever do anything about it. You may permit a fact to overwhelm you mentally before you start to deal with it actually. On the other hand, a confident and optimistic thought pattern can modify or overcome the fact altogether.

I know a man who is a tremendous asset to his organisation, not because of any extraordinary ability, but because he invariably demonstrates a triumphant thought pattern. Perhaps his associates view a proposition pessimistically, so he employs what he calls 'the vacuum-cleaner method'. That is, by a series of questions he 'sucks the dust' out of his associates' minds; he draws out their negative attitudes. Then quietly he suggests positive ideas concerning the proposition until a new set of attitudes gives them a new concept of the facts.

They often comment upon how different facts appear when this man 'goes to work on them'. It's the confidence attitude that makes the difference, nor does this rule out objectivity in an appraisal of facts. The inferiority complex victim sees all facts through discoloured attitudes. The secret of correction is simply to gain a normal view, and that is always slanted on the positive side.

So if you feel that you are defeated and have lost confidence in your ability to win, sit down, take a piece of paper and make a list, not of the factors that are against you, but of those that are for you. If you or I or anybody think constantly of the forces that seem to be against us, we will build them up into a power far beyond that which is justified. They will assume a formidable strength which they do not actually possess. But if, on the contrary, you mentally visualise and affirm and re-affirm your assets and keep your thoughts on them, emphasising them to the fullest extent, you will rise out of any difficulty regardless of what it may be. Your inner powers will reassert themselves and, with the help of God, lift you from defeat to victory.

One of the most powerful concepts, one which is a sure cure for lack of confidence, is the thought that God is actually with you and helping you. This is one of the simplest teachings in religion; namely, that Almighty God will be your companion, will stand by you, help you, and see you through. No other idea is so powerful in developing self-confidence as this simple belief when practised. To practise it simply affirm "God is with me; God is helping me; God is guiding me." Spend several minutes each day visualising His presence. Then practise believing that affirmation. Go about your business on the assumption that what you have affirmed and visualised is true. Affirm it, visualise it, believe it, and it will actualise itself. The release of power which this procedure stimulates will astonish you.

Feelings of confidence depend upon the type of thoughts that habitually occupy your mind. Think defeat and you are bound to feel defeated. But practise thinking confident thoughts, make it a dominating habit, and you will develop such a strong sense of capacity that regardless of what difficulties arise you will be able to overcome them. Feelings of confidence actually induce increased strength. Basil King once said: "Be bold, and mighty forces will come to your aid." Experience proves the truth of this. You will feel these mighty forces aiding you as your increasing faith reconditions your attitudes.

Emerson declared a tremendous truth: "They conquer who believe they can." And he added: "Do the thing you fear and the death of fear is certain." Practise confidence and faith and your fears and insecurities will soon have no power over you.

Once when Stonewall Jackson planned a daring attack, one of his generals fearfully objected, saying: "I am afraid of this," or "I fear that . . ." Putting his hand on his timorous subordinate's shoulder, Jackson said: "General, never take counsel of your fears."

The secret is to fill your mind with thoughts of faith,

confidence, and security. This will force out or expel all thoughts of doubt, all lack of confidence. To one man who for a long time had been haunted by insecurities and fears I suggested that he read through the Bible underlining in red pencil every statement it contains relative to courage and confidence. He also committed them to memory, in effect cramming his mind full of the healthiest, happiest, most powerful thoughts in the world. These dynamic thoughts changed him from cringing hopelessness to a man of compelling force. The change in him in a few weeks was remarkable. From almost complete defeat he became a confident and inspiring personality. He now radiates courage and magnetism. He regained confidence in himself and his own powers by a simple process of thought conditioning.

To sum up—what can you do *now* to build up your self-confidence? Following are ten simple, workable rules for overcoming inadequacy attitudes and learning to practise faith. Thousands have used these rules, reporting successful results. Undertake this programme and you, too, will build up confidence in your powers. You, too, will have a new feeling of power.

1. Formulate and stamp indelibly on your mind a mental picture of yourself as succeeding. Hold this picture tenaciously. Never permit it to fade. Your mind will seek to develop this picture. Never think of yourself as failing; never doubt the reality of the mental image. That is most dangerous, for the mind always tries to complete what it pictures. So *always* picture 'success' no matter how badly things seem to be going at the moment.

2. Whenever a negative thought concerning your

personal powers comes to mind, deliberately voice a positive thought to cancel it out.

3. Do not build up obstacles in your imagination. Depreciate every so-called obstacle. Minimise them. Difficulties must be studied and efficiently dealt with to be eliminated, but they must be seen for only what they are. They must not be inflated by fear thoughts.

4. Do not be awe-struck by other people and try to copy them. Nobody can be you as efficiently as YOU can. Remember also that most people, despite their confident appearance and demeanour, are often as scared as you are and as doubtful of themselves.

5. Ten times a day repeat these dynamic words: "If God be *for* us, who can be *against* us?" (Romans viii. 31.) (Stop reading and repeat them NOW slowly and confidently.)

6. Get a competent counsellor to help you understand why you do what you do. Learn the origin of your inferiority and self-doubt feelings which often begin in childhood. Self-knowledge leads to a cure.

7. Ten times each day practise the following affirmation, repeating it out loud if possible. "I can do all things through Christ which strengtheneth me." (Philippians iv. 13.) Repeat those words NOW. That magic statement is the most powerful antidote on earth to inferiority thoughts.

8. Make a true estimate of your own ability, then raise it 10 per cent. Do not become egotistical, but develop a wholesome self-respect. Believe in your own God-released powers.

9. Put yourself in God's hands. To do that simply state: "I am in God's hands." Then believe you are NOW receiving all the power you need. 'Feel' it flowing into

you. Affirm that 'the kingdom of God is within you' (Luke xvii. 21) in the form of adequate power to meet life's demands.

10. Remind yourself that God is with you and nothing can defeat you. Believe that you *now* RECEIVE power from Him.

4/10 are to do with religious belief

2 | A Peaceful Mind Generates Power

AT BREAKFAST IN A HOTEL dining-room three of us fell to discussing how well we had slept the night before, a truly momentous topic. One man complained of a sleepless night. He had tossed and turned and was about as exhausted as when he retired. "Guess I'd better stop listening to the news before going to bed," he observed. "I tuned in last night and sure got an earful of trouble."

That is quite a phrase, 'an earful of trouble'. Little wonder he had a disturbed night. "Maybe the coffee I drank before retiring had something to do with it," he mused.

The other man spoke up: "As for me, I had a grand night. I got my news from the evening paper and from an early broadcast and had a chance to digest it before I went to sleep. Of course," he continued, "I used my go-to-sleep plan, which never fails to work."

I prodded him for his plan, which he explained as follows: "When I was a boy, my father, a farmer, had the habit of gathering the family in the parlour at bedtime and he read to us out of the Bible. I can hear him yet. In fact, every time I hear those Bible verses I always seem to hear them in the tone of my father's voice. After prayers I would go up to my room and sleep like a top. But when I left home I got away from the Bible reading and prayer habit.

"I must admit that for years practically the only time I ever prayed was when I got into a jam. But some months ago my wife and I, having a number of difficult problems, decided we would try it again. We found it a very helpful practice, so now every night before going to bed she and I together read the Bible and have a little session of prayer. I don't know what there is about it, but I have been sleeping better and things have improved all down the line. In fact, I find it so helpful that even out on the road, as I am now, I still read the Bible and pray. Last night I got into bed and read the 23rd Psalm. I read it out loud and it did me a lot of good."

He turned to the other man and said: "I didn't go to bed with an ear full of trouble. I went to sleep with a mind full of peace."

Well, there are two cryptic phrases for you—'an ear full of trouble' and 'a mind full of peace'. Which do you choose?

The essence of the secret lies in a change of mental attitude. One must learn to live on a different thought basis, and even though thought change requires effort, it is much easier than to continue living as you are. The life of strain is difficult. The life of inner peace, being harmonious and without stress, is the easiest type of existence. The chief struggle then in gaining mental peace is the effort of revamping your thinking to the relaxed attitude of acceptance of God's gift of peace.

As an illustration of taking a relaxed attitude and therefore receiving peace, I always think of an experience in a certain city where I lectured one evening. Prior to going on the platform I was sitting back-stage going over my speech when a man approached and wanted to discuss a personal problem.

I informed him that at the moment it was impossible to talk as I was just about to be introduced, and asked him to wait. While speaking I noticed him in the wings nervously pacing up and down, but afterwards he was nowhere about. However, he had given me his card, which indicated that he was a man of considerable influence in that city.

Back at my hotel, although it was late, I was still troubled by this man, so I telephoned him. He was surprised at my call and explained that he did not wait because obviously I was busy. "I just wanted you to pray with me," he said. "I thought if you would pray with me, perhaps I could get some peace."

"There is nothing to prevent us from praying together on the telephone right now," I said.

Somewhat in surprise, he replied: "I have never heard of praying on the telephone."

"Why not?" I asked. "A telephone is simply a gadget of communication. You are some blocks from me, but by means of the telephone we are together. Besides," I continued, "the Lord is with each of us. He is at both ends of this line and in between. He is with you and He is with me."

"All right," he conceded. "I'd like to have you pray for me."

So I closed my eyes and prayed for the man over the telephone, and I prayed just as though we were in the same room. He could hear and the Lord could hear. When I finished I suggested: "Won't you pray?" There was no response. Then at the other end of the line I heard sobbing and finally: "I can't talk," he said.

"Go on and cry for a minute or two and then pray," I suggested. "Simply tell the Lord everything that is bothering you. I assume this is a private line, but if not, and if anybody is listening, it won't matter. As far as anyone is concerned, we are just a couple of voices. Nobody would know it is you and I."

Thus encouraged, he started to pray, hesitantly at first, and then with great impetuosity he poured out his heart, and it was filled with hate, frustration, failure—a mass of it. Finally he prayed plaintively: "Dear Jesus, I have a lot of nerve to ask you to do anything for me, because I never did anything for you. I guess you know what a no-account I am, even though I put on a big front. I am sick of all this, dear Jesus. Please help me."

So I prayed again, and asked the Lord to answer his prayer, then said: "Lord, at the other end of the telephone wire, place your hand on my friend and give him peace. Help him now to yield himself and accept your gift of peace." Then I stopped, and there was a rather long pause, and I shall never forget the tone in his voice as I heard him say: "I shall always remember this experience, and I want you to know that for the first time in months I feel clean inside and happy and peaceful." This man employed a simple technique for having a peaceful mind. He emptied his mind and he received peace as a gift from God.

As a physician said: "Many of my patients have nothing wrong with them except their thoughts. So I have a favourite prescription that I write for some. But it is not a prescription that you can fill at a drug-store. The prescription I write is a verse from the Bible: Romans xii. 2. I do not write out that verse for my patients. I make them look it up and it reads: '. . . be ye transformed by the renewing of your mind . . .' To be happier and healthier they need a renewing of their minds, that is, a change in the pattern of their thoughts. When they 'take' this prescription, they actually achieve a mind full of peace. That helps to produce health and well-being."

A primary method for gaining a mind full of peace is to practise emptying the mind. This will be emphasised in another chapter, but I mention it here to under-score the importance of a frequent mental catharsis. I recommend a mind-emptying at least twice a day, more often if necessary. Definitely practise emptying your mind of fears, hates, insecurities, regrets, and guilt feelings. The mere fact that you consciously make this effort to empty your mind tends to give relief. Haven't you experienced a sense of release when you have been able to pour out to somebody whom you can trust worrisome matters that lay heavy upon the heart? As a pastor I have often observed how much it means to people to have someone to whom they can truly and in confidence tell everything troubling their minds.

I conducted a religious service on board the s.s. *Lurline* on a recent voyage to Honolulu. In the course of my talk I suggested that people who were carrying worries in their minds might go to the stern of the vessel and imaginatively take each anxious thought out of the mind, drop it overboard, and watch it disappear in the wake of the ship. It seems an almost childlike suggestion, but a man came to me later that day and said: "I did as you suggested and am amazed at the relief it has given me. During this voyage," he said, "every evening at sunset I am going to drop all my worries overboard until I develop the psychology of casting them entirely out of my consciousness. Every day I shall watch them disappear in the great ocean of time. Doesn't the Bible say something about 'forgetting those things that are behind'?"

The man to whom this suggestion appealed is not an impractical sentimentalist. On the contrary, he is a person of extraordinary mental stature, an outstanding leader in his field.

Of course, emptying the mind is not enough. When the mind is emptied, something is bound to enter. The mind cannot long remain a vacuum. You cannot go around permanently with an empty mind. I admit that some people seem to accomplish that feat, but by and large it is necessary to refill the emptied mind or the old, unhappy thoughts which you have cast out will come sneaking in again.

To prevent that happening, immediately start filling your mind with creative and healthy thoughts. Then when the old fears, hates, and worries that have haunted you for so long try to edge back in, they will in effect find a sign on the door of your mind reading 'occupied'. They may struggle for admission, for having lived in your mind for a long time, they feel at home there. But the new and healthy thoughts which you have taken in will now be stronger and better fortified, and therefore able to repulse them. Presently the old thoughts will give up altogether and leave you alone. You will permanently enjoy a mind full of peace.

At intervals during the day practise thinking a carefully selected series of peaceful thoughts. Let mental pictures of the most peaceful scenes you have ever witnessed pass across your mind, as, for example, some beautiful valley filled with the hush of evening-time, as the shadows lengthen and the sun sinks to rest. Or recall the silvery light of the moon falling upon rippling waters, or remember the sea washing gently upon soft shores of sand. Such peaceful thought images will work upon your mind as a healing medicine. So now and then during every day allow motion pictures of peace slowly to cross your mind.

Practise the technique of suggestive articulation, that is, repeat audibly some peaceful words. Words have profound suggestive power, and there is healing in the very saying of them. Utter a series of panicky words and your mind will immediately go into a mild state of nervousness. You will perhaps feel a sinking in the pit of your stomach that will affect your entire physical mechanism. If, on the contrary, you speak peaceful, quieting words, your mind will react in a peaceful manner. Use such a word as 'tranquillity'. Repeat that word slowly several times. *Tranquillity* is one of the most beautiful and melodic of all English words, and the mere saying of it tends to induce a tranquil state.

Another healing word is 'serenity'. Picturise serenity as you say it. Repeat it slowly and in the mood of which the word is a symbol. Words such as these have a healing potency when used in this manner.

It is also helpful to use lines from poetry or passages from the Scriptures. A man of my acquaintance who achieved a remarkable peace of mind has the habit of writing on cards unusual quotations expressing peacefulness. He carries one of the cards in his wallet at all times, referring to it frequently until each quotation is committed to memory. He says that each such idea dropped into the subconscious 'lubricates' his mind with peace. A peaceful concept is indeed oil on troubled thoughts. One of the quotations which he used is from a sixteenth-century mystic: "Let nothing disturb you. Let nothing frighten you. Everything passes away except God. God alone is sufficient."

The words of the Bible have a particularly strong therapeutic value. Drop them into your mind, allowing them to 'dissolve' in consciousness, and they will spread a healing balm over your entire mental structure. This is one of the simplest processes to perform and also one of the most effective in attaining peace of mind.

A salesman told me of an incident that took place in a Mid-Western hotel room. He was one of a group of business men having a conference. One man was very much on edge. He was snappy, argumentative, high-strung. Everyone present knew him quite well and realised he was under great nervous pressure. But finally his irritating attitudes began to get on everybody's nerves. Presently this nervous individual opened his travelling-bag, took out a big bottle of brackish-looking medicine, and poured himself a large dose. Asked what this medicine was, he growled: "Oh, it's something for nerves. I feel like I'm going to break in pieces. The pressure I'm under makes me wonder if I am going to crack up. I try not to show it, but I suppose even you fellows have observed that I'm nervous. This medicine was recommended and I've swallowed several bottles of it, but I don't seem to get any better."

The other men laughed, then one said in a kindly manner: "Bill, I don't know anything about that medicine you are taking. Maybe it's all right. It probably is, but I can give you some medicine for those nerves that will do you more good than that. I know, because it cured me, and I was worse off than you are."

"What is this medicine?" snapped the other.

The other man reached into his bag and pulled out a

book. "This book will do the job, and I really mean it. I suppose you think it strange that I carry a Bible around in my bag, but I don't care who knows it. I am not a bit ashamed of it. I have been carrying this Bible in my bag for the past two years, and I have marked places in it that help keep my mind at peace. It works for me, and I think it can do something for you too. Why not give it a trial?"

The others were listening with interest to this unusual speech. The nervous man had sunk low in his chair. Seeing that he was making an impression, the speaker continued: "I had a peculiar experience in a hotel one night which got me into the habit of reading the Bible. I was getting into a pretty tense state. I was out on a business trip and late one afternoon came up to my room terribly nervous. I tried to write some letters, but couldn't get my mind on them. I paced up and down the room, tried to read the paper, but that annoyed me, so I decided to go down and get a drink—anything to get away from myself.

"While standing by the dresser, my eye happened to fall upon a Bible lying there. I had seen many such Bibles in hotel rooms, but had never read any of them. However, something impelled me, and I opened the book to one of the Psalms and started to read it. I remember that I read that one standing up, then sat down and read another. I was interested, but certainly surprised at myself—me reading the Bible! It was a laugh, but I kept on reading.

"Soon I came to the 23rd Psalm. I had learned that one as a boy in Sunday school and was surprised that I still knew most of it by heart. I tried saying it over, especially that line where it says: 'He leadeth me beside the still waters; he restoreth my soul.' I like that line. It sort of got me. I sat there repeating it over and over—and the next thing I knew I woke up.

"Apparently I had dropped off to sleep and slept soundly. I slept only about fifteen minutes, but upon awakening was as refreshed and rested as if I'd had a good night's sleep. I can remember yet the wonderful feeling of complete refreshment. Then I realised that I felt peaceful, and said to myself: 'Isn't it strange? What is wrong with me that I have missed something as wonderful as this?'

"So after that experience," he said, "I bought a Bible, a little one I could put in my bag, and I've been carrying it ever since. I honestly like to read it, and I am not nearly so nervous as I used to be. So," he added, "try that, Bill, and see if it doesn't work."

Bill did try it, and he kept on trying it. He reported that it was a bit strange and difficult for him at first, and he read the Bible on the sly when nobody was around. He didn't want to be thought holy or pious. But now he says he brings it out on trains and planes or 'any old place' and reads it, and it 'does him a world of good'.

"I no longer need to take nerve medicine," he declared.

This scheme must have worked in Bill's case, for he is easy to get along with now. His emotions are under control. These two men found that getting peace of mind isn't complicated. You merely feed your mind with thoughts that cause it to be peaceful. To have a mind full of peace merely fill it full of peace. It's as simple as that.

There are other practical ways by which you can develop serenity and quiet attitudes. One way is through your conversation. Depending upon the words we use and the tone in which we use them, we can talk ourselves into being nervous, high-strung, and upset. We can talk ourselves into either negative or positive results. By our speech we can also achieve quiet reactions. Talk gently to be peaceful.

In a group when the conversation takes a trend that is upsetting, try injecting peaceful ideas into the talk. Note how it counteracts the nervous tensions. Conversation filled with expressions of unhappy expectation, at breakfast, for example, often sets the tone of the day. Little wonder things turn out according to the unhappy specifications. Negative conversation adversely affects circumstances. Certainly talk of a tense and nervous nature enhances inner agitation.

On the contrary, start each day by affirming peaceful, contented, and happy attitudes and your days will tend to be pleasant and successful. Such attitudes are active and definite factors in creating satisfactory conditions. Watch your manner of speech then if you wish to develop a peaceful state of mind.

It is important to eliminate from conversations all negative ideas, for they tend to produce tension and annoyance inwardly. For example, when you are with a group of people at luncheon, do not comment that the 'Communists will soon take over the country'. In the first place, Communists are not going to take over the country, and by so asserting you create a depressing reaction in the minds of others. It undoubtedly affects digestion adversely. The depressing remark colours the attitude of all present, and everyone goes away with a perhaps slight but definite feeling of annoyance. They also carry away with them a mild but definite feeling that something is wrong with everything. There are times when we must face these harsh questions and deal with them objectively and vigorously, and no one has more contempt for Communism than I have, but as a general thing to have peace of mind, fill your personal and group conversations with positive, happy, optimistic, satisfying expressions.

The words we speak have a direct and definite effect upon our thoughts. Thoughts create words, for words are the vehicles of ideas. But words also affect thoughts and help to condition if not to create attitudes. In fact, what often passes for thinking starts with talk. Therefore if the average conversation is scrutinised and disciplined to be sure that it contains peaceful expressions, the result will be peaceful ideas and ultimately, therefore, a peaceful mind.

Another effective technique in developing a peaceful mind is the daily practice of silence. Everyone should insist upon not less than a quarter of an hour of absolute quiet every twenty-four hours. Go alone into the quietest place available to you and sit or lie down for fifteen minutes and practise the art of silence. Do not talk to anyone. Do not write. Do not read. Think as little as possible. Throw your mind into neutral. Conceive of your mind as quiescent, inactive. This will not be easy at first because thoughts are stirring up your mind, but practice will increase your efficiency. Conceive of your mind as the surface of a body of water and see how nearly quiet you can make it, so that there is not a ripple. When you have attained a quiescent state, then begin to listen for the deeper sounds of harmony and beauty and of God that are to be found in the essence of silence.

Americans unfortunately are not skilled in this practice, which is a pity, for as Thomas Carlyle said: "Silence is the element in which great things fashion themselves." This generation of Americans has missed something that our forefathers knew and which helped to condition their character—and that is the silence of the great forest or of the far-reaching plains.

Perhaps our lack of inner peace is due to some extent to the effect of noise upon the nervous system of modern people. Scientific experiments show that noise in the place where we work, live, or sleep reduces efficiency to a noticeable degree. Contrary to popular belief, it is doubtful if we ever completely adjust our physical, mental, or nervous mechanisms to noise. No matter how familiar a repeated sound becomes, it never passes unheard by the subconscious. Motor-car horns, the roar of aeroplanes, and other strident noises actually result in physical activity during sleep. Impulses transmitted to and through the nerves by these sounds cause muscular movements which detract from real rest. If the reaction is sufficiently severe, it partakes of the nature of shock.

On the contrary, silence is a healing, soothing, healthy practice. Starr Daily says: "No man or woman of my acquaintance who knows how to practise silence and does it has ever been sick to my knowledge. I have noticed that my own afflictions come upon me when I do not balance expression with relaxation." Starr Daily closely associates silence with spiritual healing. The sense of rest that results from a practice of complete silence is a therapy of utmost value.

In the circumstances of modern life, with its acceleration of pace, the practice of silence is admittedly not so simple as it was in the days of our forefathers. A vast number of noise-producing gadgets exist that they did not know, and our daily programme is more hectic. Space has been annihilated in the modern world, and apparently we are also attempting to annihilate the factor of time. It is only rarely possible for an individual to walk in deep woods or sit by the sea or meditate on a mountain-top or on the deck of a vessel in the midst of the ocean. But when we do have such experiences, we can print on the mind the picture of the silent place and the feel of the moment and return to it in memory to live it over again just as truly as when we were actually in that scene. In fact, when you return to it in memory the mind tends to remove any unpleasant factors present in the actual situation. The memory visit is often an improvement over the actual for the mind tends to reproduce only the beauty in the remembered scene.

For example, as I write these words, I am on a balcony of one of the most beautiful hotels in the world, the Royal Hawaiian on the famed and romantic Waikiki Beach in Honolulu, Hawaii. I am looking into a garden filled with graceful palm trees, swaying in the balmy breeze. The air is laden with the aroma of exotic flowers. Hibiscus, of which on these islands there are two thousand varieties, fill the garden. Outside my windows are papaya trees laden with ripening fruit. The brilliant colour of the royal poinciana, the flame of the forest trees, add to the glamour of the scene; and the acacia trees are hung heavily with their exquisite white flowers.

The incredible blue ocean surrounding these islands stretches away to the horizon. The white waves are surging in, and the Hawaiians and my fellow visitors are riding gracefully on surfboards and outrigger canoes. Altogether it is a scene of entrancing beauty. It has an indescribably healing effect upon me as I sit here writing about the power generated in a peaceful mind. The insistent responsibilities under which I ordinarily live seem so far away. Though I am in Hawaii to give a series of lectures and to write this book, nevertheless the peace with which this place is filled envelops me. Yet I realise that when I have returned to my home in New York, five thousand miles away, I shall only then truly savour the exquisite joy of the beauty which I now behold. It will become enshrined in memory as a prized retreat to which my mind can go in the busy days that lie ahead. Often, when far from this idyllic place, I shall return in memory to find peace along the palm-lined, foam-washed beach at Waikiki.

Fill your mind with all peaceful experiences possible, then make planned and deliberate excursions to them in memory. You must learn that the easiest way to an easy mind is to create an easy mind. This is done by practice, by the application of some such simple principles as outlined here. The mind quickly responds to teaching and discipline. You can make the mind give you back anything you want, but remember the mind can give back only what it was first given. Saturate your thoughts with peaceful experiences, peaceful words and ideas, and ultimately you will have a storehouse of peace-producing experiences to which you may turn for refreshment and renewal of your spirit. It will be a vast source of power.

I spent a night with a friend who has a very lovely home. We had breakfast in a unique and interesting dining-room. The four walls are painted in a beautiful mural picturing the countryside in which my host was reared as a boy. It is a panorama of rolling hills, gentle valleys, and singing streams, the latter clean and sun-speckled, and babbling over rocks. Winding roads meander through pleasant meadows. Little houses dot the landscape. In a central position is a white church surmounted by a tall steeple.

As we breakfasted my host talked of this region of his youth, pointing out various points of interest in the painting around the wall. Then he said: "Often as I sit in this dining-room I go from point to point in my memory and relive other days. I recall, for example, walking up that lane as a boy with bare feet, and I can remember yet how the clean dust felt between my toes. I remember fishing in that trout stream on many a summer afternoon and coasting down those hills in the winter-time.

"There is the church I attended as a boy." He grinned and said: "I sat through many a long sermon in that church but gratefully recall to mind the kindliness of the people and the sincerity of their lives. I can sit here and look at that church and think of the hymns I heard there with my mother and father as we sat together in the pew. They are long buried in that cemetery alongside the church, but in memory I go and stand by their graves and hear them speak to me as in days gone by. I get very tired and sometimes am nervous and tense. It helps to sit here and go back to the days when I had an untroubled mind, when life was new and fresh. It does something for me. It gives me peace."

Perhaps we all cannot have such murals on the dining-room walls, but you can put them around the wall of your mind: pictures of the most beautiful experiences of your life. Spend time among the thoughts which these pictures suggest. No matter how busy you may be or what responsibilities you carry, this simple, rather unique practice, having proved successful in many instances, may have a beneficial effect upon you. It is an easily practised, easy way to a peaceful mind.

There is a factor in the matter of inner peace which must be stated because of its importance. Frequently I find that people who are lacking in inner peace are victims of a self-punishment mechanism. At some time in their experience they have committed a sin and the sense of guilt haunts them. They have sincerely sought Divine forgiveness, and the good Lord will always forgive anyone who asks Him and who means it. However, there is a curious quirk within the human mind whereby sometimes an individual will not forgive himself.

He feels that he deserves punishment and therefore is constantly anticipating that punishment. As a result he lives in a constant apprehension that something is going to happen. In order to find peace under these circumstances he must increase the intensity of his activity. He feels that hard work will give him some release from his sense of guilt. A physician told me that in his practice a number of cases of nervous breakdown were traceable to a sense of guilt for which the patient had unconsciously attempted to compensate by hectic overwork. The patient attributed his breakdown not to the sense of guilt, but to his overworked condition. "But," said the physician, "these men need not have broken down from overwork if first the sense of guilt had been fully released." Peace of mind under such circumstances is available by yielding the guilt as well as the tension it produces to the healing therapy of Christ.

At a resort hotel where I had gone for a few days of quiet writing I encountered a man from New York whom I knew slightly. He was a high-pressured, hard-driving, and exceedingly nervous business executive. He was sitting in the sun in a deck-chair. At his invitation I sat down and chatted with him.

"I'm glad to see you relaxing in this beautiful spot," I commented.

He replied nervously: "I haven't any business being here. I've so much work to do at home. I'm under terrible pressure. Things have got me down, I'm nervous and can't sleep. I'm jumpy. My wife insisted that I come down here for a week. The doctors say there's nothing wrong with me if I just get to right thinking and relax. But how in the world do you do that?" he challenged. Then he gave me a piteous look. "Doctor," he said, "I would give anything if I could be peaceful and quiet. It's what I want more than anything in this world."

We talked a bit, and it came out in the conversation that he was always worrying that something sinister was going to happen. For years he had anticipated some dire event, living in constant apprehension about 'something happening' to his wife or his children or his home.

It was not difficult to analyse his case. His insecurity arose from a double source—from childhood insecurities and from later guilty experiences. His mother had always felt that 'something was going to happen', and he had absorbed her anxiety feelings. Later he committed some sins, and his subconscious mind insisted upon self-punishment. He became victim to the mechanism of self-punishment. As a result of this unhappy combination, I found him this day in a highly inflamed state of nervous reaction.

Finishing our conversation, I stood beside his chair a moment. There was no one near, so I rather hesitantly suggested: "Would you by any chance like me to pray with you?" He nodded, and I put my hand on his shoulder and prayed: "Dear Jesus, as You healed people in the long ago and gave them peace, heal this man now.

Give him fully of Thy forgiveness. Help him to forgive himself. Separate him from all his sins and let him know that You do not hold them against him. Set him free from them. Then let Thy peace flow into his mind, into his soul, and into his body."

He looked up at me with a strange look on his face and then turned away, for there were tears in his eyes and he didn't want me to see them. We were both a bit embarrassed, and I left him. Months later I met him, and he said: "Something happened to me down there that day when you prayed for me. I felt a strange sense of quietness and peace, and," he added, "healing."

He goes to church regularly now and he reads the Bible every day of his life. He follows the laws of God and he has lots of driving force. He is a healthy, happy man, for he has peace in his heart and mind.

3 | How to Have Constant Energy

A MAJOR-LEAGUE baseball pitcher once pitched a game when the temperature was over one hundred degrees. He lost several pounds as a result of his afternoon's exertion. At one stage of the game his energy sagged. His method for restoring his ebbing strength was unique. He simply repeated a passage from the Old Testament: "But they that wait upon the Lord shall renew their strength; they shall mount up with wings as eagles; they shall run, and not be weary; and they shall walk, and not faint." (Isaiah xl. 31.)

Frank Hiller, the pitcher who had this experience, told me that reciting this verse on the pitcher's mound actually gave him a renewal of strength so that he was able to complete the game with energy to spare. He explained the technique by saying: "I passed a powerful energy-producing thought through my mind."

How we think we feel has a definite effect on how we actually feel physically. If your mind tells you that you are tired, the body mechanism, the nerves, and the muscles accept the fact. If your mind is intensely interested, you can keep on at an activity indefinitely. Religion functions through our thoughts, in fact, it is a system of thought discipline. By supplying attitudes of faith to the mind it can increase energy. It helps you to accomplish prodigious activity by suggesting that you have ample support and resources of power.

A friend in Connecticut, an energetic man, full of vitality and vigour, says that he goes to church regularly to 'get his batteries recharged'. His concept is sound. God *is* the source of all energy—energy in the universe, atomic energy, electrical energy, and spiritual energy; indeed every form of energy derives from the Creator. The Bible emphasises this point when it says: "He giveth power to the faint; and to them that have no might he increaseth strength." (Isaiah xl. 29.)

In another statement the Bible describes the energising and re-energising process: ". . . in Him we live (that is, have vitality), and move (have dynamic energy, and have our being (attain completeness))." (Acts xvii. 28.)

Contact with God establishes within us a flow of the same type of energy that re-creates the world and that renews spring-time every year. When in spiritual contact with God through our thought processes, the Divine energy flows through the personality, automatically renewing the original creative act. When contact with the Divine energy is broken, the personality gradually becomes depleted in body, in mind, and spirit. An electric clock connected with an outlet does not run down and will continue indefinitely to keep accurate time. Unplug it, and the clock stops. It has lost contact with the power flowing through the universe. In general this process is operative in human experience though in a less mechanical manner.

A number of years ago I attended a lecture at which a speaker asserted before a large audience that he had not been tired in thirty years. He explained that thirty years before he had passed through a spiritual experience in which by self-surrender he had made contact with Divine power. From then on he possessed sufficient energy for all of his activities, and these were prodigious. He so obviously illustrated his teachings that everyone in that vast audience was profoundly impressed.

To me it was a revelation of the fact that in our consciousness we can tap a reservoir of boundless power as a result of which it is not necessary to suffer depletion of energy. For years I have studied and experimented with the ideas which this speaker outlined and which others have expounded and demonstrated, and it is my conviction that the principles of Christianity scientifically utilised can develop an uninterrupted and continuous flow of energy into the human mind and body.

These findings were corroborated by a prominent physician with whom I was discussing a certain man whom we both know. This man, whose responsibilities are very heavy, works from morning until night without interruption, but always seems able to assume new obligations. He has the knack of handling his work easily and with efficiency.

I commented to the physician that I hoped this man was not setting a dangerous pace that might possibly lead to a breakdown. The physician shook his head. "No," he replied, "as his physician I do not think there is any danger of a crack-up, and the reason is that he is a thoroughly well-organised individual with no energy leaks in his make-up. He operates a well-regulated machine. He handles things with easy power and carries burdens without strain. He never wastes an ounce of energy, but every effort is applied with maximum force."

"How do you account for this efficiency, this seemingly boundless energy?" I said.

The physician thought for a moment. "The answer is that he is a normal individual, emotionally well integrated, and, what is more important, he is a soundly religious person. From his religion he has learned how to avoid drainage of power. His religion is a workable and useful mechanism for preventing energy leaks. It is not hard work that drains off energy, but emotional upheaval, and this man is entirely free from that."

Increasingly people are realising that the maintenance of a sound spiritual life is important in enjoying energy and personality force.

The body is designed to produce all needed energy over an amazingly long period of time. If the individual takes reasonable care of his body from the standpoint of proper diet, exercise, sleep, no physical abuse, the body will produce and maintain astonishing energy and sustain itself in good health. If he gives similar attention to a well-balanced emotional life, energy will be conserved. But if he allows energy leaks caused by hereditary or self-imposed emotional reaction of a debilitating nature, he will be lacking in vital force. The natural state of the individual when body, mind, and spirit work harmoniously is that of a continuous replacement of necessary energy.

Mrs. Thomas A. Edison, with whom I often discussed the habits and characteristics of her famous husband, the world's greatest inventive wizard, told me that it was Mr. Edison's custom to come into the house from his laboratory after many hours of labour and lie down on his old couch. She said he would fall asleep as naturally as a child, in perfect relaxation, sinking into a deep and untroubled slumber. After three or four, or sometimes five hours he would become instantly wide awake, completely refreshed, and eager to return to his work.

Mrs. Edison, in answer to my request that she analyse her husband's ability to rest in a manner so natural and complete, said: "He was nature's man," by which she meant that he was completely in harmony with nature and with God. In him there were no obsessions, no disorganisations, no conflicts, no mental quirks, no emotional instability. He worked until he needed to sleep, then he slept soundly and arose and returned to his work. He lived for many years, and was in many respects the most creative mind ever to appear on the American continent. He drew his energy from emotional self-mastery, the ability to relax completely. His amazingly harmonious relationship with the universe caused nature to reveal to him his inscrutable secrets.

Every great personality I have ever known, and I have known many, who has demonstrated the capacity for prodigious work has been a person in tune with the Infinite. Every such person seems in harmony with nature and in contact with the Divine energy. They have not necessarily been pious people, but invariably they have been extraordinarily well organised from an emotional and psychological point of view. It is fear, resentment, the projection of parental faults upon people when they are children, inner conflicts and obsessions that throw off balance the finely equated nature, thus causing undue expenditure of natural force.

The longer I live the more I am convinced that neither age nor circumstance needs to deprive us of energy and vitality. We are at last awakening to the close relationship between religion and health. We are beginning to comprehend a basic truth hitherto neglected, that our physical condition is determined very largely by our emotional condition, and our emotional life is profoundly regulated by our thought life.

All through its pages, the Bible talks about vitality and force and life. The supreme over-all word of the Bible is life, and life means vitality—to be filled with energy. Jesus stated the key expression: ". . . I am come that they might have life, and that they might have it more abundantly." (John x. 10.) This does not rule out pain or suffering or difficulty, but the clear implication is that if a person practises the creative and re-creative principles of Christianity he can live with power and energy.

The practice of the above-mentioned principles will serve to bring a person into the proper tempo of living. Our energies are destroyed because of the high tempo, the abnormal pace at which we go. The conservation of energy depends upon getting your personality speed synchronised with the rate of God's movement. God is in you. If you are going at one rate and God at another, you are tearing yourself apart. "Though the mills of God grind slowly, yet they grind exceeding small." The mills of most of us grind very rapidly, and so they grind poorly. When we become attuned to God's rhythm we develop a normal tempo within ourselves and energy flows freely.

The hectic habits of this age have many disastrous effects. A friend of mine commented upon an observation made by her aged father. He said that in the early days when a young man came courting in the evening he sat with his intended in the parlour. Time in those days was measured by the deliberate, ponderous strokes of the grandfather clock, which has a very long pendulum. It seemed to say: "There—is—plenty—of—time. There—is—plenty—of—time. There—is—plenty—of—time." But modern clocks, having a shorter pendulum with a swifter stroke, seem to say: "Time to get busy! Time to get busy! Time to get busy! Time to get busy!"

Everything is speeded up, and for that reason many people are tired. The solution is to get into the time synchronisation of Almighty God. One way to do this is by going out some warm day and lying down on the earth. Get your ear close down to the ground and listen. You will hear all manner of sounds. You will hear the sound of the wind in the trees and the murmur of insects, and you will discover presently that there is in all these sounds a well-regulated tempo. You cannot get that tempo by listening to traffic in the city streets, for it is lost in the confusion of sound. You can get it in church where you hear the Word of God and the great hymns. Truth vibrates to God's tempo in a church. But you can also find it in a factory if you have a mind to.

A friend of mine, an industrialist in a large plant in Ohio, told me that the best workmen in his plant are those who get into harmony with the rhythm of the machine on which they are working. He declares that if a worker will work in harmony with the rhythm of his machine he will not be tired at the end of the day. He points out that the machine is an assembling of parts according to the law of God. When you love a machine and get to know it, you will be aware that it has a rhythm. It is one with the rhythm of the body, of the nerves, of the soul. It is in God's rhythm, and you can work with that machine and not get tired if you are in harmony with it. There is a rhythm of the stove, a rhythm of the typewriter, a rhythm of the office, a rhythm of a motor-car, a rhythm of your job. So to avoid tiredness and to have energy, feel your way into the essential rhythm of Almighty God and all His works.

To accomplish this, relax physically. Then conceive of your mind as likewise relaxing. Follow this mentally by visualising the soul as becoming quiescent, then pray as follows: "Dear God, You are the source of all energy. You are the source of the energy in the sun, in the atom, in all flesh, in the blood-stream, in the mind. I hereby draw energy from You as from an illimitable source." Then practise believing that you receive energy. Keep in tune with the Infinite.

Of course many people are tired simply because they are not interested in anything. Nothing ever moves them deeply. To some people it makes no difference what's going on or how things go. Their personal concerns are superior even to all crises in human history. Nothing makes any real difference to them except their own little worries, their desires, and their hates. They wear themselves out stewing around about a lot of inconsequential things that amount to nothing. So they become tired. They even become sick. The surest way not to become tired is to lose yourself in something in which you have a profound conviction.

A famous statesman who made seven speeches in one day was still boundless in energy.

"Why are you not tired after making seven speeches?" I asked.

"Because," he said, "I believe absolutely in everything I said in those speeches. I am enthusiastic about my convictions."

That's the secret. He was on fire for something. He was pouring himself out, and you never lose energy and vitality in so doing. You only lose energy when life becomes dull in your mind. Your mind gets bored and therefore tired doing nothing. You don't have to be tired. Get interested in something. Get absolutely enthralled in something. Throw yourself into it with abandon. Get out of yourself. Be somebody. Do something. Don't sit around moaning about things, reading the papers, and saying: "Why don't they do something?" The man who is out doing something isn't tired. If you're not getting into good causes, no wonder you're tired. You're disintegrating. You're deteriorating. You're dying on the vine. The more you lose yourself in something bigger than yourself, the more energy you will have. You don't have time to think about yourself and get bogged down in your emotional difficulties.

To live with constant energy it is important to get your emotional faults corrected. You will never have full energy until you do.

The late Knute Rockne, one of the greatest football coaches America ever produced, said that a football player cannot have sufficient energy unless his emotions are under spiritual control. In fact, he went so far as to say that he would not have a man on his team who did not have a genuinely friendly feeling for every fellow-player. "I have to get the most energy out of a man," he said, "and have discovered that it cannot be done if he hates another man. Hate blocks his energy and he isn't up to par until he eliminates it and develops a friendly feeling." People who lack energy are disorganised to one degree or another by their deep, fundamental emotional and psychological conflicts. Sometimes the results of this disorganisation are extreme, but healing is ever possible.

In a Mid-Western city I was asked to talk with a man, formerly a very active citizen of that community, who had suffered an acute decline in vitality. It was thought by his associates that he had had a stroke. This impression was given by the shuffling manner in which he moved, by an extraordinary lethargic attitude, and by his complete detachment of himself from the activities to which he had formerly given a large portion of his time. He sat despondently in his chair hour after hour, and often he would weep. He exhibited many of the symptoms of a nervous breakdown.

I arranged to see him in my hotel room at a certain hour. My door was open, and through it I could see the elevator. I chanced to be looking in that direction when the elevator door opened and this man came shuffling down the hall. It seemed that at any moment he would topple over, and he gave every evidence of scarcely being able to negotiate the distance. I asked him to be seated and engaged him in conversation, which conversation was rather fruitless, for it revealed little enlightenment because of his tendency to complain about his condition and his inability to give thoughtful consideration to my questions. This was apparently due to his enormous self-pity.

When I asked him if he would like to be well, he looked up at me in the most intense and pathetic manner. His desperation was revealed by his answer, which was that he would give anything in the world if he could regain the energy and the interest in life which he formerly enjoyed.

I began to draw out of him certain facts regarding his life and experience. These were all of a very intimate nature and many of them so deeply embedded in his consciousness that it was with the utmost difficulty that his personality yielded them up. They had to do with old infantile attitudes, fears that stemmed from earliest days, most of them deriving from the mother-child relationship. Not a few guilt situations appeared. It seemed that over the course of the years these factors had accumulated like drifting sand across the channel of a river. The flow of power was gradually decreased so that an insufficient amount of energy was passing through. The man's mind was in such a complete state of retreating that a process of reasoning and enlightenment seemed quite impossible.

I sought for guidance and found myself, quite to my surprise, standing beside him and placing my hand upon his head. I prayed, asking God to heal the man. I suddenly became aware of what seemed to be the passing of power through my hand which rested upon his head. I hasten to add that there is no healing power in my hand, but now and then a human being is used as a channel, and it was evidently so in this instance, for presently the man looked up with an expression of the utmost happiness and peace, and he said simply: "He was here. He touched me. I feel entirely different."

From this time on his improvement was pronounced, and at the present time he is practically his old self again, except for the fact that he now possesses a quiet and serene confidence which was not present previously. Apparently the clogged channel in his personality through which the passage of power had been impeded was opened by an act of faith and the free flow of energy was renewed.

The facts suggested by this incident are that such

healings do take place and that a gradual accumulation of psychological factors can cut off the flow of energy. The further fact is stressed that these same factors are susceptible to the power of faith to disintegrate them and thus reopen the channel of Divine human energy within an individual.

The effect of guilt and fear feelings on energy is widely recognised by all authorities having to do with the problems of human nature. The quantity of vital force required to give the personality relief from either guilt or fear or a combination of each is so great that often only a fraction of energy remains for the discharge of the functions of living. Energy drainage occasioned by fear and guilt is of such an amount as to leave little power to be applied to a person's job. The result is that he tires quickly. Not being able to meet the full requirements of his responsibility, he retreats into an apathetic, dull, listless condition and is indeed even ready to give up and fall back sleepily in a state of enervation.

A business man was referred to me by a psychiatrist whom the patient had been consulting. It appeared that the patient, generally regarded as quite morally strict and upright, had become involved with a married woman. He had attempted to break off this relationship, but was encountering resistance from his partner in infidelity, although he had earnestly besought her to abandon their practice and allow him to return to his former state of respectability.

She had threatened him with the possibility that she might enlighten her husband concerning these escapades if he insisted in his desire to cease the relationship. The patient recognised the fact that if the husband became apprised of the situation, it would result in disgrace for him in his community. He happened to be a prominent citizen and prized his high standing.

As a result of his fear of exposure and a sense of guilt he had been unable to sleep or rest. And since this had gone on for two or three months, he was in a very serious slump in energy and did not possess the vitality to perform his job efficiently. Inasmuch as some important matters were pending, the situation was serious.

When the psychiatrist suggested that he see me, a clergyman, because of his inability to sleep, he remonstrated by saying there was no way in which a clergyman could correct the condition which caused his sleeplessness, but, on the contrary, he felt that a medical doctor might supply effective medication.

When he stated his attitude to me I simply asked him how he expected to sleep when he had two very annoying and unpleasant bedfellows with whom he was attempting to sleep.

"Bedfellows?" he asked in surprise. "I have no bedfellows."

"Oh yes, you have," I said, "and there is nobody in this world who can sleep with those two, one on either side."

"What do you mean?" he asked.

I said: "You are trying to sleep every night between fear on one side and guilt on the other, and you are attempting an impossible feat. It makes no difference how many sleeping-pills you take, and you admit you have taken many such pills, but they have had no effect upon you. The reason they do not affect you is that they cannot reach the deeper levels of your mind where this sleeplessness originates and which is siphoning off your energy. You must eradicate fear and guilt before

51

you will ever be able to sleep and regain your strength."

We dealt with the fear which was of exposure by the simple expedient of getting him ready in mind to face whatever might ensue as a result of doing the right thing, which was of course to break off the relationship regardless of consequences. I assured him that whatever he did that was right would turn out right. One never does wrong by doing right. I urged him to put the matter in God's hands and simply do the right thing, leaving the outcome to God.

He did that, not without trepidation, but with considerable sincerity just the same. The woman, either through shrewdness or some expression of her own better nature or through the more doubtful expedient of transferring her affections elsewhere, released him.

The guilt was handled by seeking God's forgiveness. When this is sincerely sought it is never denied, and our patient found surcease and relief. It was astonishing how when this double weight was lifted from his mind his personality once again began to function normally. He was able to sleep. He found peace and renewal of strength. Energy quickly returned. A wiser and thankful man, he became able to carry on his normal activities.

A not infrequent case of diminishing energy is staleness. The pressure, monotony, and unceasing continuity of responsibilities dull the freshness of mind which a person must have to approach his work successfully. As an athlete goes stale, so does the individual, whatever his occupation, tend to come upon dry and arid periods. During such a condition of mind the expenditure of greater energy is required to do with difficulty what one formerly did with comparative ease. As a result the vital powers are hard put to it to supply the force required, and the individual often loses his grip and power.

A solution for this state of mind was employed by a prominent business leader, president of the board of trustees of a certain university. A professor who had formerly been outstanding and extraordinarily popular had begun to fail in teaching ability and in the power to interest students. It was the verdict of the students as well as the private opinion of the trustees that this teacher must either recover his former capacity to teach with interest and enthusiasm or it would be necessary to replace him. This latter expedient was entertained with hesitancy for the reason that there still remained a normal expectancy of several active years before he reached the age of retirement.

The business man referred to above asked the professor to come to his office and announced to him that the board of trustees was giving him a six months' leave of absence with all expenses paid and with full salary. There was only one stipulation, and that was that he go away to a place of rest and give himself over to gaining a complete renewal of strength and energy.

The business man invited him to use a cabin which he himself owned in a wilderness setting, and made the curious suggestion that he take no books except one book, the Bible. He suggested that the professor's daily programme be walking, fishing, and some manual work in the garden; that he read the Bible every day for such a period as would enable him to read the Book through three times in the six months. He further suggested that he memorise as many passages as possible for the purpose of saturating his mind with the great words and ideas which the Book contains.

53

The business man said: "I believe that if you spend six months outdoors chopping wood, digging in the soil, reading the Bible, and fishing in the deep lakes, you will become a new man."

The professor agreed to this unique proposal. His adjustment to this radically different mode of life was an easier one than he or anyone who knew him expected. In fact, he was surprised to find that he actually liked it. After he became conditioned to active outdoor living he discovered that it had an immense appeal for him. He missed his intellectual associates and his reading for a while, but forced back upon the Bible, his only book, he became immersed in it, and to his amazement found, as he put it: 'a library within itself'. In its pages he found faith and peace and power. In six months he was a new man.

The business man now tells me that this professor has become, as he puts it, 'a person of compelling power'. Staleness passed away, the old-time energy returned, power surged back, zest for living was renewed.

4 | Try Prayer Power

IN A BUSINESS OFFICE high above the city streets two men were having a serious conversation. One, heavily troubled by a business and personal crisis, paced the floor restlessly, then sat dejectedly, head in hand, a picture of despair. He had come to the other for advice, since he was considered a man of great understanding. Together they had explored the problem from every angle but seemingly without result, which only served to deepen the troubled man's discouragement. "I guess no power on earth can save me," he sighed.

The other reflected for a moment, then spoke rather diffidently. "I wouldn't look at it that way. I believe you are wrong in saying there is no power that can save you. Personally, I have found that there is an answer to every problem. There is a power that can help you." Then slowly he asked: "Why not try prayer power?"

Somewhat surprised, the discouraged man said: "Of course, I believe in prayer, but perhaps I do not know how to pray. You speak of it as something practical that fits a business problem. I never thought of it that way, but I'm willing to try prayer if you will show me how."

He did apply practical prayer techniques, and in due course got his answer. Matters ultimately turned out

55

satisfactorily. That is not to say he did not have difficulties. In fact, he had rather a hard time of it, but
ultimately he worked out of this trouble. Now he
believes in prayer power so enthusiastically that I
recently heard him say: "Every problem can be solved
and solved right if you pray."

Experts in physical health and well-being often utilise
prayer in their therapy. Disability, tension, and kindred
troubles may result from a lack of inner harmony. It
is remarkable how prayer restores the harmonious
functioning of body and soul. A friend of mine, a
physiotherapist, told a nervous man to whom he was
giving a massage: "God works through my fingers as
I seek to relax your physical body, which is the temple
of your soul. While I work on your outward being, I
want you to pray for God's relaxation inwardly." It
was a new idea to the patient, but he happened to be
in a receptive mood and he tried passing some peace
thoughts through his mind. He was amazed at the
relaxing effect this had on him.

Jack Smith, operator of a health club which is
patronised by many outstanding people, believes in the
therapy of prayer, and uses it. He was at one time a
prize-fighter, then a lorry-driver, later a taxi-driver, and
finally opened his health club. He says that while he
probes his patrons for physical flabbiness he also probes
for spiritual flabbiness, because, he declares: "You can't
get a man physically healthy until you get him spiritually
healthy."

One day Walter Huston, the actor, sat by Jack Smith's
desk. He noted a big sign on the wall on which were
pencilled the following letters: A P R P B W P R A A.
In surprise Huston asked: "What do those letters mean?"

Smith laughed and said: "They stand for 'Affirmative Prayers Release Powers By Which Positive Results Are Accomplished.'"

Huston's jaw dropped in astonishment. "Well, I never expected to hear anything like that in a health club."

"I use methods like that," said Smith, "to make people curious so they will ask what those letters mean. That gives me an opportunity to tell them that I believe affirmative prayers always get results."

Jack Smith, who helps men to keep physically fit, believes that prayer is as important, if not more important, than exercise, steam baths, and a rub down. It is a vital part of the power-releasing process.

People are doing more praying today than formerly because they find that it adds to personal efficiency. Prayer helps them to tap forces and to utilise strength not otherwise available.

A famous psychologist says: "Prayer is the greatest power available to the individual in solving his personal problems. Its power astonishes me."

Prayer power is a manifestation of energy. Just as there exist scientific techniques for the release of atomic energy, so are there scientific procedures for the release of spiritual energy through the mechanism of prayer. Exciting demonstrations of this energising force are evident.

Prayer power seems able even to normalise the ageing process, obviating or limiting infirmity and deterioration. You need not lose your basic energy or vital power or become weak and listless merely as a result of accumulating years. It is not necessary to allow your spirit to sag or grow stale or dull. Prayer can freshen you up every evening and send you out renewed each morning. You can receive guidance in problems if prayer is allowed to permeate your subconscious, the seat of the forces which determines whether you take right or wrong actions. Prayer has the power to keep your reactions correct and sound. Prayer driven deeply into your subconscious can remake you. It releases and keeps power flowing freely.

If you have not experienced this power, perhaps you need to learn new techniques of prayer. It is well to study prayer from an efficiency point of view. Usually the emphasis is entirely religious, though no cleavage exists between the two concepts. Scientific spiritual practice rules out stereotyped procedure even as it does in general science. If you have been praying in a certain manner, even if it has brought you blessings, which it doubtless has, perhaps you can pray even more profitably by varying the pattern and by experimenting with fresh prayer formulas. Get new insights; practise new skills to attain greatest results.

It is important to realise that you are dealing with the most tremendous power in the world when you pray. You would not use an old-fashioned kerosene lamp for illumination. You want the most up-to-date lighting devices. New and fresh spiritual techniques are being constantly discovered by men and women of spiritual genius. It is advisable to experiment with prayer power according to such methods as prove sound and effective. If this sounds new and strangely scientific, bear in mind that the secret of prayer is to find the process that will most effectively open your mind humbly to God. Any method through which you can stimulate the power of God to flow into your mind is legitimate and usable.

An illustration of a scientific use of prayer is the experience of two famous industrialists, whose names would be known to many readers were I permitted to mention them, who had a conference about a business and technical matter. One might think that these men would approach such a problem on a purely technical basis, and they did that and more; they also prayed about it. But they did not get a successful result. Therefore they called in a country preacher, an old friend of one of them, because, as they explained, the Bible prayer formula is: "Where two or three are gathered together in my name, there am I in the midst of them." (Matthew xviii. 20.) They also pointed to a further formula, namely: "If two of you shall agree on earth as touching any thing that they shall ask, it shall be done for them of My Father which is in heaven." (Matthew xviii. 19.)

Being schooled in scientific practice, they believe that in dealing with prayer as a phenomenon they should scrupulously follow the formulas outlined in the Bible which they described as the text-book of spiritual science. The proper method for employing a science is to use the accepted formulas outlined in the text-book of that science. They reasoned that if the Bible provides that two or three should be gathered together, perhaps the reason they were not succeeding was that they needed a third party.

Therefore the three men prayed, and to guard against error in the process they also brought to bear on the problem various other Biblical techniques such as those suggested in the statements: "According to your faith be it unto you." (Matthew ix. 29.) "What things soever ye desire, when ye pray, believe that ye receive them, and ye shall have them." (Mark xi. 24.)

After several thorough-going sessions of prayer the three men together affirmed that they had received the answer. The outcome was entirely satisfactory. Subsequent results indicated that Divine guidance was actually obtained.

These men are great enough scientists not to require precise explanation of the operation of these spiritual laws any more than in the case of naturalistic laws, but are content with the facts that the law does operate when 'proper' techniques are employed.

"While we cannot explain it," they said, "the fact remains that we were baffled by our problem and we tried prayer according to the formulas in the New Testament. That method worked and we got a beautiful result." They did add that it seemed to them that faith and harmony are important factors in the prayer process.

A man opened a small business in New York City a number of years ago, his first establishment being, as he characterised it, 'a little hole in the wall'. He had one employee. In a few years they moved into a larger room and then into extensive quarters. It became a very successful operation.

This man's method of business as he described it was 'to fill the little hole in the wall with optimistic prayers and thoughts'. He declared that hard work, positive thinking, fair dealing, right treatment of people, and the proper kind of praying always get results. This man, who has a creative and unique mind, worked out his own simple formula for solving his problems and overcoming his difficulties through prayer power. It is a curious formula, but I have practised it and personally know that it works. I have suggested it to many people who also found real value in its use. It is recommended to you.

The formula is: (1) PRAYERISE, (2) PICTURISE, (3) ACTUALISE.

By 'prayerise' my friend meant a daily system of creative prayer. When a problem arose he talked it over with God very simply and directly in prayer. Moreover, he did not talk with God as to some vast and far-off shadowy being, but conceived of God as being with him in his office, in his home, on the street, in his motor-car, always nearby as a partner, as a close associate. He took seriously the Biblical injunction to 'pray without ceasing'. He interpreted it as meaning that he should go about every day discussing with God in a natural, normal manner the questions that had to be decided and dealt with. The Presence came finally to dominate his conscious and ultimately his unconscious thinking. He 'prayerised' his daily life. He prayed as he walked or drove his car or performed other everyday activities. He filled his daily life full of prayer—that is, he lived by prayer. He did not often kneel to offer his prayers but would, for example, say to God as to a close associate: "What will I do about this, Lord?" or "Give me a fresh insight on this, Lord." He prayerised his mind and so prayerised his activities.

The second point in his formula of creative prayer is to 'picturise'. The basic factor in physics is force. The basic factor in psychology is the realisable wish. The man who assumes success tends already to have success. People who assume failure tend to have failure. When either failure or success is picturised it strongly tends to actualise in terms equivalent to the mental image pictured.

To assure something worth while happening, first pray about it and test it according to God's will; then print a picture of it on your mind as happening, holding the picture firmly in consciousness. Continue to surrender the picture to God's will—that is to say, put the matter in God's hands—follow God's guidance. Work hard and intelligently, thus doing your part to achieve success in the matter. Practise believing and continue to hold the picturisation firmly in your thoughts. Do this and you will be astonished at the strange ways in which the picturisation comes to pass. In this manner the picture 'actualises'. That which you have 'prayerised' and 'picturised' 'actualises' according to the pattern of your basic realisable wish when conditioned by invoking God's power upon it and if, moreover, you give fully of yourself to its realisation.

I have personally practised this three-point prayer method and find great power in it. It has been suggested to others, who have likewise reported that it released creative power into their experience.

For example, a woman discovered that her husband was drifting from her. Theirs had been a happy marriage, but the wife had become preoccupied in social affairs and the husband had got busy in his work. Before they knew it, the close, old-time companionship was lost. One day she discovered his interest in another woman. She lost her head and became hysterical. She consulted her minister, who adroitly turned the conversation to herself. She admitted being a careless homemaker and that she had also become self-centred, sharp-tongued, and nagging.

She then confessed that she had never felt herself the equal of her husband. She had a profound sense of inferiority regarding him, feeling unable to maintain equality with him socially and intellectually. So she retreated into an antagonistic attitude that manifested itself in petulance and criticism.

The minister saw that the woman had more talent,

ability, and charm than she was revealing. He suggested that she create an image or picture of herself as capable and attractive. He whimsically told her that "God runs a beauty parlour" and that faith techniques could put beauty on a person's face and charm and ease in her manner. He gave her instruction in how to pray and how spiritually to 'picturise'. He also advised her to hold a mental image of the restoration of the old-time companionship, to visualise the goodness in her husband, and to picture a restored harmony between the two of them. She was to hold this picture with faith. In this manner he prepared her for a most interesting personal victory.

About this time her husband informed her that he wanted a divorce. She had conquered herself to the extent of being able to receive this request with calmness. She simply replied that she was willing if he wanted it, but suggested deferment of the decision for ninety days on the ground that divorce is so final. "If at the end of ninety days you still feel that you want a divorce, I will co-operate with you." She said this calmly. He gave her a quizzical look, for he had expected an outburst.

Night after night he went out, and night after night she sat at home, but she pictured him as seated in his old chair. He was not in the chair, but she painted an image of him there comfortably reading as in the old days. She visualised him pottering around the house, painting and fixing things as he had formerly done. She even pictured him drying the dishes as he did when they were first married. She visualised the two of them playing golf together and taking hikes as they once did.

She maintained this picture with steady faith, and one night there he actually sat in his old chair. She looked twice to be sure that it was the reality rather than the picturisation, but perhaps a picturisation is a reality, for at any rate the actual man was there. Occasionally he would be gone but more and more nights he sat in his chair. Then he began to read to her as in the old days. Then one sunny Saturday afternoon he asked: "What do you say to a game of golf?"

The days went by pleasantly until she realised that the ninetieth day had arrived, so that evening she said quietly: "Bill, this is the ninetieth day."

"What do you mean," he asked, puzzled, "the ninetieth day?"

"Why, don't you remember? We agreed to wait ninety days to settle that divorce matter and this is the day."

He looked at her for a moment, then hidden behind his paper turned a page, saying: "Don't be silly. I couldn't possibly get along without you. Where did you ever get the idea I was going to leave you?"

The formula proved a powerful mechanism. She prayerised, she picturised, and the sought-for result was actualised. Prayer power solved her problem and his as well.

I have known many people who have successfully applied this technique not only to personal affairs but to business matters as well. When sincerely and intelligently brought into situations, the results have been so excellent that this must be regarded as an extraordinarily efficient method of prayer. People who take this method seriously and actually use it get astonishing results.

At an industrial convention banquet I was seated at the speaker's table next to a man who, though a bit on the rough side, was very likeable. He may have felt a bit cramped by his proximity to a preacher, which obviously wasn't his usual company. During the dinner he used a number of theological words, but they were not put together in a theological manner. After each outburst he apologised, but I advised him that I had heard all those words before.

He told me he had been a church attendant as a boy but 'had got away from it'. He gave me that old story which I have heard all my life and which even now people will get off as something entirely new, viz.: 'When I was a boy my father made me go to Sunday school and church and crammed religion down my throat. So when I got away from home I couldn't take it any more and have seldom been to church since.'

This man then observed that 'perhaps he should start going to church since he was getting old'. I commented that he would be lucky to find a seat. This surprised him for he 'did not think anybody went to church any more'. I told him that more people attend church each week than frequent any other institution in the country. This rather bowled him over.

He was head of a medium-sized business and he fell to telling me how much money his firm took in last year. I told him I knew quite a few churches whose take exceeded that. This really hit him in the solar plexus, and I noted his respect for the church mounting by leaps and bounds. I told him about the thousands of religious books that are sold, more than any other type of book. "Maybe you fellows in the church are on the ball at that," he slangily remarked.

At this moment another man came up to our table and enthusiastically told me that 'something wonderful' had happened to him. He said he had been very depressed, for things hadn't been going well with him. He decided to get away for a week or so and on this vacation read

65

one of my books* in which practical faith techniques are outlined. He said this brought him the first satisfaction and peace he had felt. It encouraged him as to his own possibilities. He began to believe that the answer to his trouble was practical religion.

"So," he said, "I began to practise the spiritual principles presented in your book. I began to believe and affirm that with God's help the objectives I was endeavouring to accomplish could be achieved. A feeling came over me that everything was going to be all right, and from then on nothing could upset me. I absolutely knew it was going to be O.K. So I began to sleep better and feel better. I felt as if I had taken a tonic. My new understanding and practise of spiritual techniques were the turning point."

When he left us my table companion, who had listened in on this recital, said: "I never heard anything like that before. That fellow talks about religion as happy and workable. It was never presented to me that way. He also gives the impression that religion is almost a science, that you can use it to improve your health and do better in your job. I never thought of religion in that connection."

Then he added: "But do you know what struck me? It was the look on that guy's face."

Now the curious fact is that when my table companion made that statement a semblance of the same look was on his own face. For the first time he was getting the idea that religious faith is not something piously stuffy but is a scientific procedure for successful living. He was observing at first-hand the practical working of prayer power in personal experience.

* *A Guide to Confident Living.* (The World's Work (1913) Ltd)

Personally, I believe that prayer is a sending out of vibrations from one person to another and to God. All of the universe is in vibration. There are vibrations in the molecules of a table. The air is filled with vibrations. The reaction between human beings is also in vibration. When you send out a prayer for another person, you employ the force inherent in a spiritual universe. You transport from yourself to the other person a sense of love, helpfulness, support—a sympathetic, powerful understanding—and in this process you awaken vibrations in the universe through which God brings to pass the good objectives prayed for. Experiment with this principle and you will know its amazing results.

For example, I have a habit, which I often use, of praying for people as I pass them. I remember being on a train travelling through West Virginia when I had a curious thought. I saw a man standing on a station platform, then the train moved on and he passed from sight. It occurred to me that I was seeing him for the first and last time. His life and mine touched lightly for just a fraction of an instant. He went his way and I went mine. I wondered how his life would turn out.

Then I prayed for that man, sending out an affirmative prayer that his life would be filled with blessings. Then I began praying for other people I saw as the train passed. I prayed for a man ploughing in the field and asked the Lord to help him and give him a good crop. I saw a mother hanging up clothes, and that line of freshly-washed garments told me she had a large family. A glimpse of her face and the way in which she handled the clothes of the children told me she was a happy woman. I prayed for her, that she would have a happy life, that her husband would always be true to her and that she would be true to him. I prayed that they might be a religious family and that the children would grow up strong, honourable young people.

In one station I saw a man leaning half asleep against a wall, and I prayed that he would wake up and get off relief and amount to something.

Then we stopped at a station, and there was a lovable little kid, one trouser leg longer than the other, shirt open at the neck, wearing a too-big sweater, hair tousled, face dirty. He was sucking a lollipop and working hard on it. I prayed for him, and as the train started to move he looked up at me and gave me the most wonderful smile. I knew my prayer had caught him, and I waved to him, and he waved back at me. I shall never see that boy again in all likelihood, but our lives touched. It had been a cloudy day up to that point, but suddenly the sun came out and I think there was a light in the boy's heart, for it was revealed on his face. I know that my heart felt happy. I am sure it was because the power of God was moving in a circuit through me, to the boy and back to God; and we were all under the spell of prayer power.

One of the important functions of prayer is as a stimulus to creative ideas. Within the mind are all of the resources needed for successful living. Ideas are present in consciousness which, when released and given scope together with proper implementation, can lead to the successful operation of any project or undertaking. When the New Testament says: "The kingdom of God is within you." (Luke xvii. 21), it is informing us that God our Creator has laid up within our minds and personalities all the potential powers and ability we need for constructive living. It remains for us to tap and develop these powers.

For example, a man of my acquaintance is connected with a business where he is the chief of four executives. At regular intervals these men have what they call an 'idea session', the purpose of which is to tap all the creative ideas lurking in the minds of any of the four. For this session they use a room without telephones, buzzers, or other usual office equipment. The double window is fully insulated so that street noises are for the most part eliminated.

Before starting the session the group spends ten minutes in silent prayer and meditation. They conceive of God as creatively working in their minds. Each in his own way silently prays, affirming that God is about to release from his mind the proper ideas needed in the business.

Following the quiet period all start talking, pouring out ideas that have come to their minds. Memos of the ideas are written upon cards and thrown on the table. No one is permitted to criticise any idea at this particular juncture for argument might stop the flow of creative thought. The cards are gathered up and each one is evaluated at a later session; but this is the idea-tapping session, stimulated by prayer power.

When this practice was inaugurated a high percentage of the ideas suggested proved to be without particular value, but as the session continued the percentage of good ideas increased. Now many of the best suggestions which have later demonstrated their practical value were evolved in the 'idea session'.

As one of the executives explained: "We have come up with insights that not only show on our balance sheet but we have also gained a new feeling of confidence. Moreover, there is a deeper feeling of fellowship among the four of us and this has spread to others in the organisation."

Where is the old-fashioned business man who says that religion is theoretical and has no place in business? Today any successful and competent business man will employ the latest and best-tested methods in production, distribution, and administration, and many are discovering that one of the greatest of all efficiency methods is prayer power.

Alert people everywhere are finding that by trying prayer power they feel better, work better, do better, sleep better, are better.

My friend Grove Patterson, editor of the Toledo *Blade*, is a man of remarkable vigour. He says that his energy results, in part at least, from his methods of prayer. For example, he likes to fall asleep while praying, for he believes that his subconscious is most relaxed at that time. It is in the subconscious that our life is largely governed. If you drop a prayer into the subconscious at the moment of its greatest relaxation, the prayer has a powerful effect. Mr. Patterson chuckled as he said: "Once it worried me because I would fall asleep while praying. Now I actually try to have it so."

Many unique methods of prayer have come to my attention, but one of the most effective is that advocated by Frank Laubach in his excellent book, *Prayer, the Mightiest Power in the World*.* I regard this as one of the most practical books on prayer, for it outlines fresh prayer techniques that work. Dr. Laubach believes that actual power is generated by prayer. One of his methods is to walk down the street and 'shoot' prayers at people. He calls this type of praying 'flash prayers'. He bombards

* Lutterworth Press

passers-by with prayers, sending out thoughts of goodwill and love. He says that people passing him on the street as he 'shoots' prayers at them often turn around and look at him and smile. They feel the emanation of a power like electrical energy.

In a bus he 'shoots' prayers at his fellow passengers. Once he was sitting behind a man who seemed to be very gloomy. He had noticed when he entered the bus that the man had a scowl on his face. He began to send out towards him prayers of goodwill and faith, conceiving of these prayers as surrounding him and driving into his mind. Suddenly the man began to stroke the back of his head, and when he left the bus the scowl was gone and a smile had replaced it. Dr. Laubach believes that he has often changed the entire atmosphere of a car or bus full of people by the process of 'swishing love and prayers all around the place'.

In a Pullman club car a half-intoxicated man was quite boorish and rude, talking in an overbearing manner and generally making himself obnoxious. I felt that everyone in the car took a dislike to him. Half-way down the car from him I determined to try Frank Laubach's method. So I started to pray for him, meanwhile visualising his better self and sending out thoughts of goodwill towards him. Presently, for no seemingly apparent reason, the man turned in my direction, gave me a most disarming smile, and raised his hand in the gesture of salute. His attitude changed and he became quiet. I have every reason to believe that the prayer thoughts effectively reached out towards him.

It is my practice before making a speech to any audience to pray for the people present and to send out thoughts of love and goodwill towards them. Sometimes

I select out of the audience one or two people who seem to be either depressed or even antagonistic and send my prayer thoughts and goodwill attitude specifically towards them. Recently addressing a Chamber of Commerce annual dinner in a south-western city, I noted a man in the audience who seemed to be scowling at me. It was altogether possible that his facial expression was not in any way related to me, but he seemed antagonistic. Before starting to speak I prayed for him and 'shot' a series of prayers and goodwill thoughts in his direction. As I spoke, I continued to do this.

When the meeting was over, while shaking hands with those around me, suddenly my hand was caught in a tremendous clasp and I was looking into the face of this man. He was smiling broadly. "Frankly I did not like you when I came to this meeting," he said. "I do not like preachers and saw no reason for having you, a minister, as speaker at our Chamber of Commerce dinner. I was hoping that your speech would not be successful. However, as you spoke something seemed to touch me. I feel like a new person. I had a strange sense of peace— and doggone it, I like you!"

It was not my speech that had this effect. It was the emanation of prayer power. In our brains we have about two billion little storage batteries. The human brain can send off power by thoughts and prayer. The human body's magnetic power has actually been tested. We have thousands of little sending stations, and when these are tuned up by prayer it is possible for a tremendous power to flow through a person and to pass between human beings. We can send off power by prayer which acts as both a sending and receiving station.

There was a man, an alcoholic, with whom I had been

working. He had been 'dry' (as the Alcoholics Anonymous term it) for about six months. He was on a business trip, and one Tuesday afternoon about four o'clock I had a strong impression that he was in trouble. This man dominated my thoughts. I felt something drawing me so I dropped everything and started praying for him. I prayed for about half an hour, then the impression seemed to let up and I discontinued my prayers.

A few days later he telephoned me. "I have been in Boston all week," he said, "and I want you to know I'm still 'dry', but early in the week I had a very hard time."

"Was it on Tuesday at four o'clock?" I asked.

Astonished, he replied: "Why, yes, how did you know? Who told you?"

"Nobody told me," I replied. "That is, no human told me." I described my feeling concerning him on Tuesday at four o'clock and told about praying for him for half an hour.

He was astounded, and explained: "I was at the hotel and stopped in front of the bar. I had a terrible struggle with myself. I thought of you, for I needed help badly right then, and I started to pray."

Those prayers starting out from him reached me, and I began to pray for him. Both of us joining in prayer completed the circuit and reached God, and the man got his answer in the form of strength to meet the crisis. And what did he do?

He went to a drug-store, bought a box of candy, and ate all of it without stopping. That pulled him through, he declared—"prayer and candy."

A young married woman admitted she was filled with hates, jealousy, and resentment towards neighbours and friends. She was also very apprehensive, always worrying

73

about her children, whether they would be sick or get into an accident or fail in school. Her life was a pathetic mixture of dissatisfaction, fear, hate, and unhappiness. I asked her if she ever prayed. She said: "Only when I get so up against it that I am just desperate; but I must admit that prayer doesn't mean anything to me, so I don't pray very often."

I suggested that the practice of real prayer could change her life and gave her some instructions in sending out love thoughts instead of hate thoughts and confidence thoughts instead of fear thoughts. I suggested that every day at the time for the children to come home from school she pray, and make her prayers an affirmation of God's protective goodness. Doubtful at first, she became one of the most enthusiastic advocates and practisers of prayer I have ever known. She avidly reads books and pamphlets and practises every effective prayer-power technique. This procedure changed her life, as is illustrated by the following letter which she wrote me recently:

"I feel that my husband and I have both made wonderful progress in the last few weeks. My greatest progress dates from the night you told me that 'every day is good if you pray'. I began to put into practice the idea of affirming that this would be a good day the minute I woke up in the morning, and *I can positively say that I have not had a bad or upsetting day since that time*. The amazing thing is that my days actually haven't been any smoother or any more free from petty annoyances than they ever were, but they just don't seem to have the power to upset me any more. Every night I begin my prayers by listing all the things for which I am grateful, little things that happened during the day which added to the happiness of my day. I know that this habit had geared my mind to pick out the nice things and forget the unpleasant ones. The fact that for six weeks I have not had a single bad day and have refused to get downhearted with anyone is really marvellous to me."

She discovered amazing power in trying prayer power.

You can do the same. Following are ten rules for getting effective results from prayer:

1. Set aside a few minutes every day. Do not say anything. Simply practise thinking about God. This will make your mind spiritually receptive.

2. Then pray orally, using simple, natural words. Tell God anything that is on your mind. Do not think you must use stereotyped pious phrases. Talk to God in your own language. He understands it.

3. Pray as you go about the business of the day, on the subway or bus or at your desk. Utilise minute prayers by closing your eyes to shut out the world and concentrating briefly on God's presence. The more you do this every day the nearer you will feel God's presence.

4. Do not always ask when you pray, but instead affirm that God's blessings are being given, and spend most of your prayers giving thanks.

5. Pray with the belief that sincere prayers can reach out and surround your loved ones with God's love and protection.

6. Never use a negative thought in prayer. Only positive thoughts get results.

7. Always express willingness to accept God's will. Ask for what you want, but be willing to take what God gives you. It may be better than what you ask for.

8. Practise the attitude putting everything in God's hands. Ask for the ability to do your best and to leave the results confidently to God.

9. Pray for people you do not like or who have mistreated you. Resentment is blockade number one of spiritual power.

10. Make a list of people for whom to pray. The more you pray for other people, especially those not connected with you, the more prayer results will come back to you.

5 | How to Create Your Own Happiness

Who decides whether you shall be happy or unhappy? The answer—you do!

A television celebrity had as a guest on his programme an aged man. And he was a very rare old man indeed. His remarks were entirely unpremeditated and of course absolutely unrehearsed. They simply bubbled up out of a personality that was radiant and happy. And whenever he said anything, it was so naïve, so apt, that the audience roared with laughter. They loved him. The celebrity was impressed, and enjoyed it with the others.

Finally he asked the old man why he was so happy. "You must have a wonderful secret of happiness," he suggested.

"No," replied the old man, "I haven't any great secret. It's just as plain as the nose on your face. When I get up in the morning," he explained, "I have two choices—either to be happy or to be unhappy, and what do you think I do? I just choose to be happy, and that's all there is to it."

That may seem an over-simplification, and it may appear that the old man was superficial, but I recall that Abraham Lincoln, whom nobody could accuse of being superficial, said that people were just about as happy as they made up their minds to be. You can be unhappy if you want to be. It is the easiest thing in the world to accomplish. Just choose unhappiness. Go around telling yourself that things aren't going well, that nothing is satisfactory, and you can be quite sure of being unhappy. But say to yourself: "Things are going nicely. Life is good. I choose happiness," and you can be quite certain of having your choice.

Children are more expert in happiness than adults. The adult who can carry the spirit of a child into middle and old age is a genius, for he will preserve the truly happy spirit with which God endowed the young. The subtlety of Jesus Christ is remarkable, for He tells us that the way to live in this world is to have the childlike heart and mind. In other words, never get old or dull or jaded in spirit. Don't become super-sophisticated.

My little daughter Elizabeth, aged nine, has the answer to happiness. One day I asked her: "Are you happy, honey?"

"Sure I'm happy," she replied.

"Are you always happy?" I asked.

"Sure," she answered, "I'm always happy."

"What makes you happy?" I asked her.

"Why, I don't know," she said, "I'm just happy."

"There must be something that makes you happy," I urged.

"Well," she said, "I'll tell you what it is. My playmates, they make me happy. I like them. My school makes me happy. I like to go to school. (I didn't say anything, but she never got that from me.) I like my teachers. And I like to go to church. I like Sunday school and my Sunday school teacher. I love my sister Margaret and my brother John. I love my mother and father. They take care of me when I'm sick, and they love me and are good to me."

This is Elizabeth's formula for happiness, and it seems to me that it's all there—her playmates (that's her associates), her school (the place where she works), her church and Sunday school (where she worships), her sister, brother, mother and father (that means the home circle where love is found). There you have happiness in a nutshell, and the happiest time of your life is in relation to those factors.

A group of boys and girls were asked to list the things that made them happiest. Their answers were rather touching. Here is the boys' list: 'A swallow flying; looking into deep, clear water; water being cut at the bow of a boat; a fast train rushing; a builder's crane lifting something heavy; my dog's eyes.'

And here is what the girls said made them happy: 'Street lights on the river; red roofs in the trees; smoke rising from a chimney; red velvet; the moon in the clouds.' There is something in the beautiful essence of the universe that is expressed, though only half articulated, by these things. To become a happy person have a clean soul, eyes that see romance in the commonplace, a child's heart, and spiritual simplicity.

Many of us manufacture our own unhappiness. Of course not all unhappiness is self-created, for social conditions are responsible for not a few of our woes. Yet it is a fact that to a large extent by our thoughts and attitudes we distil out of the ingredients of life either happiness or unhappiness for ourselves.

"Four people out of five are not so happy as they can be," declares an eminent authority, and he adds: "Unhappiness is the most common state of mind." Whether

79

human happiness strikes as low a level as this, I would hesitate to say, but I do find more people living unhappy lives than I would care to compute. Since a fundamental desire of every human being is for that state of existence called happiness, something should be done about it. Happiness is achievable and the process for obtaining it is not complicated. Anyone who desires it, who wills it, and who learns and applies the right formula may become a happy person.

In a railway dining-car I sat across from a husband and wife, strangers to me. The lady was expensively dressed, as the furs, diamonds, and costume which she wore indicated. But she was having a most unpleasant time with herself. Rather loudly she proclaimed that the car was dingy and draughty, the service abominable, and the food most unpalatable. She complained and fretted about everything.

Her husband, on the contrary, was a genial, affable, easy-going man who obviously had the capacity to take things as they came. I thought he seemed a bit embarrassed by his wife's critical attitude and somewhat disappointed, too, as he was taking her on this trip for pleasure.

To change the conversation he asked what business I was in, and then said that he was a lawyer. Then he made a big mistake, for with a grin he added: "My wife is in the manufacturing business."

This was surprising, for she did not seem to be the industrial or executive type, so I asked: "What does she manufacture?"

"Unhappiness," he replied. "She manufactures her own unhappiness."

Despite the icy coolness that settled upon the table

following this ill-advised observation, I was grateful for his remark, for it describes exactly what so many people do—'They manufacture their own unhappiness.'

It is a pity, too, for there are so many problems created by life itself that dilute our happiness that it is indeed most foolish to distil further unhappiness within your own mind. How foolish to manufacture personal unhappiness to add to all the other difficulties over which you have little or no control!

Rather than to emphasise the manner in which people manufacture their own unhappiness, let us proceed to the formula for putting an end to this misery-producing process. Suffice it to say that we manufacture our unhappiness by thinking unhappy thoughts, by the attitudes which we habitually take, such as the negative feeling that everything is going to turn out badly, or that other people are getting what they do not deserve and we are failing to get what we do deserve.

Our unhappiness is further distilled by saturating the consciousness with feelings of resentment, ill-will, and hate. The unhappiness-producing process always makes important use of the ingredients of fear and worry. Each of these matters is dealt with elsewhere in this book. We merely want to make the point at the present time, and stress it forcefully, that a very large proportion of the unhappiness of the average individual is self-manufactured. How, then, may we proceed to produce not unhappiness but happiness?

An incident from one of my railway journeys may suggest an answer. One morning in an old-style Pullman car approximately half a dozen of us were shaving in the men's lounge. As always in such close and crowded quarters after a night on the train, this group of strangers was not disposed to be gay, and there was little conversation and that little was mostly mumbled.

Then a man came in wearing on his face a broad smile. He greeted us all with a cheery good morning, but received rather unenthusiastic grunts in return. As he went about his shaving he was humming, probably quite unconsciously, a gay little tune. It got a bit on the nerves of some of the men. Finally one said rather sarcastically: "You certainly seem to be happy this morning! Why all the cheer?"

"Yes," the man answered, "as a matter of fact, I am happy. I do feel cheerful." Then he added: "I make it a habit to be happy."

That is all that was said, but I am sure that each man in that lounge left the train with those interesting words in mind: 'I make it a habit to be happy.'

The statement is really very profound, for our happiness or unhappiness depends to an important degree upon the habit of mind we cultivate. That collection of wise sayings, the book of Proverbs, tells us that ". . . he that is of a merry heart hath a continual feast." (Proverbs xv. 15.) In other words, cultivate the merry heart; that is, develop the happiness habit, and life will become a continual feast, which is to say you can enjoy life every day. Out of the happiness habit comes a happy life. And because we can cultivate a habit, we therefore have the power to create our own happiness.

The happiness habit is developed by simply practising happy thinking. Make a mental list of happy thoughts and pass them through your mind several times every day. If an unhappiness thought should enter your mind, immediately stop, consciously eject it, and substitute a happiness thought. Every morning before arising, lie relaxed in bed and deliberately drop happy thoughts into your conscious mind. Let a series of pictures pass across your mind of each happy experience you expect to have during the day. Savour their joy. Such thoughts will help cause events to turn out that way. Do not affirm that things will not go well that day. By merely saying that, you can actually help to make it so. You will draw to yourself every factor, large and small, that will contribute to unhappy conditions. As a result, you will find yourself asking: "Why does everything go badly for me? What is the matter with everything?"

The reason can be directly traced to the manner in which you began the day in your thoughts.

Tomorrow try this plan instead. When you arise, say out loud three times this one sentence: "This is the day which the Lord hath made; we will rejoice and be glad in it." (Psalm cxviii. 24.) Only personalise it and say: "I will rejoice and be glad in it." Repeat it in a strong, clear voice and with positive tone and emphasis. The statement, of course, is from the Bible and it is a good cure for unhappiness. If you repeat that one sentence three times before breakfast and meditate on the meaning of the words, you will change the character of the day by starting off with a happiness psychology.

While dressing or shaving or getting breakfast, say aloud a few such remarks as the following: 'I believe this is going to be a wonderful day. I believe I can successfully handle all problems that will arise today. I feel good physically, mentally, emotionally. It is wonderful to be alive. I am grateful for all that I have had, for all that I now have, and for all that I shall have. Things aren't going to fall apart. God is here and He is with me and He will see me through. I thank God for every good thing.'

I once knew an unhappy sort of fellow who always said to his wife at breakfast: "This is going to be another tough day." He didn't really think so, but he had a mental quirk whereby if he said it was going to be a tough day, it might turn out pretty well. But things really started going badly with him, which was not surprising, for if you visualise and affirm an unhappy outcome, you tend thereby to create just that type of condition. So affirm happy outcomes at the start of every day, and you will be surprised at how often things will turn out so.

But it is not sufficient to apply to the mind even such an important affirmation therapy as I have just suggested unless throughout the day you also base your actions and attitudes upon fundamental principles of happy living.

One of the most simple and basic of such principles is that of human love and goodwill. It is amazing what happiness a sincere expression of compassion and tenderness will induce.

My friend Dr. Samuel Shoemaker once wrote a moving story about a mutual friend. Ralston Young is famous as Porter No. 42 in the Grand Central Station in New York. He carries bags for a living, but his real job is living the spirit of Christ as a porter in one of the world's greatest railway stations. As he carries a man's suitcase, he tries to share a little Christian fellowship with him. He carefully watches a customer to see if there is any way in which he can give him more courage and hope. He is very skilful in the way he goes about it too.

One day, for example, he was asked to take a little old lady to her train. She was in a wheel-chair, so he took her down on the elevator. As he wheeled her into the elevator he noticed that there were tears in her eyes. Ralston Young stood there as the elevator descended, closed his eyes, and asked the Lord how he could help her, and the Lord gave him an idea. As he wheeled her off the elevator, he said with a smile: "Ma'am, if you don't mind my saying so, that is a mighty pretty hat you are wearing."

She looked up at him and said: "Thank you."

"And I might add," he said, "that sure is a pretty dress you have on. I like it so much."

Being a woman, this appealed to her, and despite the fact that she was not feeling well, she brightened up and asked: "Why in the world did you say those nice things to me? It is very thoughtful of you."

"Well," he said, "I saw how unhappy you were. I saw that you were crying, and I just asked the Lord how I could help you. The Lord said: 'Speak to her about her hat.' The mention of the dress," he added, "was my own idea." Ralston Young and the Lord together knew how to get a woman's mind off her troubles.

"Don't you feel well?" he then asked.

"No," she replied. "I am constantly in pain. I am never free from it. Sometimes I think I can't stand it. Do you, by any chance, know what it means to be in pain all the time?"

Ralston had an answer. "Yes, ma'am, I do, for I lost an eye, and it hurts like a hot iron day and night."

"But," she said, "you seem to be happy now. How did you accomplish it?"

By this time he had her in her seat in the train, and he said: "Just by prayer, ma'am, just by prayer."

Softly she asked: "Does prayer, just prayer, take your pain away?"

"Well," answered Ralston, "perhaps it doesn't always take it away. I can't say that it does, but it always helps to overcome it so it doesn't seem like it hurts so much. Just keep on prayin', ma'am, and I'll pray for you too."

Her tears were dried now, and she looked up at him with a lovely smile, took him by the hand, and said: "You've done me so much good."

A year passed, and one night in Grand Central Station Ralston Young was paged to come to the Information booth. A young woman was there who said: "I bring you a message from the dead. Before she died my mother told me to find you and to tell you how much you helped her last year when you took her to the train in her wheelchair. She will always remember you, even in eternity. She will remember you, for you were so kind and loving and understanding." Then the young woman burst into tears and sobbed in her grief.

Ralston stood quietly watching her. Then he said: "Don't cry, missy, don't cry. You shouldn't cry. Give a prayer of thanksgiving."

Surprised, the girl said: "Why should I give a prayer of thanksgiving?"

"Because," said Ralston, "many people have become orphans much younger than you. You had your mother for a long, long time, and besides, you still have her. You will see her again. She is near to you now and she always will be near to you. Maybe," he said, "she is right with us now—the two of us, as we talk."

The sobs ended and the tears dried. Ralston's kindness had the same effect on the daughter as it had had on the mother. In this huge station, with thousands of people passing by, the two of them felt the presence of one who inspired this wonderful porter to go around this way, spreading love.

"Where love is," said Tolstoy, "God is," and, we

might add, where God and love are, there is happiness. So a practical principle in creating happiness is to practise love.

A genuinely happy man is a friend of mine, H. C. Mattern, who with his equally happy wife, Mary, travels throughout the country in the course of his work. Mr. Mattern carries a unique business card on the reverse side of which is stated the philosophy which has brought happiness to him and his wife and to hundreds of others who have been so fortunate as to feel the impact of their personalities.

The card reads as follows: 'The way to happiness: keep your heart free from hate, your mind from worry. Live simply, expect little, give much. Fill your life with love. Scatter sunshine. Forget self, think of others. Do as you would be done by. Try this for a week and you will be surprised.'

As you read these words you may say: "There is nothing new in that." Indeed, there is something new in it if you have never tried it. When you start to practise it you will find it the newest, freshest, most astonishing method of happy and successful living you have ever used. What is the value of having known these principles all your life if you have never made use of them? Such inefficiency in living is tragic. For a man to have lived in poverty when all the time right on his doorstep is gold indicates an unintelligent approach to life. This simple philosophy is the way to happiness. Practise these principles for just one week, as Mr. Mattern suggests, and if it has not brought you the beginnings of real happiness, then your unhappiness is very deep-seated indeed.

Of course, in order to give power to these principles of happiness and make them work it is necessary to support them with a dynamic quality of mind. You are not likely to secure effective results even with spiritual principles without spiritual power. When one experiences a dynamic spiritual change inwardly, success with happiness-producing ideas becomes extraordinarily easy. If you begin to use spiritual principles, however awkwardly, you will gradually experience spiritual power inwardly. I can assure you that this will give you the greatest surge of happiness you have ever known. It will stay with you, too, as long as you live a God-centred life.

In my travels about the country I have been encountering an increasing number of genuinely happy individuals. These are persons who have been practising the techniques described in this book and which I have presented in other volumes, and in other writings and talks and which other writers and speakers have likewise been giving to receptive people. It is astonishing how people can become inoculated with happiness through an inner experience of spiritual change. People of all types everywhere are having this experience today. In fact, it has become one of the most popular phenomena of our times, and if it continues to develop and expand, the person who has not had a spiritual experience will soon be considered old-fashioned and behind the times. Nowadays it is smart to be spiritually alive. It is old-fogyism to be ignorant of that happiness-producing transformation which people everywhere are enjoying at this time.

Recently, after finishing a lecture in a certain city, a big, strapping, fine-looking man came up to me. He slapped me on the shoulder with such force that it almost bowled me over.

"Doctor," he said in a booming voice, "how about coming out with the gang? We are having a big party at the Smiths' house, and we would like you to come along. It's going to be a whale of a shindig and you ought to get in on it." So ran his racy invitation.

Well, obviously this didn't sound like a proper party for a preacher, and I was hesitant. I was afraid I might cramp everyone's style, so I began to make excuses.

"Oh, forget it," my friend told me. "Don't worry, this is your kind of party. You will be surprised. Come on along. You will get the kick of your life out of it."

So I yielded and went along with my buoyant and racy friend, and he was certainly one of the most infectious personalities I had encountered in quite a while. Soon we came to a big house set back among trees with a wide, sweeping driveway up to the front door. From the noise issuing from the open windows there was no question but that quite a party was in progress, and I wondered what I was getting myself into. My host, with a great shout, dragged me into the room, and we had quite a hand-shaking time, and he introduced me to a large group of gay and exuberant people. They were a happy, joyous lot of folk.

I looked around for a bar, but there wasn't any. All that was being served was coffee, fruit juice, ginger ale, sandwiches, and ice-cream, but there was lots of those.

"These people must have stopped somewhere before coming here," I remarked to my friend.

He was shocked, and said: "Stopped somewhere? Why, you don't understand. These people have got the spirit all right, but not the kind of 'spirit' you are thinking about. I am surprised at you," he said. "Don't you realise what makes this crowd so happy? They have been renewed spiritually. They have got something. They have been set free from themselves. They have found God as a living, vital, honest-to-goodness reality. Yes," he said, "they have got spirit all right, but it isn't that kind that you get out of a bottle. They have got spirit in their hearts."

Then I saw what he meant. This wasn't a crowd of sad-faced, stodgy people. They were the leaders of that town—business men, lawyers, doctors, teachers, society people, and a lot of simpler folk besides, and they were having a wonderful time at this party—talking about God, and they were doing it in the most natural manner imaginable. They were telling one another about the changes that had occurred in their lives through re-vitalised spiritual power.

Those who have the naïve notion that you can't laugh and be gay when you are religious should have been in on that party.

Well, I went away from that party with a Bible verse running through my mind: "In Him was life; and the life was the light of men." (John i. 4.) That was the light I saw on the faces of those happy people. An inner light was reflected outwardly on their faces, and it came from an effervescent spiritual something that they had taken into themselves. Life means vitality, and these people obviously were getting their vitality from God. They had found the power that creates happiness.

This is no isolated incident. I venture the assertion that in your own community, if you will look around for them, you will find lots of people just like those described above. If you don't find them in your own home town, come to the Marble Collegiate Church in New York

City and you will find them by the score. But you can get the same spirit by reading this book if you practise the simple principles set forth.

As you read this book believe what you read, because it is true; then start working on the practical suggestions the book contains and you, too, will have the spiritual experience that produces this quality of happiness. I know this is so, because many of those to whom I have referred and shall refer in later chapters got their vital new life in the same way. Then, having been changed inwardly, you will begin to create out of yourself not unhappiness, but a happiness of such quality and character that you will wonder if you are living in the same world. As a matter of fact, it won't be the same world because you are not the same, and what you are determines the world in which you live, so as you change, your world changes also.

If happiness is determined by our thoughts it is necessary to drive off the thoughts which make for depression and discouragement. This can be done first by simply determining to do it; second, by utilising an easily employed technique which I suggested to a business man. I met him at a luncheon and have seldom heard such gloom as he got off. His conversation would have been ultra-depressing had I permitted it to affect me. It reeked with pessimism. To hear him talk you would think everything was headed for ruin. Of course the man was tired. Accumulated problems had swamped his mind which was seeking release in retreat from a world which was too much for his depleted energy. His principal trouble was in his depressed thought pattern. He needed an infusion of light and faith.

So rather boldly I said: "If you want to feel better and

stop being miserable, I can give you something that will fix you up."

"What can you do?" he snorted. "Are you a miracle worker?"

"No," I replied, "but I can put you in touch with a miracle worker who will drain off that unhappiness of yours and give you a new slant on life. I mean that," I concluded, as we separated.

Apparently he became curious, for he got in touch with me later and I gave him a little book of mine called *Thought Conditioners*.* It contains forty health- and happiness-producing thoughts. Inasmuch as it is a pocket-sized booklet, I suggested that he carry it for easy consultation and that he drop one of the suggested thoughts in his mind every day for forty days. I further suggested that he commit each thought to memory, thus allowing it to dissolve in consciousness, and that he visualise this healthy thought sending a quieting and healing influence through his mind. I assured him that if he would follow this plan, these healthy thoughts would drive off the diseased thoughts that were sapping his joy, energy and creative ability.

The idea at first impressed him as being a bit queer and he had his doubts, but he followed directions. After about three weeks he called me on the telephone and shouted: "Boy, this sure works! It is wonderful. I have snapped out of it, and I wouldn't have believed it possible."

He remains 'snapped out of it' and is a genuinely happy person. This pleasant condition resulted because he became skilled in the power to create his own

* *Thought Conditioners*, published by Sermon Publications, Inc., Marble Collegiate Church, 1 West 29th Street, New York 1, New York

happiness. He later commented that his first mental hurdle was honestly to face the fact that while his un-happiness made him miserable, yet he was at home in self-pity and self-punishment thoughts. He knew that these sick thoughts were the cause of his trouble, but he shrank from the effort required to want to change sufficiently actually to go about changing. But when he began systematically to insert healthy spiritual thoughts into his mind as directed, he began first to want new life, then to realise the thrilling fact that he could have it, then the even more amazing fact that he was getting it. The result was that after some three weeks of a self-improvement process new happiness 'burst' upon him.

Nearly everywhere in the world today are groups of people who have found the happy way. If we can have even one such group in every city, town, and hamlet in the country, we can change the life of this country within a very short time. And what kind of group do we mean? Let me explain.

I was speaking in a Western city and returned to my hotel room rather late. I wanted to get a little sleep, for I was to be up at five-thirty next morning to catch a plane. As I was preparing for bed, the telephone rang, and a lady said: "There are about fifty of us at my house wait-ing for you."

I explained that I could not come due to the early hour of my departure in the morning.

"Oh," she said, "two men are on their way to get you. We have been praying for you, and we want you to come and pray with us before you leave the city."

I am glad I went, though I had very little sleep that night.

The men who came for me were a couple of alcoholics

who had been healed by the power of faith. They were two of the happiest, most lovable fellows you can imagine.

The home to which they took me was packed. People were sitting on the stairways, on the tables, on the floor. One man was even perched on the grand piano. And what were they doing? They were having a prayer meeting. They told me that sixty such prayer groups were going on in that city all the time.

I was never in such a meeting. They were anything but a stuffy group. They were a released, happy crowd of real people. I found myself strangely moved. The spirit in that room was tremendous in its lifting force. The group would burst into song, and I never heard such singing. The room was filled with a wonderful spirit of laughter.

Then a woman stood up. I saw that she had braces on her legs, and she said: "They told me I would never walk again. Do you want to see me walk?" And she walked up and down the room.

"What did it?" I asked.

"Jesus," she replied simply.

Then another fine-looking girl said: "Did you ever see a victim of the narcotics habit? Well, I was one and I was healed." There she sat, a beautiful, modest, charming young woman, and she, too, said: "Jesus did it."

Then a couple who had drifted apart told me that they had been brought together and they were happier than ever before.

"How did it come about?" I asked. And their reply was: "Jesus did it."

A man said he had been a victim of alcohol, that he had dragged his family down until they were living in abject poverty and he was a complete failure. And now as he stood before me he was a strong, healthy personality. I started to ask how, but he nodded and said: "Jesus did it."

Then they burst into another song, and then someone dimmed the lights and we all held hands around in a great circle. I had a feeling as though I had hold of an electric wire. Power was flowing around that room. Without any question I was the least spiritually developed person in that group. I knew in that moment that Jesus Christ was right there in that house and those people had found Him. They had been touched by His power. He had given them new life. This life bubbled up in an irrepressible effervescence.

This is the secret of happiness. All else is secondary. Get this experience and you've got real, unalloyed happiness, the best the world offers. Don't miss it whatever you do in this life, for this is it.

6 | Stop Fuming and Fretting

MANY PEOPLE MAKE life unnecessarily difficult for themselves by dissipating power and energy through fuming and fretting.

Do you ever 'fume' and 'fret'? Here is a picture of yourself if you do. The word 'fume' means to boil up, to blow off, to emit vapour, to be agitated, to be distraught, to seethe. The word 'fret' is equally descriptive. It is reminiscent of a sick child in the night, a petulant half-cry, half-whine. It ceases, only to begin again. It has an irritating, annoying, penetrating quality. To fret is a childish term, but it describes the emotional reaction of many adults.

The Bible advises us to "Fret not thyself . . ." (Psalm xxxvii. 1.) This is sound advice for the people of our time. We need to stop fuming and fretting and get peaceful if we are to have power to live effectively. And how do we go about doing so?

A first step is to reduce your pace or at least the tempo of your pace. We do not realise how accelerated the rate of our lives has become, or the speed at which we are driving ourselves. Many people are destroying their physical bodies by this pace, but what is even more tragic, they are tearing their minds and souls to shreds as well. It is possible for a person to live a quiet existence physically and yet maintain a high tempo emotionally. Even an invalid can live at too high a pace from that standpoint. The character of our thoughts determines pace. When the mind goes rushing on pell-mell from one feverish attitude to another it becomes feverish and the result is a state bordering on petulance. The pace of modern life must be reduced if we are not to suffer profoundly from its debilitating over-stimulation and super-excitement. This over-stimulation produces toxic poisons in the body and creates emotional illness. It produces fatigue and a sense of frustration so that we fume and fret about every-thing from our personal troubles to the state of the nation and the world. If the effect of this emotional disquiet is so pronounced physically, what must its effect be on that deep inner essence of the personality known as the soul?

It is impossible to have peace of soul if the pace is so feverishly accelerated. God won't go that fast. He will not endeavour to keep up with you. He says in effect: 'Go ahead if you must with this foolish pace and when you are worn out I will offer my healing. But I can make your life so rich if you will slow down now and live and move and have your being in me. God moves imperturbably, slowly, and with perfect organisation. The only wise rate at which to live is God's rate. God gets things done and they are done right and He does them without hurry. He neither fumes nor frets. He is peaceful and therefore efficient. This same peace is offered to us—"Peace I leave with you, my peace I give unto you . . ." (John xiv. 27.)

In a sense this is a pathetic generation, especially in the great cities, because of the effect of nervous tension, synthetic excitement, and noise; but the malady extends into the country districts also, for the air waves transmit tension.

I was amused by an old lady who, in talking about this matter, said: "Life is so daily." That remark certainly spoke volumes about the pressure, responsibilities, and tension of daily life. Its persistent, insistent demand upon us is provocative of pressure.

One wonders whether this generation is not so accustomed to tension that many are in the unhappy state of not being comfortable without it. The deep quietness of woods and valleys so well known to our forefathers is an unaccustomed state to them. The tempo of their lives is such that in many instances they have an incapacity to draw upon the sources of peace and quietness which the physical world offers.

One summer afternoon my wife and I went for a long walk in the woods. We were stopping at the beautiful Lake Mohonk Mountain House which is set in one of the finest natural parks in America, 7,500 acres of virgin mountain-side in the middle of which is a lake lying like a gem in the forest. The word *mohonk* means 'lake in the sky'. Æons ago some giant upheaval of the earth cast up these sheer cliffs. You come out of the deep woods on to some noble promontory and rest your eyes on great valleys set among hills, rock-ribbed and ancient as the sun. These woods, mountains, and valleys constitute what ought to be a sure retreat from every confusion of this world.

On this afternoon as we walked there was a mixture of summer showers and sunlit hours. We were drenched and started to fret about it a bit because it took the press out of our clothes. Then we told each other that it doesn't hurt a human being to get drenched with clean rain water, that the rain feels cool and fresh on one's face, and that you can always sit in the sun and dry yourself out. We walked under the trees and talked and then fell silent.

We were listening, listening deeply to the quietness. In a strict sense, the woods are never still. There is tremendous activity always in process, but nature makes no strident noises, regardless of the vastness of its operation. Nature's sounds are quiet, harmonious.

On this beautiful afternoon, nature was laying its hand of healing quietness upon us, and we could actually feel the tension being drawn off.

Just as we were falling under this spell, the faint sound of what passes for music came to us. It was nervous, high-strung music of the jitterbug variety. Presently through the woods came three young people, two young women and a young man, and the latter was lugging a portable radio.

They were three young city people out for a walk in the woods and tragically enough were bringing their noise along with them. They were nice young folk, too, for they stopped and we had a pleasant talk with them. It occurred to me to ask them to turn that thing off and listen to the music of the woods, but I didn't feel it was my business to instruct them, and finally they went on their way.

We commented on the loss they were incurring, that they could pass through this peacefulness and not give ear to the music that is as old as the world, harmony and melody the like of which man has never equalled: the song of the wind through the trees, the sweet notes of birds singing their hearts out, the whole background of the music of the spheres.

This is still to be found in the country, in our woods and

great plains, in our valleys, in our mountain majesties, where the ocean foams on soft shores of sand. We should avail ourselves of its healing. Remember the words of Jesus: "Come ye yourselves apart into a desert place, and rest awhile." (Mark vi. 31.) Even as I write these words and give you this good advice, I recall instances where it has been necessary to remind myself to practise the same truth, which emphasises that we must everlastingly discipline ourselves to quietness if we expect its benefits in our lives.

One autumn day Mrs. Peale and I took a trip into Massachusetts to see our son John at Deerfield Academy. We told him we would arrive at 11 a.m., and we pride ourselves on the good old-fashioned custom of promptness. Therefore, being a bit behind schedule, we were driving at breakneck speed through the autumnal landscape. My wife said: "Norman, did you see that radiant hillside?"

"What hillside?" I asked.

"It just went by on the other side," she explained. "Look at that beautiful tree."

"What tree?" I was already a mile past it.

"This is one of the most glorious days I have ever seen," my wife said. "How could you possibly imagine such amazing colours as these New England hillsides in October? In fact," she said, "it makes me happy inside."

That remark of hers so impressed me that I stopped the car and went back a quarter of a mile to a lake backed by towering hills dressed in autumn colours. We sat and looked and meditated. God with His genius and skill had painted that scene in the varied colours which He alone can mix. In the still waters of the lake lay a reflected vision of His glory, for the hillside was unforgettably pictured in that mirror-like pond.

For quite a while we sat without a word until finally my wife broke the silence by the only appropriate statement that one could make: "He leadeth me beside the still waters." (Psalm xxiii. 2.) We arrived at Deerfield at 11 a.m. but we were not tired. In fact, we were deeply refreshed.

To help reduce this tension which seems to dominate our people everywhere, you can start by reducing your own pace. To do that you will need to slow down, quiet down. Do not fume. Do not fret. Practise being peaceful. Practise ". . . the peace of God which passeth all understanding." (Philippians iv. 7.) Then note the quiet power sense that wells up within you.

A friend of mine who was compelled to take an enforced rest as a result of 'pressure' wrote me: 'Many lessons have been learned during this enforced retreat. Now I know better than before that in the quiet we become aware of His presence. Life can get muddled. But "muddied water", says Lao-tse, "let stand, will become clear".'

A physician gave some rather whimsical advice to a patient, an aggressive, go-getter type of business man. Excitedly he told the doctor what an enormous amount of work he had to do and that he had to get it done right away, quick, or else.

"I take my brief-case home every night and it's packed with work," he said with nervous inflexion.

"Why do you take work home with you at night?" the doctor asked quietly.

"I have to get it done," he fumed.

"Cannot someone else do it, or help you with it?" asked the doctor.

"No," the man snapped. "I am the only one who can do it. It must be done just right, and I alone can do it as it must be done, and it has to be done quickly. Everything depends upon me."

"If I write you a prescription, will you follow it?" asked the doctor.

This, believe it or not, was the prescription. His patient was to take two hours off every working day and go for a long walk. Then he was to take a half-day off a week and spend that half-day in a cemetery.

In astonishment the patient demanded: "Why should I spend that half-day in a cemetery?"

"Because," answered the doctor, "I want you to wander around and look at the gravestones of men who are there permanently. I want you to meditate on the fact that many of them are there because they thought even as you do, that the whole world rested on their shoulders. Meditate on the solemn fact that when you get there permanently the world will go on just the same and, as important as you are, others will be able to do the work you are now doing. I suggest that you sit on one of those tombstones and repeat this statement: '. . . a thousand years in Thy sight are but as yesterday when it is past, and as a watch in the night'." (Psalm xc. 4.)

The patient got the idea. He slowed his pace. He learned to delegate authority. He achieved a proper sense of his own importance. He stopped fuming and fretting. He got peaceful. And, it might be added, he does better work. He is developing a more competent organisation and he admits that his business is in better condition.

A prominent manufacturer was afflicted with tension, in fact, he was in a very high-strung frame of mind. As he himself described it: 'he leapt out of bed every morning and immediately got himself into high gear. He was in such a rush and dither that he "made his breakfast on soft-boiled eggs because they slid down fast".' This hectic pace left him fagged and worn at about midday. He sank into bed every night exhausted.

It so happens that his home is situated in a grove of trees. Very early one morning, unable to sleep, he rose and sat by the window. He became interested in watching a bird emerge from his night's sleep. He noticed that a bird sleeps with his head under his wing, the feathers pulled all around himself. When he awakened, he pulled his bill out from under his feathers, took a sleepy look around, stretched one leg to its full length, meanwhile stretching the wing over the leg until it spread out like a fan. He pulled the leg and wing back and then repeated the same process with the other leg and wing, whereupon he put his head down in his feathers again for a delicious little cat nap (only in this case a bird nap), then the head came out again. This time the bird looked around eagerly, threw his head back, gave his wings and legs two more big stretches, then he sent up a song, a thrilling, melodic song of praise to the day, wherewith he hopped down off the limb, got himself a drink of cold water, and started looking for food.

My high-strung friend said to himself: "If that's the way the birds get up, sort of slow and easy like, why wouldn't it be a good method for me to start the day that way?" He actually went through the same performance, even to singing, and noticed that the song was an especially beneficial factor, that it was a releasing mechanism.

"I can't sing," he chuckled, "but I practised sitting quietly in a chair and singing. Mostly I sang hymns and happy songs. Imagine me singing, but I did. My wife thought I was bereft of my senses. The only thing I had on the bird was that I did a little praying, too, then, like the bird, I felt like some food, and I wanted a good breakfast—bacon and eggs. And I took my time eating it. After that I went to work in a released frame of mind. It surely did start me off for the day minus the tension, and it helped me go through the day in a peaceful and relaxed manner."

A former member of a championship university crew told me that their shrewd crew coach often reminded them: "To win this or any race, row slowly." He pointed out that rapid rowing tends to break the stroke and when the stroke is broken it is with the greatest difficulty that a crew recovers the rhythm necessary to win. Meanwhile other crews pass the disorganised group. It is indeed wise advice—'To go fast, row slowly.'

In order to row slowly or to work slowly and maintain the steady pace that wins, the victim of high tempo will do well to get the co-ordinating peace of God into his mind, his soul, and, it might be added, into his nerves and muscles also.

Have you ever considered the importance of having the peace of God in your muscles, in your joints? Perhaps your joints will not pain so much when they have the peace of God in them. Your mucles will work with correlation when the peace of God who created them governs their action. Speak to your muscles every day and to your joints and to your nerves, saying: "Fret not thyself." (Psalm xxxvii. 1.) Relax on a couch or bed, think of each important muscle from head to feet, and say to each: "The peace of God is touching you." Then practise 'feeling' that peace throughout your entire body. In due course your muscles and joints will take heed.

Slow down, for whatever you really want will be there when you get there if you work towards it without stress, without pressing. If, proceeding under God's guidance and in His smooth and unhurried tempo, it is not there, then it was not supposed to be there. If you miss it, perhaps you should have missed it. So definitely seek to develop a normal, natural, God-ordered pace. Practise and preserve mental quiet. Learn the art of letting go all nervous excitement. To do this, stop at intervals and affirm: 'I now relinquish nervous excitement—it is flowing from me. I am at peace.' Do not fume. Do not fret. Practise being peaceful.

To attain this efficient state of living, I recommend the practise of thinking peaceful thoughts. Every day we perform a series of acts designed to care for the body properly. We bathe, brush the teeth, take exercise. In similar fashion we should give time and planned effort to keeping the mind in a healthy state. One way to do this is to sit quietly and pass a series of peaceful thoughts through the mind. For example, pass through the thoughts the memory of a lofty mountain, a misty valley, a sun-speckled trout stream, silver moonlight on water.

At least once in every twenty-four hours, preferably in the busiest part of the day, deliberately stop whatever you are doing for ten or fifteen minutes and practise serenity.

There are times when it is essential resolutely to check our headlong pace, and it must be emphasised that the only way to stop is to stop.

I went to a certain city on a lecture date and was met at

the train by a committee. I was rushed to a book-store where I had an autographing party and then to another book-store where another autographing party was held. Then they rushed me to a luncheon. After rushing through the luncheon I was rushed to a meeting. After the meeting I was rushed back to the hotel where I changed my clothes and was rushed to a reception where I met several hundred people and drank three glasses of fruit punch. Then I was rushed back to the hotel and told I had twenty minutes to dress for dinner. When I was getting dressed the telephone rang and somebody said: "Hurry, hurry, we must rush down to dinner."

Excitedly I chattered: "I will rush right down."

I rushed from the room and was so excited that I could scarcely get the key into the lock. Hastily I felt myself, to be sure that I was completely dressed, and rushed towards the elevator. All of a sudden I stopped. I was out of breath. I asked myself: "What is this all about? What is the meaning of this ceaseless rush? This is ridiculous!"

Then I declared independence, and said: "I do not care if I go to dinner. I do not care whether I make a talk. I do not have to go to this dinner and I do not have to make a speech." So deliberately and slowly I walked back to my room and took my time about unlocking the door. I telephoned the man downstairs and said: "If you want to eat, go ahead. If you want to save a place for me, I will be down after a while, but I am not going to rush any more."

So I removed my coat, sat down, took off my shoes, put my feet up on the table, and just sat. Then I opened the Bible and very slowly read aloud the 121st Psalm: "I will lift up mine eyes unto the hills from whence cometh my help." I closed the book and had a little talk with myself, saying: "Come on now, start living a slower and more relaxed life," and then I affirmed: "God is here and His peace is touching me.

"I do not need anything to eat," I reasoned. "I eat too much anyway. Besides, the dinner will probably not be very good, and if I am quiet now I will give a better speech at eight o'clock."

So I sat there resting and praying for fifteen minutes. I shall never forget the sense of peace and personal mastery I had when I walked out of that room. I had the glorious feeling of having overcome something, of having taken control of myself emotionally, and when I reached the dining-room the others had just finished the first course. All I had missed was the soup, which by general consent was no great loss.

This incident was an amazing experience of the healing presence of God. I gained these values by simply stopping, by quietly reading the Bible, by sincerely praying, and by thinking some peaceful thoughts for a few moments.

Physicians generally seem to feel that much physical trouble could be avoided or overcome by practising the philosophy of not fuming or fretting.

A prominent citizen of New York told me that his doctor suggested that he come to our clinic at the church "because," said the physician, "you need to develop a calm philosophy of living. Your power resources are played out."

"My doctor says I am pushing myself to the limit. He tells me I'm too tense, too high-strung, that I fume and fret too much, and," he concluded, "my doctor declares the only sure cure is for me to develop what he calls a calm philosophy of living."

My visitor arose and paced the floor, then demanded: "But how in the world can I do that? It's a lot easier said than done."

Then this excited gentleman went on to say that his doctor had given him certain suggestions for developing this calm philosophy of living. The suggestions as outlined were indeed wise. "But then," he explained, "the doctor suggested that I see you people here at the church, for he feels that if I learn to use religious faith in a practical manner it will give me peace of mind and bring down my blood pressure. Then I will feel better physically. While I realise the doctor's prescription is sensible," he complained, "how can a man of fifty years old, of a high-strung nature such as mine, suddenly change the habits of a lifetime and develop this so-called calm philosophy of living?"

That did indeed seem to be a problem, for he was a bundle of excitable and explosive nerves. He paced the floor, he thumped the table, his voice was high-pitched. He gave the impression of a thoroughly disturbed and baffled man. Obviously he was showing up at his worst, but he was clearly revealing the inner state of his personality, and the insight thus gained gave us a chance to help him through understanding him better.

As I listened to his words and observed his attitude, I again understood why Jesus Christ retains his remarkable hold on men. It is because He has the answer to such problems as this, and I proved that fact by suddenly changing the line of the conversation. Without any introductory words I began to recite certain Bible texts such as: "Come unto me, all that labour and are heavy laden, and I will give you rest." (Matthew xi. 28.) And again: "Peace I leave with you, my peace I give unto you: not as the world giveth, give I unto you. Let not your heart be troubled, neither let it be afraid." (John xiv. 27.) And still again: "Thou wilt keep him in perfect peace, whose mind is stayed on thee." (Isaiah xxvi. 3.)

I recited these words slowly, deliberately, reflectively. As this reciting went on, I noticed that my visitor stopped being agitated. Quietness came over him and then we both sat in silence. It seemed that we sat so for several minutes. Perhaps it wasn't that long, but finally he took a deep breath.

"Why, that's funny," he said. "I feel a lot better. Isn't that queer? I guess it was those words that did it."

"No, not the words alone," I answered, "though they do have a remarkable effect upon the mind, but something deeper happened just then. He touched you a minute ago—the Physician with the healing touch. He was present in this room."

My visitor evinced no surprise at this assertion, but eagerly and impetuously agreed—and conviction was written on his face. "That's right, He sure was. I felt Him. I see what you mean. Now I understand—Jesus Christ will help me develop a calm philosophy of living."

This man found what increasing thousands are presently discovering, that a simple faith in and practice of the principles and techniques of Christianity bring peace and quietness and therefore new power to body, mind, and spirit. It is the perfect antidote to fuming and to fretting. It helps a person to become peaceful and thus to tap new resources of strength.

Of course it was necessary to teach this man a new pattern of thinking and acting. This was done in part by suggesting literature written by experts in the field of spiritual culture. For example, we gave him lessons in the skill of church-going. We showed him how to make church worship a therapy. He was instructed in the scientific use of prayer and relaxation. And as a result of this practice eventually became a healthy man. Anyone willing to follow this programme and sincerely put these principles into day-by-day practice can, I believe, develop inner peace and power. Many of these techniques are outlined in this book.

In attaining emotional control the daily practice of healing techniques is of first importance. Emotional control cannot be gained in any magical or easy way. You cannot develop it by merely reading a book, although that is often helpful. The only sure method is by working at it regularly, persistently, scientifically, and by developing creative faith.

I suggest that you begin with such a primary procedure as simply the practice of keeping physically still. Don't pace the floor. Don't wring your hands. Don't pound or shout or argue or walk up and down. Don't let yourself get worked up into a dither. In excitement one's physical movements become accentuated. Therefore begin at the simplest place, that is by ceasing physical movement. Stand still, sit down, lie down. Certainly keep the voice down to a low pitch.

In developing a calm control it is necessary to think calmness, for the body responds sensitively to the type of thoughts that pass through the mind. It is also true that the mind can be quieted by first making the body quiet. That is to say, a physical attitude can induce desired mental attitudes.

In a speech I related the following incident which occurred in a committee meeting I attended. A gentleman who heard me tell this story was greatly impressed by it and took its truth to heart. He tried the technique suggested and reports that it has been very effective in controlling his fuming and fretting.

I was in a meeting where a discussion was going on which finally became rather bitter. Tempers were becoming frayed and some of the participants were decidedly on edge. Sharp remarks were passed. Suddenly one man arose, deliberately took off his coat, opened his collar, and lay down upon a couch. All were astonished, and someone asked if he felt ill.

"No," he said, "I feel fine, but I am beginning to get mad, and I have learned that it is difficult to get mad lying down."

We all laughed, and the tension was broken. Then our whimsical friend went on to explain that he had 'tried a little trick' with himself. He had a quick temper, and when he felt himself getting mad he found that he was clenching his fist and raising his voice, so he deliberately extended his fingers, not allowing them to form into a fist. In proportion to the rising of his tension or anger, he depressed his voice and talked in exaggerated low tones. "You cannot carry on an argument in a whisper," he said with a grin.

This principle can be effective in controlling emotional excitements, fretting, and tension, as many have discovered by experimentation. A beginning step, therefore, in achieving calmness is to discipline your physical reactions. You will be surprised at how quickly this can reduce the heat of your emotions, and when emotional heat is driven off, fuming and fretting subside. You will be amazed at the energy and power you will save. You will be much less tired.

It is, moreover, a good procedure to practise being

phlegmatic or apathetic, even indifferent. To a certain extent even practise being sluggish. People thus constituted are less likely to emotional breaks. Highly organised individuals may do well to cultivate these reactions to a degree at least.

Naturally one does not want to lose the keen, sensitive responsiveness characteristic of the highly organised individual. But the practice of being phlegmatic tends to bring such a keyed-up personality to a balanced emotional position.

Following is a technique consisting of six points which I have personally found of great helpfulness in reducing the tendency to fume and fret. I have suggested its use to countless people who practise it and find it of great value:

1. Sit relaxed in a chair. Completely yield yourself to the chair. Starting with your toes and proceeding to the top of your head, conceive of every portion of the body as relaxing. Affirm relaxation by saying: "My toes are relaxed—my fingers—my facial muscles."

2. Think of your mind as the surface of a lake in a storm, tossed by waves and in tumult. But now the waves subside, and the surface of the lake is placid and unruffled.

3. Spend two or three minutes thinking of the most beautiful and peaceful scenes you have ever beheld, as, for example, a mountain at sunset, or a deep valley filled with the hush of early morning, or a wood at noonday, or moonlight upon rippling waters. In memory relive these scenes.

4. Repeat slowly, quietly, bringing out the melody in each, a series of words which express quietness and peace, as, for example: (a) tranquillity (say it very deliberately and in a tranquil manner); (b) serenity;

(c) quietness. Think of other such words and repeat them.

5. Make a mental list of times in your life when you have been conscious of God's watchful care and recall how, when you were worried and anxious, He brought things out right and took care of you. Then recite aloud this line from an old hymn: 'So long Thy power hath kept me, sure it STILL will lead me on.'

6. Repeat the following, which has an amazing power to relax and quiet the mind: "Thou wilt keep him in perfect peace, whose mind is stayed on thee." (Isaiah xxvi. 3.) Repeat this several times during the day, whenever you have a fraction of a moment. Repeat it aloud if possible, so that by the end of the day you will have said it many times. Conceive of these words as active, vital substances permeating your mind, sending into every area of your thinking a healing balm. This is the best-known medicine for taking tension from the mind.

As you work with the techniques suggested in this chapter, the tendency to fume and fret will gradually be modified. In direct proportion to your progress the power heretofore drawn off by this unhappy habit will be felt in your increased ability to meet life's responsibilities.

7 | Expect the Best and Get It

"Why does my boy fail in every job he gets?" asked a puzzled father about his thirty-year-old son.

It was indeed difficult to understand the failure of this young man, for seemingly he had everything. Of good family, his educational and business opportunities were beyond the average. Nevertheless, he had a tragic flair for failure. Everything he touched went wrong. He tried hard enough, yet somehow he missed success. Presently he found an answer, a curiously simple but potent answer. After practising this new-found secret for a while he lost the flair for failure and acquired the touch of success. His personality began to focus, his powers to fuse.

Not long ago at a luncheon I could not help admiring the dynamic man at the height of his power. "You amaze me," I commented. "A few years ago you were failing at everything. Now you have worked up an original idea into a fine business. You are a leader in your community. Please explain this remarkable change in you."

"Really it was quite simple," he replied. "I merely learned the magic of believing. I discovered that if you expect the worst you will get the worst and if you expect the best you will get the best. It all happened through actually practising a verse from the Bible."

114

"And what is that verse?"

" 'If thou canst believe, all things are possible to him that believeth.' (Mark ix. 23.) I was brought up in a religious home," he explained, "and heard that verse many times, but it never had any effect upon me. One day in your church I heard you emphasise those words in a talk. In a flash of insight I realised that the key I had missed was that my mind was not trained to believe, to think positively, to have faith in either God or myself. I followed your suggestion of putting myself in God's hands and practised your outlined techniques of faith. I trained myself to think positively about everything. Along with that I try to live right." He smiled and said: "God and I struck up a partnership. When I adopted that policy, things began to change almost at once for me. I got into the habit of expecting the best, not the worst, and that is the way my affairs have turned out lately. I guess it's a kind of miracle, isn't it?" he asked as he concluded his fascinating story.

But it wasn't miraculous at all. Actually what had happened was that he had learned to use one of the most powerful laws in this world, a law recognised alike by psychology and religion, namely, change your mental habits to belief instead of disbelief. Learn to expect, not to doubt. In so doing you bring everything into the realm of possibility.

This does not mean that by believing you are necessarily going to get everything you want or think you want. Perhaps that would not be good for you. When you put your trust in God, He guides your mind so that you do not want things that are not good for you or that are inharmonious with God's will. But it does definitely mean that when you learn to believe, then that which has seemingly been impossible moves into the area of the possible. Every great thing at last becomes for you a possibility.

William James, the famous psychologist, said: "Our belief at the beginning of a doubtful undertaking is the one thing (now get that—*is the one thing*) that insures the successful outcome of your venture." To learn to believe is of primary importance. It is the basic factor of succeeding in any undertaking. When you expect the best, you release a magnetic force in your mind which by a law of attraction tends to bring the best to you. But if you expect the worst, you release from your mind the power of repulsion which tends to force the best from you. It is amazing how a sustained expectation of the best sets in motion forces which cause the best to materialise.

An interesting illustration of this fact was described some years ago by Hugh Fullerton, a famous sports writer of a bygone era. As a boy, Hugh Fullerton was my favourite writer of sports stories. One story which I have never forgotten concerned Josh O'Reilly, one-time manager of the San Antonio Club of the Texas league. O'Reilly had a roster of great players, seven of whom had been hitting over three hundred, and everybody thought his team would easily take the championship. But the club fell into a slump and lost seventeen of the first twenty games. The players simply couldn't hit anything, and each began to accuse the other of being a 'jinx' to the team.

Playing the Dallas Club, a rather poor team that year, only one San Antonio player got a hit, and that, strangely enough, was the pitcher. O'Reilly's team was badly beaten that day. In the club-house after the game the players were a disconsolate lot. Josh O'Reilly knew that he had an aggregation of stars and he realised that their trouble was simply that they were thinking wrong. They didn't expect to get a hit. They didn't expect to win. They expected to be defeated. They were thinking not victory but defeat. Their mental pattern was not one of expectation but of doubt. This negative mental process inhibited them, froze their muscles, threw them off their timing, and there was no free flow of easy power through the team.

It so happened that a preacher named Schlater was popular in that neighbourhood at that time. He claimed to be a faith-healer, and apparently was getting some astounding results. Throngs crowded to hear him, and almost everybody had confidence in him. Perhaps the fact that they did believe in his power enabled Schlater to achieve results.

O'Reilly asked each player to lend him his two best bats. Then he asked the members of the team to stay in the club-house until he returned. He put the bats in a wheelbarrow and went off with them. He was gone for an hour. He returned jubilantly to tell the players that Schlater, the preacher, had blessed the bats and that these bats now contained a power that could not be overcome. The players were astounded and delighted.

The next day they overwhelmed Dallas, getting 37 base hits and 20 runs. They hammered their way through the league to a championship, and Hugh Fullerton said that for years in the South-West a player would pay a large sum for a 'Schlater bat'.

Regardless of Schlater's personal power, the fact remains that something tremendous happened in the minds of those ball-players. Their thought pattern was changed. They began thinking in terms of expectation, not doubt. They expected not the worst, but the best. They expected hits, runs, victories, and they got them. They had the power to get what they wanted. There was no difference in the bats themselves, I am quite sure of that, but there was certainly a difference in the minds of the men who used them. Now they knew they could make hits. Now they knew they could get runs. Now they knew they could win. A new thought pattern changed the minds of those men so that the creative power of faith could operate.

Perhaps you have not been doing so well in the game of life. Perhaps you stand up to bat and cannot make a hit, You strike out time and again and your batting average is lamentably low. Let me give you a suggestion. I guarantee that it will work. The basis for my assurance is the fact that thousands of people have been trying it with very great results. Things will be very different for you if you give this method a real trial.

Start reading the New Testament and notice the number of times it refers to faith. Select a dozen of the strongest statements about faith, the ones that you like the best. Then memorise each one. Let these faith concepts drop into your conscious mind. Say them over and over again, especially just before going to sleep at night. By a process of spiritual osmosis they will sink from your conscious into your subconscious mind and in time will modify and reslant your basic thought pattern. This process will change you into a believer, into an expecter, and when you become such, you will in due course become an achiever. You will have new power to get what God and you decide you really want from life.

The most powerful force in human nature is the

spiritual-power technique taught in the Bible. Very astutely the Bible emphasises the method by which a person can make something of himself, when it refers to "The shield of faith, wherewith ye shall be able to quench all the fiery darts of the wicked." (Ephesians vi. 16.) Faith, belief, positive thinking, faith in God, faith in other people, faith in yourself, faith in life. This is the essence of the technique that it teaches. "If thou canst believe," it says, "all things are possible to him that believeth." (Mark ix. 23.) "If ye have faith . . . nothing shall be impossible unto you." (Matthew xvii. 21.) "According to your faith be it unto you." (Matthew ix. 29.) Believe—believe—so it drives home the truth that faith moves mountains.

Some sceptical person who has never learned this powerful law of the effect of right thinking may doubt my assertions regarding the amazing results which happen when this technique is employed.

Things become better when you expect the best instead of the worst, for the reason that being freed from self-doubt, you can put your whole self into your endeavour, and nothing can stand in the way of the man who focuses his entire self on a problem. When you approach a difficulty as a personal unity, the difficulty, which itself is a demonstration of disunity, tends to deteriorate.

When the entire concentration of all your force—physical, emotional, and spiritual—is brought to bear, the consolidation of these powers properly employed is quite irresistible.

Expecting the best means that you put your whole heart (i.e., the central essence of your personality) into what you want to accomplish. People are defeated in life not because of lack of ability, but for lack of whole-heartedness. They do not whole-heartedly expect to succeed. Their heart isn't in it, which is to say they themselves are not fully given. Results do not yield themselves to the person who refuses to give himself to the desired results.

A major key to success in this life, at attaining that which you deeply desire, is to be completely released and throw all there is of yourself into your job or any project in which you are engaged. In other words, whatever you are doing, give it all you've got. Give every bit of yourself. Hold nothing back. Life cannot deny itself to the person who gives life his all. But most people, unfortunately, don't do that. In fact, very few people do, and this is a tragic cause of failure, or, if not failure, it is the reason we only half attain.

A famous Canadian athletic coach, Ace Percival, says that most people, athletes as well as non-athletes, are 'hold-outs', that is to say, they are always keeping something in reserve. They do not invest themselves 100 per cent in competition. Because of that fact they never achieve the highest of which they are capable.

Red Barber, famous baseball announcer, told me that he had known few athletes who completely give themselves.

Don't be a 'hold-out'. Go all out. Do this, and life will not hold out on you.

A famous trapeze artiste was instructing his students how to perform on the high trapeze bar. Finally, having given full explanations and instruction in this skill, he told them to demonstrate their ability.

One student, looking up at the insecure perch from which he must perform, was suddenly filled with fear.

He froze completely. He had a terrifying vision of himself falling to the ground. He couldn't move a muscle, so deep was his fright. "I can't do it! I can't do it!" he gasped.

The instructor put his arm around the boy's shoulder and said: "Son, you can do it, and I will tell you how." Then he made a statement which is of inestimable importance. It is one of the wisest remarks I have ever heard. He said: "Throw your heart over the bar and your body will follow."

Copy that one sentence. Write it on a card and put it in your pocket. Place it under the glass on your desk top. Tack it up on your wall. Stick it in your shaving-mirror. Better still, write it on your mind, you who really want to do something with life. It's packed with power, that sentence. 'Throw your heart over the bar and your body will follow.'

Heart is the symbol of creative activity. Fire the heart with where you want to go and what you want to be. Get it so deeply fixed in your unconscious that you will not take no for an answer, then your entire personality will follow where your heart leads. 'Throw your heart over the bar' means to throw your faith over your difficulty, throw your affirmation over every barrier, throw your visualisation over your obstacles. In other words, throw the spiritual essence of you over the bar and your material self will follow in the victory groove thus pioneered by your faith-inspired mind. Expect the best, not the worst, and you will attain your heart's desire. It is what is in the heart of you, either good or bad, strong or weak, that finally comes to you. Emerson said: "Beware of what you want for you will get it."

That this philosophy is of practical value is illustrated

by the experience of a young woman whom I interviewed a number of years ago. She made an appointment to see me in my office at two o'clock on a certain afternoon. Being quite busy that day, I had got a little behind schedule, and it was about five minutes after two when I walked into the conference-room where she was waiting. It was obvious that she was displeased, for her lips were pressed firmly together.

"It's five minutes after two, and we had an appointment at 2 p.m.," she said. "I always admire promptness."

"So do I. I always believe in being prompt, and I hope you will forgive me for my unavoidable delay," I said with a smile.

But she was not in a smiling mood, for she said crisply: "I have a very important problem to present to you and I want an answer, and I expect an answer." Then she shot out at me: "I might as well put it to you bluntly. I want to get married."

"Well," I replied, "that is a perfectly normal desire, and I should like to help you."

"I want to know why I can't get married," she continued. "Every time I form a friendship with a man, the next thing I know he fades out of the picture and another chance is gone by, and," she added, speaking frankly, "I am not getting any younger. You conduct a personal-problem clinic to study people and you have had some experience, and I am putting my problem right up to you. Tell me, why can't I get married?"

I studied her to see if she was the kind of person to whom one could speak frankly, for certain things had to be said if she really meant business. Finally I decided that she was of big enough calibre to take the medicine that would be required if she was to correct her personality difficulties, so I said: "Well, now, let's analyse the situation. Obviously you have a good mind and a fine personality, and, if I may say so, you are a very handsome lady."

All of these things were true. I congratulated her in every way that I honestly could, but then I said: "I think that I see your difficulty, and it is this. You took me to task because I was five ·minutes late for our appointment. You were really quite severe with me. Has it ever occurred to you that your attitude represents a pretty serious fault? I think a husband would have a very difficult time if you checked him up that closely all the time. In fact, you would so dominate him that, even if you did marry, your marital life would be unsatisfactory. Love cannot live under domination."

Then I said: "You have a very firm way of pressing your lips together, which indicates a domineering attitude. The average male, I might as well tell you, does not like to be dominated, at least so that he knows it." Then I added: "I think you would be a very attractive person if you got those too-firm lines out of your face. You must have a little softness, a little tenderness, and those lines are too firm to be soft." Then I observed her dress, which was obviously quite expensive, but she didn't wear it very well, and so I said: "This may be a bit out of my line, and I hope you won't mind, but perhaps you could get that dress to hang a little better." I know my description was awkward, but she was a good sport about it and laughed right out loud.

She said: "You certainly don't use style phraseology, but I get the idea."

Then I suggested: "Perhaps it might help to get your

hair fixed up a little. It's a little—floaty. Then you might also add a little sweet-smelling perfume—just a whiff of it. But the really important thing is to get a new attitude that will change the lines on your face and give you that indefinable quality known as spiritual joy. This I am certain will release charm and loveliness in you."

"Well," she burst out, "never did I expect to get this combination of advice in a minister's office."

"No," I chuckled, "I suppose not, but nowadays we have to cover the whole field in a human problem."

Then I told her about an old professor of mine at Ohio Wesleyan University, 'Rolly' Walker, who said: "God runs a beauty parlour." He explained that some girls when they came to college were very pretty, but when they came back to visit the campus thirty years later their beauty had faded. The moonlight-and-roses loveliness of their youth did not last. On the other hand, other girls came to college who were very plain, but when they returned thirty years later they were beautiful women. "What made the difference?" he asked. "The latter had the beauty of an inner spiritual life written on their faces," and then he added: "God runs a beauty parlour."

Well, this young lady thought about what I told her for a few minutes, and then she said: "There's a lot of truth in what you say. I'll try it."

Here is where her strong personality proved effective, for she did try it.

A number of years went by and I had forgotten her. Then in a certain city, after making a speech, a very lovely-looking lady with a fine-looking man and a little boy about ten years of age came up to me. The lady asked smilingly: "Well, how do you think it hangs?"

"How do I think what hangs?" I asked, puzzled.

"My dress," she said. "Do you think it hangs right?"

Bewildered, I said: "Yes, I think it hangs all right, but just why do you ask?"

"Don't you know me?" she asked.

"I see a great many people in my life," I said.

"Frankly, no, I don't think I have ever seen you before."

Then she reminded me of our talk of years ago which I have described.

"Meet my husband and my little boy. What you told me was absolutely true," she said very earnestly. "I was the most frustrated, unhappy individual imaginable when I came to see you, but I put into practice the principles you suggested. I really did, and they worked."

Her husband then spoke up and said: "There was never a sweeter person in the world than Mary here," and I must say that she looked the part. She had evidently visited 'God's beauty parlour'.

Not only did she experience a softening and mellowing of her inner spirit, but she properly used a great quality which she possessed, namely, the driving force to get what she wanted. This led her to the point where she was willing to change herself so that her dreams could be realised. She had that quality of mind whereby she took herself in hand, she applied the spiritual techniques, and she had a profound and yet simple faith that what her heart told her she wanted could be obtained by the proper creative and positive procedures.

So the formula is to know what you want, test it to see if it is a right thing, change yourself in such a manner that it will naturally come to you, and always have faith. With the creative force of belief you stimulate that particular gathering together of circumstances which brings your cherished wish to pass.

Students of modern dynamic thought are realising more and more the practical value of the ideas and teachings of Jesus, especially such truths as the dictum: "According to your faith, be it unto you." (Matthew ix. 29.) According to your faith in yourself, according to your faith in your job, according to your faith in God this far will you get and no farther. If you believe in your job and in yourself and in the opportunities of your country, and if you believe in God and will work hard and study and put yourself into it—in other words, if you 'throw your heart over the bar', you can swing up to any high place to which you want to take your life and your service and your achievement. Whenever you have a bar, that is to say a barrier, in front of you, stop, close your eyes, visualise everything that is above the bar and nothing that is below it, then imaginatively 'throw your heart' over the bar and see yourself as being given lifting power to rise above it. Believe that you are experiencing this up-thrust of force. You will be amazed at the lifting force you will receive. If in the depth of your mind you visualise the best and employ the powers of faith and energy, you will get the best.

Naturally in this process of achieving the best it is important to know where you want to go in life. You can reach your goal, your best dreams can come true, you can get where you want to go only if you know what your goal is. Your expectation must have a clearly defined objective. Lots of people get nowhere simply because they do not know where they want to go. They have no clear-cut, precisely defined purpose. You cannot expect the best if you think aimlessly.

A young man of twenty-six consulted me because he was dissatisfied with his job. He was ambitious to fill a bigger niche in life and wanted to know how to improve his circumstances. His motive seemed unselfish and entirely worth while.

"Well, where do you want to go?" I asked.

"I just don't know exactly," he said hesitantly. "I have never given it any thought. I only know I want to go somewhere other than where I am."

"What can you do best?" I then asked. "What are your strong points?"

"I don't know," he responded. "I never thought that over either."

"But what would you like to do if you had your choice? What do you really want to do?" I insisted.

"I just can't say," he replied dully. "I don't really know what I would like to do. I never thought it over. Guess I ought to figure that one out too."

"Now, look here," I said, "you want to go somewhere from where you are, but you don't know where you want to go. You don't know what you can do or what you would like to do. You will have to get your ideas organised before you can expect to start getting anywhere."

That is the failure point with many people. They never get anywhere because they have only a hazy idea where they want to go, what they want to do. No objective leads to no end.

We made a thorough analysis, testing this young man's capabilities, and found some assets of personality he did not know he possessed. But it was necessary to supply a dynamic to move him forward, so we taught him the techniques of practical faith. Today he is on the way to achievement.

Now he knows where he wants to go and how to get there. He knows what the best is and he expects to attain it, and he will—nothing can stop him.

I asked an outstanding newspaper editor, an inspiring personality: "How did you get to be the editor of this important paper?"

"I wanted to be," he replied simply.

"Is that all there is to it?" I asked. "You wanted to be, and so there you are."

"Well, that may not be all of it, but that was a large part of the process," he explained. "I believe that if you want to get somewhere, you must decide definitely where you want to be or what you want to accomplish. Be sure it is a right objective, then photograph this objective on your mind and hold it there. Work hard, believe in it, and the thought will become so powerful that it will tend to assure success. There is a deep tendency," he declared, "to become what your mind pictures, provided you hold the mental picture strongly enough and if the objective is sound."

So saying, the editor pulled a well-worn card from his wallet and said: "I repeat this quotation every day of my life. It has become my dominating thought."

I copied it and am giving it to you: 'A man who is self-reliant, positive, optimistic, and undertakes his work with the assurance of success magnetises his condition. He draws to himself the creative powers of the universe.'

It is indeed a fact that the person who thinks with positive self-reliance and optimism does magnetise his condition and releases power to attain his goal. So expect the best at all times. Never think of the worst.

Drop it out of your thought, relegate it. Let there be no thought in your mind that the worst will happen. Avoid entertaining the concept of the worst, for whatever you take into your mind can grow there. Therefore take the best into your mind, and only that. Nuture it, concentrate on it, emphasise it, visualise it, prayerise it, surround it with faith. Make it your obsession. Expect the best, and spiritually creative mind-power aided by God power will produce the best.

It may be that as you read this book you are down to what you think is the worst, and you may remark that no amount of thinking will affect your situation. The answer to that objection is that it simply isn't so. Even if you may be down to the worst, the best is potentially within you. You have only to find it, release it, and rise up with it. This requires courage and character, to be sure, but the main requirement is faith. Cultivate faith and you will have the necessary courage and character.

A woman was compelled by adversity to go into sales work, a type of activity for which she had no training. She undertook to demonstrate vacuum-cleaners from house to house. She took a negative attitude towards herself and her work. She 'just didn't believe she could do this job'. She 'knew' she was going to fail. She feared to approach a house, even though she came for a requested demonstration. She believed that she could not make the sale. As a result, as is not surprising, she failed in a high percentage of her interviews.

One day she chanced to call upon a woman who evinced consideration beyond the average. To this customer the saleswoman poured out her tale of defeat and powerlessness. The other woman listened patiently, then said quietly: "If you expect failure, you will get failure, but if you expect to succeed, I am sure you will succeed." And she added: "I will give you a formula which I believe will help you. It will re-style your thinking, give you new confidence, and help you to accomplish your goals. Repeat this formula before every call. Believe in it and then marvel at what it will do for you. This is it. 'If God be for us, who can be against us?' (Romans viii. 31.) But change it by personalising it so that you say: 'If God be for *me*, who can be against *me*? If God be for me, then I know that with God's help I can sell vacuum-cleaners.' God realises that you want security and support for your little children and yourself, and by practising the method I suggest you will be given power to get what you want."

She learned to utilise this formula. She approached each house expecting to make a sale, affirming and picturising positive, not negative, results. As the saleswoman employed this principle she presently acquired new courage, new faith, and deeper confidence in her own ability. Now she declares: "God helps me sell vacuum-cleaners," and who can dispute it?

It is a well-defined and authentic principle that what the mind profoundly expects it tends to receive. Perhaps this is true because what you really expect is what you actually want. Unless you really want something sufficiently to create an atmosphere of positive factors by your dynamic desire, it is likely to elude you. 'If with all your heart'—that is the secret. 'If with all your heart,' that is to say, if with the full complement of your personality, you reach out creatively towards your heart's desire, your reach will not be in vain.

Let me give you four words as a formulation of a great law—*faith power works wonders*. Those four words are packed with dynamic and creative force. Hold them in your conscious mind. Let them sink into the unconscious and they can help you to overcome any difficulty. Hold them in your thoughts, say them over and over again. Say them until your mind accepts them, until you believe them—*faith power works wonders*.

I have no doubt about the effectiveness of this concept, for I have seen it work so often that my enthusiasm for faith power is absolutely boundless.

You can overcome any obstacle. You can achieve the most tremendous things by faith power. And how do you develop faith power? The answer is: to saturate your mind with the great words of the Bible. If you will spend one hour a day reading the Bible and committing its great passages to memory, thus allowing them to recondition your personality, the change in you and in your experience will be little short of miraculous.

Just one section of the Bible will accomplish this for you. The eleventh chapter of Mark is enough. You will find the secret in the following words, and this is one of the greatest formulas the Book contains: "Have faith in God (that's positive, isn't it?). For verily I say unto you, that whosoever shall say unto *this* mountain (that's specific) be thou removed (that is, stand aside) and be thou cast into the sea; (that means out of sight—anything you threw into the sea is gone for good. The *Titanic* lies at the bottom of the sea. And the sea bottom is lined with ships. Cast your opposition called a 'mountain' into the sea) and shall not doubt in his heart, (Why does this statement use the word heart? Because it means you are not to doubt in your subconscious, in the inner essence of you. It isn't so superficial as a doubt in the conscious mind. That is a normal, intelligent questioning. It's deep fundamental doubt that is to be avoided) but shall believe that those things which he saith shall come to pass; he shall have whatsoever he saith." (Mark xi. 22–23.)

This is not some theory that I have thought up. It is taught by the most reliable book known to man. Generation after generation, no matter what develops in the way of knowledge and science, the Bible is read by more people than any other book. Humanity rightly has more confidence in it than any other document ever written, and the Bible tells us that faith powers work wonders.

The reason, however, that great things do not happen to some people is that they are not specific in their application of faith power. We are told: 'Ye shall say to *this* mountain.' That is to say, do not address your efforts to the entire mountain range of all your difficulties, but attack one thing that may be defeating you at the moment. Be specific. Take them one by one.

If there is something you want, how do you go about getting it? In the first place, ask yourself: 'Should I want it?' Test that question very honestly in prayer to be sure you should want it and whether you should have it. If you can answer that question in the affirmative, then ask God for it and don't be backward in asking Him. And if God, having more insight, believes that you shouldn't have it, you needn't worry—He won't give it to you. But if it is a right thing, ask Him for it, and when you ask, do not doubt in your heart. Be specific.

The validity of this law was impressed upon me by something that a friend of mine, a Mid-Western business man told me. This man is a big, extrovertish, outgoing, lovable gentleman, a truly great Christian. He teaches the largest Bible class in his state. In the town where he lives he is Mr. 'Town' himself. He is head of a plant employing forty thousand people.

His office desk is full of religious literature. He even has some of my sermons and pamphlets there. In his plant, one of the biggest in the United States, he manufactures refrigerators.

He is one of those whole-souled, rugged individuals who has the capacity to have faith. He believes that God is right there in his office with him.

My friend said: "Preach a big faith—not any little old watered-down faith. Don't be afraid that faith isn't scientific enough. I am a scientist," he said. "I use science in my business every day, and I use the Bible every day. The Bible will work. Everything in the Bible works if you believe in it."

When he was made general manager of this plant it was whispered around town: 'Now that Mr. —— is general manager, we'll have to bring our Bibles to work with us.' After a few days he called into his office some of the men who were making this remark. He uses language they understand, and he said: "I hear you guys are going around town saying that now I am general manager, you will have to bring your Bibles to work with you."

"Oh, we didn't mean that," they said in embarrassment.

He said: "Well, you know, that's a —— good idea, but I don't want you to come lugging them under your arms. Bring them here in your hearts and in your minds. If you come with a spirit of goodwill and faith in your hearts and minds, believe me, we'll do business.

"So," he said, "the kind of faith to have is the specific

kind, the kind that moves this particular mountain."

Suddenly he said to me: "Did you ever have a toe bother you."

I was rather astonished by that, but before I could answer he said: "I had a toe that bothered me and I took it to the doctors here in town, and they are wonderful doctors, and they said there wasn't anything wrong with the toe that they could see. But they were wrong, because it hurt. So I went out and got a book on anatomy and read up on toes. It is really a simple construction. There's nothing but a few muscles and ligaments and a bony structure. It seemed that anybody who knows anything about a toe could fix it, but I couldn't get anybody to fix that toe, and it hurt me all the time. So I sat down one day and took a look at that toe. Then I said: 'Lord, I'm sending this toe right back to the plant. You made that toe. I make refrigerators, and I know all there is to know about a refrigerator. When we sell a refrigerator, we guarantee the customer service. If this refrigerator doesn't work right and if our service agents can't fix it, he brings it back to the plant and we fix it, because we know how.' So I said: 'Lord, you made this toe. You manufactured it, and your service agents, the doctors, don't seem to know how to get it working right, and if you don't mind, Lord, I would like to have it fixed up as soon as possible, because it's bothering me.'"

"How is the toe now?" I asked.

"Perfect," he replied.

Perhaps this is a foolish kind of story, and I laughed when he told it, but I almost cried, too, for I saw a wonderful look on that man's face as he related that incident of a specific prayer.

Be specific. Ask God for any right thing, but, as a

little child, don't doubt. Doubt closes the power flow. Faith opens it. The power of faith is so tremendous that there is nothing that Almighty God cannot do for us, with us, or through us if we let Him channel His power through our minds.

So roll those words around on your tongue. Say them over and over again until they lodge deeply in your mind, until they get down into your heart, until they take possession of the essence of you: ". . . whosoever shall say unto this mountain, be thou removed, and be thou cast into the sea, and shall not doubt in his heart, but shall believe that those things which he saith shall come to pass; he shall have whatsoever he saith." (Mark xi. 23.)

I suggested these principles some months ago to an old friend of mine, a man who perpetually expects the worst. Up to the time of our discussion, never did I hear him say anything other than that things would not turn out right. He took this negative attitude towards every project or problem. He expressed vigorous disbelief in the principles outlined in this chapter and offered to make a test to prove that I am wrong in my conclusions. He is an honest man, and he faithfully tried these principles in connection with several matters and actually kept a score card. He did this for six months. He volunteered the information at the end of that period that eighty-five per cent of the matters under investigation had turned out satisfactorily.

"I am now convinced," he said, "although I wouldn't have believed it possible, but it is evidently a fact, that if you expect the best, you are given some strange kind of power to create conditions that produce the desired results. From now on I am changing my mental attitude and shall expect the best, not the worst. My test indicates that this is not theory, but a scientific way to meet life's situations."

I might add that even the high percentage he attained can be raised with practice, and of course practice in the art of expectation is as essential as practice on a musical instrument or with a golf club. Nobody ever mastered any skill except through intensive, persistent, and intelligent practice. Also it should be noted that my friend approached this experiment at first in a spirit of doubt which would tend adversely to affect his earlier results.

Every day as you confront the problems of life, I suggest that you affirm as follows: 'I believe God gives me power to attain what I really want.'

Never mention the worst. Never think of it. Drop it out of your consciousness. At least ten times every day affirm: 'I expect the best and with God's help will attain the best.'

In so doing your thoughts will turn towards the best and become conditioned to its realisation. This practice will bring all of your powers to focus upon the attainment of the best. It will bring the best to you.

8 | I Don't Believe in Defeat

IF YOU ARE thinking thoughts of defeat, I urge you to rid yourself of such thoughts, for as you think defeat you tend to get it. Adopt the 'I don't believe in defeat' attitude.

I want to tell you about some people who have put this philosophy into effect with excellent results and shall explain the techniques and formulas which they used so successfully. If you read these incidents carefully and thoughtfully and believe as they did and think positively and put these techniques into operation, you, too, can overcome defeats which at the present moment may seem inevitable.

I hope you are not like an 'obstacle man' of whom I was told. He was called an obstacle man because, regardless of whatever suggestion was advanced, his mind instantly went to all possible obstacles in connection with it, but he met his match and learned a lesson which helped to change his negative attitude. It came about in the following manner.

The directors of his firm had a project under consideration which involved considerable expense and some definite hazards as well as success possibilities. In the discussion regarding this venture the obstacle man would invariably say, and always with a scholarly air (invariably this type acts wise, probably a cover-up for inner doubt feelings): "Now just a moment. Let's consider the obstacles involved."

Another man, who said very little but who was respected by his associates for his ability and achievements and for a certain indomitable quality which characterised him, presently spoke up and asked: "Why do you constantly emphasise the obstacles in this proposition instead of the possibilities?"

"Because," replied the obstacle man, "to be intelligent one must always be realistic, and it is a fact that there are certain definite obstacles in connection with this project. What attitude would you take towards these obstacles, may I ask?"

The other man unhesitatingly replied: "What attitude would I take towards these obstacles? Why, I would just remove them, that's all, and then I would forget them."

"But," said the obstacle man, "that is easier said than done. You say you would remove them and then you would forget them. May I ask if you have any technique for removing obstacles and for forgetting them that the rest of us have never discovered?"

A slow smile came over the face of the other man as he said: "Son, I have spent my entire life removing obstacles and I never yet saw one that could not be removed provided you had enough faith and guts and were willing to work. Since you want to know how it's done, I will show you."

He then reached into his pocket and took out his wallet. Under the isinglass window was a card on which were written some words. He shoved the wallet across the table and said: "There, son, read that. That is my formula, and don't give me the song and dance that it won't work either. I know better from experience."

The obstacle man picked up the wallet and with a strange look on his face read the words to himself.

"Read them out loud," urged the owner of the wallet.

This is what he read in a slow, dubious voice: "I can do all things through Christ which strengtheneth me." (Philippians iv. 13.)

The owner of the wallet put it back in his pocket and said: "I have lived a long time and have faced a lot of difficulties in my time, but there is power in those words —actual power—and with them you can remove any obstacle."

He said this with confidence and everybody knew he meant it. This positiveness, together with the facts of his experience which were known to all, for he was a remarkable man who had overcome many odds, and because of the further fact that he was not in any sense 'holier than thou', made his words convincing to the men around the table. At any rate, there was no more negative talk. The project was put into operation and, despite difficulties and risks, turned out successfully.

The technique used by this man is based on the primary fact about an obstacle which is—don't be afraid of it. Practise believing that God is with you and that in combination with Him you have the power to handle it.

So the first thing to do about an obstacle is simply to stand up to it and not complain about it or whine under it but forthrightly attack it. Don't go crawling through life on your hands and knees half-defeated. Stand up to your obstacles and do something about them. You will find that they haven't half the strength you think they have.

A friend in England sent me a book by Winston Churchill entitled *Maxims and Reflections*.* In this book Churchill tells of the British General Tudor, who commanded a division of the British Fifth Army which faced the great German assault in March 1918. The odds were heavily against him, but General Tudor knew how to meet an apparently immovable and undefeatable obstacle. His method was simple. He merely stood and let the obstacle break on him and he, in turn, broke the obstacle.

Here is what Churchill said about General Tudor. This is a very great sentence and it is filled with power: 'The impression I had of Tudor was of an iron peg, hammered into the frozen ground, immovable.'

General Tudor knew how to stand up to an obstacle. Just stand up to it, that's all, and don't give way under it, and it will finally break. You will break it. Something has to break, and it won't be you, it will be the obstacle.

You can do this when you have faith, faith in God and faith in yourself. Faith is the chief quality you need. It is enough. In fact, it is more than enough.

Use that formula which the business man suggested and you will develop this brand of powerful faith in God and in yourself. You will learn to know yourself, your own ability, your power to do things. To the degree to which your attitude shifts from negative to positive the mastery touch will come to you. Then, with assurance, you can say to yourself under any and all circumstances and mean it: 'I don't believe in defeat.'

Take the story of Gonzales, who won the national tennis championship a few years ago in a gruelling battle. He had been practically unknown, and because

* Eyre and Spottiswoode

of wet weather he had not been able to perfect his game prior to the tournament. The sports writer of a metropolitan newspaper in analysing Gonzales said that there were certain defects in his techniques, and gave it as his opinion that probably greater champions had played on the courts, however, he credited Gonzales with a marvellous service and a skilful volley. But the factor that won the championship, said the writer, was his staying power and the further fact that 'he was never defeated by the discouraging vicissitudes of the game'.

That is one of the most subtle lines I have ever read in any sports story—'He was never defeated by the discouraging vicissitudes of the game.'

It means, does it not, that when the game seemed to go against him he did not let discouragement creep in nor negative thoughts dominate and thus lose the power needed to win. This mental and spiritual quality made that man a champion. He was able to face obstacles, to stand up to them and overcome them.

Faith supplies staying power. It contains dynamic to keep one going when the going is hard. Anybody can keep going when the going is good, but some extra ingredient is needed to enable you to keep fighting when it seems that everything is against you. It is a great secret, that of never being 'defeated by the discouraging vicissitudes of the game'.

You may counter: "But you don't know my circumstances. I am in a different situation than anybody else and I am as far down as a human being can get."

In that case you are fortunate, for if you are as far down as you can get there is no farther down you can go. There is only one direction you can take from this position, and that is up. So your situation is quite encouraging. However, I caution you not to take the attitude that you are in a situation in which nobody has ever been before. There is no such situation.

Practically speaking, there are only a few human stories and they have all been enacted previously. This is a fact that you must never forget—there are people who have overcome every conceivable difficult situation, even the one in which you now find yourself and which to you seems utterly hopeless. So did it seem to some others, but they found an out, a way up, a path over, a pass through.

One of the most inspiring illustrations of this fact is the story of Amos Parrish who twice every year brings together hundreds of leading department-store executives and style experts into two huge sessions held in the Grand Ballroom of the Waldorf-Astoria Hotel in New York City. At these sessions Mr. Parrish gives advice to the merchants and their associates on business trends, on merchandise, on selling methods, and other matters important to the conduct of their business. Having attended a number of the sessions, however, I am convinced that the greatest values Mr. Parrish transmits to his customers are courage and positive thinking, a deep belief in themselves, and the confidence that they can overcome all difficulties.

He seems a living example of the philosophy which he teaches. As a boy he was sickly. Moreover, he stuttered. He was sensitive and a victim of an inferiority complex. It was thought that he would not live because of his weakened physical condition, but one day Amos Parrish had a spiritual experience. Faith dawned in his mind, and from then on he knew that with the help of God and the utilisation of his own powers he could achieve.

He developed a unique idea of service to business men, and so highly do they rate it that they are willing to pay large fees to attend a two-day session twice a year under the business wisdom and inspiration of Amos Parrish. To me it is a moving experience to sit with that big crowd in a hotel ballroom and listen to 'A.P.', as he is affectionately called, talk positive thinking to those important business men and women.

Sometimes he has the greatest difficulty with his stuttering, but he is never discouraged. He refers to it frankly and with a sense of humour. One day, for example, he was trying to say the word Cadillac. He tried several times and was unable to get it out, and finally did so with a powerful effort. Then he commented: "I can't even say C-C-C-Cadillac, let alone buy one." The audience roared with laughter, but I noted that they looked up at him with affection written on their faces. Everyone leaves a meeting at which he speaks with the conviction that they, too, can turn their obstacles into assets.

Again I repeat, there is no difficulty you cannot overcome. A wise and philosophical negro man once said to me, when asked how he overcame his difficulties: "How do I get through a trouble? Well, first I try to go around it, and if I can't go around it, I try to get under it, and if I can't get under it, I try to go over it, and if I can't get over it, I just plough right through it." Then he added: "God and I plough right through it."

Take seriously that formula of a business man given earlier in this chapter. Stop reading for a moment and repeat it over to yourself five times, and each time you say it conclude with this affirmation: 'I believe that.' Here is the formula again. "I can do all things through Christ which strengtheneth me." (Philippians iv. 13.)

Say that five times every day and it will release indomitable power in your mind.

Your subconscious, which always resents any change, may say to you: 'You don't believe any such thing.' But remember that your subconscious mind in a sense is one of the greatest liars in existence. It concurs in and sends back to you your own errors about your abilities. You have created the negative attitude in your subconscious and it gives this error back to you. So just turn on your subconscious and say to it: 'Now look here, I do believe that. I insist upon believing it.' If you talk to your subconscious mind with that positiveness, in due course it will be convinced. One reason is because you are now feeding it positive thoughts. In other words, you are at last telling the truth to your subconscious. After a while your subconscious mind will begin to send back the truth to you, the truth being that with the help of Jesus Christ there isn't any obstacle you cannot overcome.

An effective method for making your subconscious positive in character is to eliminate certain expressions of thought and speech which we may call the 'little negatives'. These so-called 'little negatives' clutter up the average person's conversation, and while each one is seemingly unimportant in itself, the total effect of these attitudes is to condition the mind negatively. When this thought of 'little negatives' first occurred to me, I began to analyse my own conversation habits and was shocked by what I found. I discovered that I was making such statements as: 'I'm afraid I'll be late,' or 'I wonder if I'll have a flat tyre,' or 'I don't think I can do that,' or 'I'll never get through this job. There's so much to do.' If something turned out badly, I might say: 'Oh, that's just what I expected.' Or, again, I might observe a few clouds in the sky and would gloomily state: 'I knew it was going to rain.'

These are 'little negatives' to be sure, and a big thought is of course more powerful than a little one, but it must never be forgotten that 'mighty oaks from little acorns grow', and if a mass of 'little negatives' clutter up your conversation, they are bound to seep into your mind. It is surprising how they accumulate in force, and presently, before you know it, they will grow into 'big negatives'. So I determined to go to work on the 'little negatives' and root them out of my conversation. I found that the best way to eliminate them was deliberately to say a positive word about everything. When you keep asserting that things are going to work out well, that you can do the job, that you will not have a flat tyre, that you will get there on time, by talking up good results you invoke the law of positive effects and good results occur. Things do turn out well.

On a roadside hoarding I saw an advertisement of a certain brand of motor oil. The slogan read: 'A clean engine always delivers power.' So will a mind free of negatives produce positives, that is to say, a clean mind will deliver power. Therefore flush out your thoughts, give yourself a clean mental engine, remembering that a clean mind, even as a clean engine, always delivers power.

So to overcome your obstacles and live the 'I don't believe in defeat' philosophy, cultivate a positive-idea pattern deeply in your consciousness. What we do with obstacles is directly determined by our mental attitude. Most of our obstacles, as a matter of fact, are mental in character.

'Ah,' you may object, 'mine are not mental, mine are real.'

Perhaps so, but your attitude towards them is mental. The only possible way you can have an attitude is by the mental process, and what you think about your obstacles largely determines what you do about them. Form the mental attitude that you cannot remove an obstacle and you will not remove it, not if you think you can't. But get the idea firmly fixed that the obstacle is not so great as you previously considered it to be. Hold the idea that it is removable, and however faintly you entertain this positive thought, from the very moment you begin to think in this manner, the process is inaugurated which will lead to its ultimate removal.

If you have been long defeated by a difficulty, it is probably because you have told yourself for weeks, months, and even for years that there is nothing you can do about it. You have so emphasised your inability to yourself that your mind gradually accepted the conclusion upon which you have insisted, and when your mind is convinced, you are convinced, for as you think so are you.

But, on the contrary, when you employ this new and creative concept: 'I can do all things through Christ,' then you develop a new mental slant. Emphasise and re-emphasise that positive attitude and you will finally convince your own consciousness that you can do something about difficulties. When at last your mind becomes convinced, astonishing results will begin to happen. Of a sudden you discover that you have the power you would never acknowledge.

I played golf with a man who was not only an excellent golfer but a philosopher as well. As we went around the golf-course the game itself drew out of him certain gems of wisdom for one of which I shall ever be grateful.

I hit a ball into the rough, into some high grass. When we came up to my ball, I said in some dismay: "Now just look at that. I certainly am in the rough. I have a bad lie. It is going to be tough getting out of here."

My friend grinned and said: "Didn't I read something about positive thinking in your books?"

Sheepishly I acknowledged that such was the case.

"I wouldn't think negatively about that lie of yours," he said. "Do you think you could get a good hit if this ball were lying out on the fairway on the short grass?"

I said I thought so.

"Well," he continued, "why do you think you could do better out there than here?"

"Because," I replied, "the grass is cut short on the fairway and the ball can get away better."

Then he did a curious thing. "Let's get down on our hands and knees," he suggested, "and examine the situation. Let's see just how this ball does lie."

So we got down on our hands and knees, and he said: "Observe that the relative height of the ball here is about the same as it would be on the fairway, the only difference being that you have about five or six inches of grass above the ball."

Then he did an even more whimsical thing. "Notice the quality and character of this grass," he said. He pulled off a blade and handed it to me. "Chew it," he said.

I chewed, and he asked: "Isn't that tender?"

"Why, yes," I replied. "It certainly does seem to be tender grass."

"Well," he continued, "an easy swing of your number

147

five iron will cut through that grass almost like a knife."
And then he gave me this sentence which I am going
to remember as long as I live, and I hope you will also.

"The rough is only mental. In other words," he continued, "it is rough because you think it is. In your
mind you have decided that there is an obstacle which
will cause you difficulty. The power to overcome this
obstacle is in your mind. If you visualise yourself lifting
that ball out of the rough, believing you can do it, your
mind will transfer flexibility, rhythm, and power to your
muscles and you will handle that club in such a manner
that the ball will rise right out of there in a beautiful
shot. All you need to do is to keep your eye on that ball
and tell yourself that you are going to lift it out of that
grass with a lovely stroke. Let the stiffness and tension
go out of you. Hit it with exhilaration and power.
Remember, the rough is only mental."

To this day I remember the thrill, the sense of power
and delight I had in the clean shot that dropped the ball
to the edge of the green.

That is a very great fact to remember in connection
with difficult problems—'the rough is only mental'.

Your obstacles are present all right. They are not
fanciful, but they are not actually so difficult as they
seem. Your mental attitude is the most important factor.
Believe that Almighty God has put in you the power to
lift yourself out of the rough by keeping your eye firmly
fixed on the source of your power. Affirm to yourself
that through this power you can do anything you have
to do. Believe that this power is taking the tension out
of you, that this power is flowing through you. Believe
this, and a sense of victory will come.

Now take another look at that obstacle that has been

bothering you. You will find that it isn't so formidable as you thought. Say to yourself: 'The rough is only mental. I think victory—I get victory.' Remember that formula. Write it on a piece of paper, put it in your wallet, stick it up on your mirror where you shave each morning, put it over the kitchen sink, put it on your dressing-table and on your desk—keep looking at it until its truth drives into the depths of your consciousness, until it permeates your whole mental attitude, until it becomes a positive obsession—'I can do all things through Christ which strengtheneth me.'

What may seem to be a difficult proposition is, as I have pointed out, hard or easy in proportion to how we think about it. It may be said that three men vitally affected the thought processes of Americans—Emerson, Thoreau, and William James. Analyse the American mind even to this late date and it is evident that the teachings of these three philosophers combined to create that particular genius of the American who is not defeated by obstacles and who accomplishes 'impossibles' with amazing efficiency.

A fundamental doctrine of Emerson is that the human personality can be touched with Divine power and thus greatness can be released from it. William James pointed out that the greatest factor in any undertaking is one's belief about it. Thoreau told us that the secret of achievement is to hold a picture of a successful outcome in mind.

Still another wise American was Thomas Jefferson, who, like Franklin, set for his guidance a series of rules. Franklin had thirteen daily rules; Jefferson only ten. One of Jefferson's rules was this, and I think it is priceless: 'Always take hold of things by the smooth handle.'

That is, go at a job or at your difficulty by the use of a method that will encounter the least resistance. Resistance causes friction in mechanics, therefore it is necessary in mechanics to overcome or reduce friction. The negative attitude is a friction approach. That is why negativism develops such great resistance. The positive approach is the 'smooth handle' technique. It is in harmony with the flow of the universe. It not only encounters less resistance, but actually stimulates assistance forces. It is remarkable how from early life until the end of your earthly existence the application of this philosophy will enable you to attain successful results in areas where otherwise you would be defeated.

For example, a woman sent her fifteen-year-old son to us. She said she wanted him 'straightened out'. It annoyed her no end that her boy could never get over seventy in any of his studies. "This boy has a great mind potentially," she declared proudly.

"How do you know he has a great mind?" I asked.

"Because he is my son," she said. "I graduated from college *magna cum laude*."

The boy came in very glumly, so I asked: "What's the matter, son?"

"I don't know. My mother sent me to see you."

"Well," I commented, "you don't seem to be burning with enthusiasm. Your mother says you get only seventies."

"Yes," he said, "that's all I get, and," he added, "that isn't the worst of it. I've even received less than that."

"Do you think you have a good mind, son?" I asked.

"My mother says I have. I don't know—I think I'm awful dumb. Dr. Peale," he said earnestly, "I study the stuff. At home I read it over once and then close the book and try to remember it. I repeat this process about three times, and then I think that if three times doesn't get it into my head, how am I ever going to get it into my head? And then I go to school thinking maybe I have it, and the teacher calls on me to say something, and I stand up and can't remember a thing. Then," he said, "examinations come along and I sit there and just get hot and cold all over and I can't think of the answers. I don't know why," he continued. "I know that my mother was a great scholar. I guess I just haven't got it in me."

This negative thought pattern combined with the inferiority feeling stimulated by his mother's attitude was, of course, defeating him. He froze up in his mind. His mother had never told him to go to school and study for the wonder and glory of learning knowledge. She was not wise enough to encourage him to compete with himself rather than with others. And she was constantly insisting that he duplicate her success in scholarship. Little wonder that under this pressure he froze mentally.

I gave him some suggestions that proved helpful. 'Before you read your lessons, pause a moment and pray in this manner: "Lord, I know I have a good mind and that I can get through my work." Then get relaxed and read the book without strain. Imagine you are reading a story. Do not read it twice unless you wish. Simply believe that you got it on the first reading. Visualise the material as soaking in and germinating. Then next morning, as you go to school, say to yourself: "I have a wonderful mother. She is very pretty and sweet, but she must have been an old bookworm to get those high marks. And who wants to be an old bookworm, anyway? I don't want to become magna cum nothing. I only want to get through school creditably."

'In class, when the teacher calls on you, quickly pray before answering. Then believe the Lord will at that moment help your mind to deliver. When an examination is given, affirm in prayer that God is releasing your mind and that the right answers are given you.'

The boy followed these ideas, and what marks do you think he got the following half-year? Ninety! I am sure that this boy, having discovered the amazing workability of the 'I don't believe in defeat philosophy', will employ the amazing power of positive thinking in all the affairs of his life.

I could use so many illustrations of the manner in which men's lives have been revamped by these procedures that this book would grow to unwieldy size. Moreover, these are incidents and experiences out of everyday life that are in no way theoretical, but are entirely practical. My mail is literally filled with testimonials sent by people who, having heard or read accounts I have told of victorious life experiences, have felt moved to relate similar occurrences in their own lives.

Such a letter came from a gentleman who tells about his father as follows. I know several people who have used the plan in this letter with amazing results.

'My father was a travelling salesman. One time he sold furniture, another time hardware, sometimes it was leather goods. He changed his line every year.

'I would hear him telling Mother that this was his last trip in stationery or in bed lamps or whatever it was he was selling at the moment. Next year everything would be different; we would be on Easy Street. He had a chance to go with a firm that had a product that sold itself. It was always the same. My father never had a product that sold. He was always tense, always afraid of himself, always whistling in the dark.

'Then one day a fellow-salesman gave Father a copy of a little three-sentence prayer. He was told to repeat it just before calling on a customer. Father tried it, and the results were almost miraculous. He sold 85 per cent of all calls made during the first week, and every week thereafter the results were wonderful. Some weeks the percentage ran as high as 95, and Father had sixteen weeks in which he sold every customer called on.

'Father gave this prayer to several other salesmen, and in each case it brought astounding results.

'The prayer my father used is as follows:

' "I believe I am always divinely guided.

' "I believe I will always take the right turn of the road.

' "I believe God will always make a way where there is no way." '

The head of a small firm who had a great many difficulties in establishing his business told me that he was immeasurably helped by a technique which he invented. He had trouble, he said, with the tendency to 'blow up' a small difficulty into a seemingly insurmountable obstacle. He knew that he was approaching his problems in a defeatist attitude, and had common sense enough to realise that these obstacles were not so difficult as he made them appear to be. As he told the story, I wondered if he did not have that curious psychological difficulty known as the will to fail.

He employed a device which reconditioned his mental attitude, and after a time had a noticeable effect on his business. He simply placed a large wire basket on his office desk. The following words were printed on a card and wired to this basket: 'With God all things are possible.' Whenever a problem came up which the old mechanism of defeat began to develop into a big difficulty, he threw the paper pertaining to it into the basket marked 'With God all things are possible' and let it rest there for a day or two. 'It is queer how each matter when I took it out of that basket again didn't seem difficult at all,' he reported.

In this act he dramatised the mental attitude of putting the problem in God's hands. As a result he received power to handle the problem normally and therefore successfully.

As you finish this chapter, please say the following line aloud: 'I don't believe in defeat.' Continue to affirm that until the idea dominates your subconscious attitudes.

9 | How to Break the Worry Habit

You do not need to be a victim of worry. Reduced to its simplest form, what is worry? It is simply an unhealthy and destructive mental habit. You were not born with the worry habit. You acquired it. And because you can change any habit and any acquired attitude, you can cast worry from your mind. Since aggressive, direct action is essential in the elimination process, there is just one proper time to begin an effective attack on worry, and that is now. So let us start breaking your worry habit at once.

Why should we take the worry problem thus seriously? The reason is clearly stated by Dr. Smiley Blanton, eminent psychiatrist: 'Anxiety is the great modern plague.'

A famous psychologist asserts that 'fear is the most disintegrating enemy of human personality', and a prominent physician declares that 'worry is the most subtle and destructive of all human diseases'. Another physician tells us that thousands of people are ill because of 'dammed-up anxiety'. These sufferers have been unable to expel their anxieties which have turned inward on the personality, causing many forms of ill-health. The destructive quality of worry is indicated by the fact that the word itself is derived from an old Anglo-Saxon word meaning 'to choke'. If someone were to put his fingers around your throat and press hard, cutting off the flow of vital power, it would be a dramatic demonstration of what you do to yourself by long-held and habitual worry.

We are told that worry is not infrequently a factor in arthritis. Physicians who have analysed the causes of this prevalent disease assert that the following factors, at least some of them, are nearly always present in arthritic cases: financial disaster, frustration, tension, apprehension, loneliness, grief, long-held ill will, and habitual worry.

A clinic staff is said to have made a study of 176 American executives of the average age of forty-four years and discovered that one half had high blood pressure, heart disease, or ulcers. It was notable in every case of those thus afflicted that worry was a prominent factor.

The worrier, so it seems, is not likely to live as long as the person who learns to overcome his worries. The *Rotarian* magazine carried an article entitled 'How Long Can You Live?' The author says that the waistline is the measure of your life-line. The article also declares that if you want to live long, observe the following rules: (1) Keep calm. (2) Go to church. (3) Eliminate worry.

A survey shows that Church members live longer than non-Church members (better join the Church if you don't want to die young). Married people, according to the article, live longer than single people. Perhaps this is because a married couple can divide the worry. When you are single, you have to do it all alone.

A scientific expert on length of life made a study of some 450 people who lived to be one hundred years of age. He found that these people lived long and contented lives for the following reasons: (1) They kept busy. (2) They used moderation in all things. (3) They ate lightly and simply. (4) They got a great deal of fun out of life. (5) They were early to bed and early up. (6) They were free from worry and fear, especially fear of death. (7) They had serene minds and faith in God.

Haven't you often heard a person say: "I am almost sick with worry," and then add with a laugh: "But I guess worry never really makes you ill." But that is where he is wrong. Worry can make you ill.

Dr. George W. Crile, famous American surgeon, said: "We fear not only in our minds but in our hearts, brains, and viscera, that whatever the cause of fear and worry, the effect can always be noted in the cells, tissues, and organs of the body."

Dr. Stanley Cobb, neurologist, says that worry is intimately connected with the symptoms of rheumatoid arthritis.

A doctor recently stated that there is an epidemic of fear and worry in America. "All doctors," he declared, "are having cases of illness which are brought on directly by fear, and aggravated by worry and a feeling of insecurity."

But do not be discouraged, for you can overcome your worries. There is a remedy that will bring you sure relief. It can help you break the worry habit. And the first step to take in breaking it is simply to believe you can. Whatever you believe you can do, you can do, with God's help.

Here, then, is a practical procedure which will help to eliminate abnormal worry from your experience.

Practise emptying the mind daily. This should be

done preferably before retiring at night to avoid the retention by the consciousness of worries while you sleep. During sleep, thoughts tend to sink more deeply into the subconscious. The last five minutes before going to sleep are of extraordinary importance, for in that brief period the mind is most receptive to suggestion. It tends to absorb the last ideas that are entertained in waking consciousness.

This process of mind drainage is important in overcoming worry, for fear thoughts, unless drained off, can clog the mind and impede the flow of mental and spiritual power. But such thoughts can be emptied from the mind and will not accumulate if they are eliminated daily. To drain them, utilise a process of creative imagination. Conceive of yourself as actually emptying your mind of all anxiety and fear. Picture all worry thoughts as flowing out as you would let water flow from a basin by removing the stopper. Repeat the following affirmation during this visualisation: 'With God's help I am now emptying my mind of all anxiety, all fear, all sense of insecurity.' Repeat this slowly five times, then add: 'I believe that my mind is now emptied of all anxiety, all fear, all sense of insecurity.' Repeat that statement five times, meanwhile holding a mental picture of your mind as being emptied of these concepts. Then thank God for thus freeing you from fear. Then go to sleep.

In starting the curative process the foregoing method should be utilised in mid-morning and mid-afternoon as well as at bedtime. Go into some quiet place for five minutes for this purpose. Faithfully perform this process and you will soon note beneficial results.

The procedure may be further strengthened by

imaginatively thinking of yourself as reaching into your mind and one by one removing your worries. A small child possesses an imaginative skill superior to that of adults. A child responds to the game of kissing away a hurt or throwing away a fear. This simple process works for the child because in his mind he believes that that is actually the end of it. The dramatic act is a fact for him, and so it proves to be the end of the matter. Visualise your fears as being drained out of your mind and the visualisation will in due course be actualised.

Imagination is a source of fear, but imagination may also be the cure of fear. 'Imagineering' is the use of mental images to build factual results, and it is an astonishingly effective procedure. Imagination is not simply the use of fancy. The word imagination derives from the idea of imagining. That is to say, you form an image either of fear or of release from fear. What you 'image' (imagine) may ultimately become a fact if held mentally with sufficient faith.

Therefore hold an image of yourself as delivered from worry and the drainage process will in time eliminate abnormal fear from your thoughts. However, it is not enough to empty the mind, for the mind will not long remain empty. It must be occupied by something. It cannot continue in a state of vacuum. Therefore, upon emptying the mind, practise refilling it. Fill it with thoughts of faith, hope, courage, expectancy. Say aloud such affirmations as the following: 'God is now filling my mind with courage, with peace, with calm assurance. God is now protecting me from all harm. God is now protecting my loved ones from all harm. God is now guiding me to right decisions. God will see me through this situation.'

A half-dozen times each day crowd your mind with such thoughts as these until the mind is overflowing with them. In due course these thoughts of faith will crowd out worry. Fear is the most powerful of all thoughts with one exception, and that one exception is faith. Faith can always overcome fear. Faith is the one power against which fear cannot stand. Day by day, as you fill your mind with faith, there will ultimately be no room left for fear. This is the one great fact that no one should forget. Master faith and you will automatically master fear.

So the process is—empty the mind and cauterise it with God's grace, then practise filling your mind with faith and you will break the worry habit.

Fill your mind with faith, and in due course the accumulation of faith will crowd out fear. It will not be of much value merely to read this suggestion unless you practise it. And the time to begin practising it is now, while you think of it and while you are convinced that the number one procedure in breaking the worry habit is to drain the mind daily of fear and fill the mind daily with faith. It is just as simple as that. Learn to be a practiser of faith until you become an expert in faith. Then fear cannot live in you.

The importance of freeing your mind of fear cannot be over-emphasised. Fear something over a long period of time and there is a real possibility that by fearing you may actually help bring it to pass. The Bible contains a line which is one of the most terrible statements ever made—terrible in its truth: "For the thing which I greatly feared is come upon me . . ." (Job iii. 25.) Of course it will, for if you fear something continuously you tend to create conditions in your mind propitious to the development of that which you fear. An atmosphere is encouraged in which it can take root and grow. You tend to draw it to yourself.

But do not be alarmed. The Bible also constantly reiterates another great truth: 'That which I have greatly believed has come upon me.' It does not make that statement in so many words, and yet again and again and still again the Bible tells us that if we have faith 'nothing is impossible' unto us, and 'according to your faith be it done unto you'. So if you shift your mind from fear to faith you will stop creating the object of your fear and will, instead, actualise the object of your faith. Surround your mind with healthy thoughts, thoughts of faith, and not fear, and you will produce faith results instead of fear results.

Strategy must be used in the campaign against the worry habit. A frontal attack on the main body of worry with the expectation of conquering it may prove difficult. Perhaps a more adroit plan is to conquer the outer fortifications one by one, gradually closing in on the main position.

To change the figure, it might be well to snip off the little worries on the farthest branches of your fear. Then work back and finally destroy the main trunk of worry.

At my farm it was necessary to take down a large tree, much to my regret. Cutting down a great old tree is fraught with sadness. Men came with a motor-driven saw, and I expected them to start by cutting through the main trunk near the ground. Instead, they put up ladders and began snipping off the small branches, then the larger ones, and finally the top of the tree. Then all that remained was the huge central trunk, and in a few moments my tree lay neatly stacked as though it had not spent fifty years in growing.

"If we had cut the tree at the ground before trimming off the branches, it would have broken nearby trees in falling. It is easier to handle a tree the smaller you can make it," so explained the tree man.

The vast tree of worry which over long years has grown up in your personality can best be handled by making it as small as possible. Thus it is advisable to snip off the little worries and expressions of worry. For example, reduce the number of worry words in your conversation. Words may be the result of worry, but they also create worry. When a worry thought comes to mind, immediately remove it with a faith thought and expression. For example: 'I'm worried that I will miss the train.' Then start early enough to be sure you get there on time. The less worrying you do, the more likely you are to start promptly, for the uncluttered mind is systematic and is able to regulate time.

As you snip off these small worries you will gradually cut back to the main trunk of worry. Then with your developed greater power you will be able to eliminate basic worry, i.e., the worry habit, from your life.

My friend Dr. Daniel A. Poling gives a valuable suggestion. He says that every morning before he arises he repeats these two words: 'I believe', three times. Thus at the day's beginning he conditions his mind to faith, and it never leaves him. His mind accepts the conviction that by faith he is going to overcome his problems and difficulties during the day. He starts the day with creative positive thoughts in his mind. He 'believes', and it is very difficult to hold back the man who believes.

I related Dr. Poling's 'I believe' technique in a radio talk, and had a letter from a woman who told me that she had not been very faithful to her religion, which happened to be the Jewish faith. She said their home was filled with contention, bickering, worry, and unhappiness. Her husband, she declared, 'drank far too much for his own good' and sat around all day doing no work. He weakly complained that he couldn't find a job. This woman's mother-in-law lived with her, and the latter 'whined and complained of her aches and pains all the while'.

This woman said that Dr. Poling's method impressed her, and she decided to try it herself. So the next morning upon awakening she affirmed: "I believe, I believe, I believe." In her letter she excitedly reported: 'It has been only ten days since I started this plan and my husband came home last night and told me he had a job paying $80 a week. And he also says that he is going to quit drinking. I believe he means it. What is even more wonderful, my mother-in-law has practically stopped complaining of her aches and pains. It is almost as if a miracle has happened in this house. My worries seem to have just about disappeared.'

That does indeed seem almost magical, and yet that miracle happens every day to people who shift over from negative fear thoughts to positive faith thoughts and attitudes.

My good friend, the late Howard Chandler Christy, the artist, had many a sound anti-worry technique. Scarcely ever have I known a man so filled with the joy and delight of life. He had an indomitable quality, and his happiness was infectious.

My church has a policy of having the minister's portrait painted some time during his pastorate. This portrait hangs in the minister's home until his death, when it reverts to the church and is placed in a gallery along with pictures of his predecessors. It is usually the policy of the Board of Elders and Deacons to have a portrait painted when in their wise judgment the minister is at the height of his good looks (mine was painted several years ago).

While sitting for Mr. Christy, I asked: "Howard, don't you ever worry?"

He laughed. "No, not on your life. I don't believe in it."

"Well," I commented, "that is quite a simple reason for not worrying. In fact, it seems to me too simple—you just don't believe in it, therefore you don't do it. Haven't you ever worried?" I asked.

He replied: "Well, yes, I tried it once. I noticed that everybody else seemed to worry, and I figured I must be missing something, so one day I made up my mind to try it. I set aside a day and said: 'That is to be my worry day.' I decided I would investigate this worry business and do some worrying just to see what it was like.

"The night before the day came I went to bed early to get a good night's sleep to be rested up to do a good job of worrying the next day. In the morning I got up, ate a good breakfast—for you can't worry successfully on an empty stomach—and then decided to get to my worrying. Well, I tried my best to worry until along about noon, but I just couldn't make heads nor tails of it. It didn't make sense to me, so I just gave it up."

He laughed one of these infectious laughs of his.

"But," I said, "you must have some other method of overcoming worry." He did indeed, and it is perhaps the best method of all.

"Every morning I spend fifteen minutes filling my mind full of God," he said. "When your mind is full of

God, there is no room for worry. I fill my mind full of God every day, and I have the time of my life all day long."

Howard Christy was a great artist with a brush, but he was an equally great artist with life because he was able to take a great truth and simplify it down to its basic fact, namely, that only that comes out of the mind which originally you put into the mind. Fill the mind with thoughts of God rather than with thoughts of fear, and you will get back thoughts of faith and courage.

Worry is a destructive process of occupying the mind with thoughts contrary to God's love and care. Basically that is all worry is. The cure is to fill the mind with thoughts of God's power, His protection, and His goodness. So spend fifteen minutes daily filling your mind full of God. Cram your mind full of the 'I believe' philosophy, and you will have no mental room left to accommodate thoughts of worry and lack of faith.

Many people fail to overcome such troubles as worry because, unlike Howard Christy, they allow the problem to seem complicated and do not attack it with some simple technique. It is surprising how our most difficult personal problems often yield to an uncomplicated methodology. This is due to the fact that it is not enough to know what to do about difficulties. We must also know how to do that which should be done.

The secret is to work out a method of attack and keep working at it. There is value in doing something that dramatises to our own minds that an effective counter-attack is in progress. In so doing we bring spiritual forces to bear upon the problem in a manner both understandable and usable.

One of the best illustrations of this technique strategy

against worry was a scheme developed by a business man. He was a tremendous worrier. In fact, he was fast getting himself into a bad state of nerves and ill-health. His particular form of worry was that he was always doubtful as to whether he had done or said the right thing. He was always rehashing his decisions and getting himself unnerved about them. He was a post-mortem expert. He is an exceptionally intelligent man, in fact a graduate of two universities, in both instances with honours. I suggested that he ought to work out some simple method that would help him to drop the day when it was over and go ahead into the future and forget it. I explained the gripping effectiveness of simple, dramatised spiritual truth.

It is always true that the greatest minds have the best ability to be simple, that is, they have the capacity to work out some simple plans for putting profound truths into operation, and this man did that in connection with his worries. I noticed that he was improving and commented on it.

"Oh yes," he said, "I finally got the secret and it has worked amazingly well." He said that if I would drop into his office some time towards the close of the day he would show me how he had broken the worry habit. He telephoned me one day and asked me to have dinner that evening. I met him at his office at closing time. He explained that he had broken his worry habit by working out 'a little ritual' that he performed every night before leaving his office. And it was unique. It made a lasting impression upon me.

We picked up our hats and coats and started towards the door. By the door of his office stood a waste-basket, and above it on the wall was a calendar. It was not one of those calendars where you see a week or a month, or three months, it was a one-day calendar. You could see only one date at a time, and that date was in large print. He said: "Now I will perform my evening ritual, the one that has helped me break the worry habit."

He reached up and tore off the calendar page for that particular day. He rolled it into a small ball, and I watched with fascination as his fingers slowly opened and he dropped that 'day' into the waste-basket. Then he closed his eyes and his lips moved, and I knew that he was praying, so was respectfully silent. Upon finishing his prayer he said aloud: "Amen. O.K., the day is over. Come on, let's go out and enjoy ourselves."

As we walked down the street I asked: "Would you mind telling me what you said in that prayer?"

He laughed and said: "I don't think it is your kind of prayer." But I persisted, and he said: "Well, I pray something like this: 'Lord, you gave me this day. I didn't ask for it, but I was glad to have it. I did the best I could with it and you helped me, and I thank you. I made some mistakes. That was when I didn't follow your advice, and I am sorry about that. Forgive me. But I had some victories and some successes, too, and I am grateful for your guidance. But now, Lord, mistakes or successes, victories or defeats, the day is over and I'm through with it, so I'm giving it back to you. Amen.' "

Perhaps that isn't an orthodox prayer, but it certainly proved to be an effective one. He dramatised the finishing of the day and he set his face to the future, expecting to do better the next day. He co-operated with God's method. When the day is over, God blacks it out by bringing down the curtain of night. By this method this man's past mistakes and failures, his sins of omission and commission gradually lost their hold on him. He was released from the worries that accumulated from his yesterdays. In this technique this man was practising one of the most effective anti-worry formulas, which is described in these words: ". . . but this one thing I do, forgetting those things which are behind, and reaching forth unto those things which are before, I press towards the mark for the prize of the high calling of God in Christ Jesus." (Philippians iii. 13–14.)

Other practical anti-worry techniques may suggest themselves to you, and I should like to hear of those which after careful use prove effective. I believe that all of us who are interested in self-improvement are fellow-students in God's great spiritual laboratory. Together we work out practical methods of successful living. People from everywhere are kind enough to write me about their methods and the results attained. I try to be helpful in making tested methods available to others through books, sermons, newspaper columns, radio, television, and other media. In this manner there can be developed a great many people who have the know-how for overcoming not only worry but other personal problems as well.

To conclude this chapter in a manner designed to help you go to work *now* to break the worry habit, I list a ten-point worry-breaking formula.

1. Say to yourself: 'Worry is just a very bad mental habit. And I can change any habit with God's help.'

2. You become a worrier by practising worry. You can become free of worry by practising the opposite and stronger habit of faith. With all the strength and perseverance you can command, start practising faith.

3. How do you practise faith? First thing every morning before you arise say out loud: 'I believe', three times.

4. Pray, using this formula: 'I place this day, my life, my loved ones, my work in the Lord's hand. There is no harm in the Lord's hands, only good. Whatever happens, whatever results, if I am in the Lord's hands it is the Lord's will, and it is good.'

5. Practise saying something positive concerning everything about which you have been talking negatively. Talk positively. For example, don't say: 'This is going to be a terrible day.' Instead, affirm: 'This is going to be a glorious day.' Don't say: 'I'll never be able to do that.' Instead, affirm: 'With God's help I will do that.'

6. Never participate in a worry conversation. Shoot an injection of faith into all your conversations. A group of people talking pessimistically can infect every person in the group with negativism. But by talking things up rather than down, you can drive off that depressing atmosphere and make everyone feel hopeful and happy.

7. One reason you are a worrier is that your mind is literally saturated with apprehension thoughts, defeat thoughts, gloomy thoughts. To counteract, mark every passage in the Bible that speaks of faith, hope, happiness, glory, radiance. Commit each to memory. Say them over and over again until these creative thoughts saturate your subconscious mind. Then the subconscious will return to you what you have given it, namely, optimism, not worry.

8. Cultivate friendships with hopeful people. Surround yourself with friends who think positive, faith-producing thoughts and who contribute to a creative

atmosphere. This will keep you re-stimulated with faith attitudes.

9. See how many people you can help to cure their own worry habit. In helping another to overcome worry you get greater power over it within yourself.

10. Every day of your life conceive of yourself as living in partnership and companionship with Jesus Christ. If He actually walked by your side, would you be worried or afraid? Well, then, say to yourself: 'He is with me.' Affirm aloud: 'I am with you always.' Then change it to say: 'He is with me now.' Repeat that affirmation three times every day.

10 | Power to
Solve Personal Problems

I WANT TO tell you about some fortunate people who found the right solution to their problems.

They followed a simple but highly practical plan and in each case the outcome was a happy and successful one. These people are in no sense different from you. They had the same problems and difficulties that you have, but they found a formula which helped them to get the right answers to the difficult questions facing them. This same formula applied by you can get similar results.

First, let me tell you the story of a husband and wife, long-time friends of mine. For years Bill, the husband, worked hard until he finally reached the rung next to the top of the ladder in his company. He was in line for the presidency of the firm and felt certain that upon retirement of the president he would be advanced to that position. There was no apparent reason why his ambition should not be realised, for by ability, training, and experience he was qualified. Besides, he had been led to believe he was to be chosen.

However, when the appointment was made he was by-passed. A man was brought in from the outside to fill the post.

I arrived in his city just after the blow had fallen. The

wife, Mary, was in an especially vindictive state of mind. At dinner she bitterly outlined all that she would 'like to tell them'. The intense disappointment, humiliation, frustration, focused in a burning anger which she poured out to her husband and me.

Bill, on the contrary, was quiet. Obviously hurt, disappointed, and bewildered, he took it courageously. Being essentially a gentle person, it was not surprising that he failed to become angry or violent in his reaction. Mary wanted him to resign immediately. She urged him to 'tell them off and tell them plenty, then quit'.

He seemed disinclined to take this action, saying perhaps it was for the best that he would go along with the new man and help him in any way that he could.

That attitude admittedly might be difficult, but he had worked for the company for so long that he would not be happy elsewhere, and besides, he felt that in the secondary position the company could continue to use him.

The wife then turned to me and asked what I would do. I told her that I would, like herself, undoubtedly feel disappointed and hurt, but that I would try not to allow hate to creep in, for animosity not only corrodes the soul, but disorganises thought processes as well.

I suggested that what we needed was Divine guidance, a wisdom beyond ourselves in this situation. There was such an emotional content in the problem that we might possibly be incapable of thinking the matter through objectively and rationally.

I suggested, therefore, that we have a few minutes of quietness, no one saying anything, that we sit quietly in an attitude of fellowship and prayer, turning our thoughts to the One who said: "Where two or three are gathered together in my name, there am I in the midst of them." (Matthew xviii. 18–20.) I pointed out that there were three of us, and if we sought to achieve the spirit of being gathered in 'His' name, He would be present to quiet us and show us what to do.

It was not easy for the wife to accommodate herself to the mood suggested, but basically she was an intelligent, fine type of person, and she joined in the plan.

Presently, after a few quiet minutes, I suggested that we join hands, and even though we were in a public restaurant I would quietly offer a prayer. In the prayer I asked for guidance. I requested peace of mind for Bill and Mary, and I went a step farther and even asked God's blessing upon the new appointee. I also prayed that Bill would be able to fit in with the new administration and give more effective service than before.

After the prayer we sat silent for a time, then with a sigh the wife said: "Yes, I guess that is the way to do it. When I knew you were coming to dinner with us I feared that you would tell us to take a Christian position on this. Frankly, I didn't feel like doing that. I was boiling inwardly, but of course I realise that the right answer to this problem is to be found through that approach. I will try it, faithfully, as difficult as it may be." She smiled wanly, but the animus was gone.

From time to time I checked with my friends, and found that while everything was not entirely as they desired, they gradually became fairly contented under the new arrangement. They were able to overcome their disappointment and ill will.

Bill even confided to me that he liked the new man and in a way enjoyed working with him. He told me that the new president often called him in for consultation and seemed to lean on him.

Mary was nice to the president's wife, and in fact they went to the fullest extent to be co-operative.

Two years passed. One day I arrived in their city and telephoned them.

"Oh, I am so excited I can hardly speak," Mary said.

I commented that anything that could put her in that state must be of unusual importance.

Ignoring this remark, she cried: "Oh, the most wonderful thing has happened. Mr. So-and-So," naming the president, "has been selected by another company at a big promotion for a special job which will take him out of our organisation into a much better position and" —she poised the question—"guess what? Bill has just been notified that he is now president of this company. Come over right away and let the three of us give thanks together."

Later, as we sat together, Bill said: "Do you know, I am beginning to realise that Christianity isn't theoretical after all. We have solved a problem according to well-defined spiritually scientific principles. I shudder to think," he said, "of the terrible mistake we would have made had we not gone at this problem according to the formula contained in the teachings of Jesus.

"Who in the world," he asked, "is responsible for the silly idea that Christianity is impractical? Never again will I let a problem come up without attacking it in just the way the three of us solved this one."

Well, several years have passed, and Mary and Bill have had other problems, and to each of them they have applied this same technique, invariably with good results. By the 'put it in God's hands' method they have learned to solve their problems right.

Another effective technique in problem solving is the simple device of conceiving of God as a partner. One of the basic truths taught by the Bible is that God is with us. In fact, Christianity begins with that concept, for when Jesus Christ was born He was called Immanuel, meaning 'God with us'.

Christianity teaches that in all the difficulties, problems, and circumstances of this life God is close by. We can talk to Him, lean upon Him, get help from Him, and have the inestimable benefit of His interest, support and help. Practically everybody believes in a general way that this is true, and many have experienced the reality of this faith.

In getting correct solutions to your problems, however, it is necessary to go a step further than believing this, for one must actually practise the idea of presence. Practise believing that God is as real and actual as your wife, or your business partner, or your closest friend. Practise talking matters over with Him; believe that He hears and gives thought to your problem. Assume that He impresses upon your mind through consciousness the proper ideas and insights necessary to solve your problems. Definitely believe that in these solutions there will be no error, but that you will be guided to actions according to truth which results in right outcomes.

A business man stopped me one day following a Rotary Club meeting in a Western city at which I had made a speech. He told me that something he had read in one of my newspaper columns had, as he put it: 'completely revolutionised his attitude and saved his business'.

Naturally I was interested and pleased that any little

thing I had said would bring about such a splendid result.

"I had been having quite a difficult time in my business," he said. "In fact, it was beginning to be a very serious question as to whether I could save my business. A series of unfortunate circumstances together with market conditions, regulatory procedures, and dislocations to the economy of the country generally affected my line profoundly. I read this article of yours in which you advanced the idea of taking God in as a partner. I think you used the phrase: 'effect a merger with God'.

"When I first read that, it seemed to me a rather 'cracked-brain idea'. How could a man on earth, a human being, take God as a partner? Besides, I had always thought of God as a vast being, so much bigger than man that I was like an insect in His sight, and yet you were saying that I should take Him as a partner. The idea seemed preposterous. Then a friend gave me one of your books and I found similar ideas scattered all through it. You told actual life stories about people who followed this advice. They all seemed to be sensible people, but still I was unconvinced. I always had the idea that ministers are idealistic theorists, that they know nothing about business and practical affairs. So I sort of 'wrote you off'," he said with a smile.

"However, a funny thing happened one day. I went to my office so depressed that I actually thought perhaps the best thing for me to do would be to blow my brains out and get away from all these problems which seemed completely to floor me. Then into my mind came this idea of taking God as a partner. I shut the door, sat in my chair, and put my head on my arms on the desk. I might as well confess to you that I hadn't prayed more than a dozen times in as many years. However, I certainly did pray on this occasion. I told the Lord that I had heard this idea about taking Him in as a partner, that I wasn't actually sure what it meant, or how one did it. I told Him I was sunk, that I couldn't get any ideas except panicky ones, that I was baffled, bewildered, and very discouraged. I said: 'Lord, I can't offer You much in the way of a partnership, but please join with me and help me. I don't know how You can help me, but I want to be helped. So I now put my business, myself, my family, and my future in Your hands. Whatever You say goes. I don't even know how You are going to tell me what to do, but I am ready to hear and will follow Your advice if You will make it clear.'

"Well," he continued, "that was the prayer. After I finished praying I sat at my desk. I guess I expected something miraculous to happen, but nothing did. However, I did suddenly feel quiet and rested. I actually had a feeling of peacefulness. Nothing out of the ordinary occurred that day, nor that night, but next day when I went to my office I had a brighter and happier feeling than usual. I began to feel confident that things would turn out right. It was hard to explain why I felt that way. Nothing was any different. In fact, you might say things were a shade worse, but I was different, at least a little different.

"This feeling of peacefulness stayed with me and I began to feel better. I kept praying each day and talked to God as I would to a partner. They were not churchy prayers—just plain man-to-man talk. Then one day in my office, all of a sudden an idea popped up in my mind. It was like toast popping up in a toaster. I said to myself:

'Well, what do you know about that?' for it was something that had never occurred to me, but I knew instantly that it was just the method to follow. Why I had never thought of it before I haven't the slightest idea. My mind was too tied up, I guess. I hadn't been functioning mentally.

"I immediately followed the hunch." Then he stopped. "No, it was no hunch, it was my partner talking to me. I immediately put this idea into operation and things began to roll. New ideas began to flow out of my mind, and despite conditions I began to get the business back on an even keel. Now the general situation has improved considerably, and I'm out of the woods."

Then he said: "I don't know anything about preaching or about writing the kind of books you write, or any books for that matter, but let me tell you this—whenever you get a chance to talk to business men tell them that if they will take God as a partner in their business they will get more good ideas than they can ever use, and they can turn those ideas into assets. I don't merely mean money," he said, "although a way to get a good return on your investments, I believe, is to get God-guided ideas. But tell them that the God-partnership method is the way to get their problems solved right."

This incident is just one of many similar demonstrations of the law of Divine-human relationship working itself out in practical affairs. I cannot emphasise too strongly the effectiveness of this technique of problem solving. It has produced amazing results in the many cases coming under my observation.

In the very necessary business of solving personal problems, it is important, first of all, to realise that the power to solve them correctly is inherent within you. Second, it is necessary to work out and actualise a plan. Spiritual and emotional planlessness is a definite reason for the failure of many people to meet their personal problems successfully.

A business executive told me that he puts his dependence upon the 'emergency powers of the human brain'. It is his theory, and a sound one, that a human being possesses extra powers that may be tapped and utilised under emergency situations. In the ordinary conduct of day-by-day living, these emergency powers lie dormant, but under extraordinary circumstances the personality is able, when called upon, to deliver extra power if needed.

A person who develops a working faith does not allow these powers to lie dormant, but in proportion to his faith brings many of them into play in connection with normal activity. This explains why some people demonstrate greater force than others in daily requirements and in a crisis. They have made it a habit normally to draw upon powers that would otherwise be ignored except in some dramatic necessity.

When a difficult situation arises, do you know how to meet it? Have you any clearly defined plan for solving unusually difficult problems as they develop? Many people proceed on a hit-or-miss method and, sadly enough, most frequently they miss. I cannot urge too strongly the importance of a planned use of your greater powers in meeting problems.

In addition to the method of two or three praying together in the 'surrender of God' technique and that of establishing a partnership with God and the importance of a plan to tap and utilise emergency inner powers, there is still another tremendous technique—that of practising faith attitudes. I read the Bible for years before it ever dawned on me that it was trying to tell me that if I would have faith—and really have it—that I could overcome all of my difficulties, meet every situation, rise above every defeat, and solve all of the perplexing problems of my life. The day that realisation dawned on me was one of the greatest, if not the greatest, of my life. Undoubtedly many people will read this book who have never got the faith idea of living. But I hope you will get it now, for the faith technique is without question one of the most powerful truths in the world having to do with the successful conduct of human life.

Throughout the Bible the truth is emphasised again and again that "If ye have faith as a grain of mustard seed . . . nothing shall be impossible unto you." (Matthew xvii. 20.) The Bible means this absolutely, factually, completely and literally. It isn't an illusion, it isn't a fantasy. It is not an illustration, nor a symbol, nor a metaphor, but the absolute fact—'Faith, even as a grain of mustard seed', will solve your problems, any of your problems, all of your problems, if you believe it and practise it. "According to your faith, be it unto you." (Matthew ix. 29.) The requirement is faith, and directly in proportion to the faith that you have and use will you get results. Little faith gives you little results, medium faith gives you medium results, great faith gives you great results. But in the generosity of Almighty God, if you have only the faith symbolised by a grain of mustard seed, it will do amazing things in solving your problems.

For example, let me tell you the thrilling story of my friends Maurice and Mary Alice Flint. I became acquainted with them when a previous book of mine, *A Guide to Confident Living*, was condensed in *Liberty* magazine. Maurice Flint at that time was failing, and failing badly. Not only was he failing in his job, but as a person as well. He was filled with fear and resentment and was one of the most negative persons I have ever encountered. He was endowed with a nice personality and at heart was a wonderful fellow, but he had simply messed life up as he himself admitted.

He read the condensation of the book in which is emphasised the idea of 'mustard-seed faith'. At this time he was living in Philadelphia with his family, a wife and two sons. He telephoned my church in New York, but for some reason did not make contact with my secretary. I mention this to show his already changing mental attitude, for normally he would never have called the second time, because it was his pathetic habit to give up everything after a feeble effort, but in this instance he persevered until he got through and secured the information relative to the time of church services. The next Sunday he drove from Philadelphia to New York with his family to attend church, which he continued to do even in the most inclement weather.

In an interview later he told me his life story in full detail and asked if I thought he could ever make anything of himself. The problems of money, of situations, of debts, of the future, and primarily of himself were so complicated and he was so overwhelmed with difficulty that he regarded the situation as completely hopeless.

I assured him that if he would get himself personally straightened out and get his mental attitudes attuned to God's pattern of thought, and if he would learn and utilise the technique of faith, all of his problems could be solved.

One attitude that both he and his wife had to clear out of their minds was that of resentment. They were dully mad at everybody and acutely so at some. They were in their present unhappy condition, so they reasoned in their diseased thoughts, not because of any failure on their part but because of 'dirty deals' other people had given them. They actually used to lie in bed at night telling each other what they would like to say to other people by way of insult. In this unhealthy atmosphere they tried to find sleep and rest, but with no successful result.

Maurice Flint really took to the faith idea. It gripped him as nothing ever had. His reactions were weak, of course, for his will-power was disorganised. At first he was unable to think with any power or force due to his long habit of negativism, but he held on tenaciously, even desperately, to the idea that if you have 'faith as a grain of mustard seed, nothing is impossible'. With what force he did have he absorbed faith. Of course, his capacity to have faith gradually increased as he practised it.

One night he went into the kitchen where his wife was washing dishes. He said: "The faith idea is comparatively easy on Sunday in church, but I can't hold it. It fades. I was thinking that if I could carry a mustard seed in my pocket, I could feel it when I begin to weaken and that would help me to have faith." He then asked his wife: "Do we have any of those mustard seeds, or are they just something mentioned in the Bible? Are there mustard seeds today?"

She laughed and said: "I have some right here in a pickle-jar."

She fished one out and gave it to him. "Don't you know, Maurice," Mary Alice said, "that you don't need an actual mustard seed. That is only the symbol of an idea."

"I don't know about that," he replied. "It says mustard seed in the Bible and that's what I want. Maybe I need the symbol to get faith."

He looked at it in the palm of his hand and said wonderingly: "Is that all the faith I need—just a small amount like this tiny grain of mustard seed?" He held it for a while and then put it in his pocket, saying: "If I can just get my fingers on that during the day, it will keep me working on this faith idea." But the seed was so small he lost it, and he would go back to the pickle-jar for another one, only to lose it also. One day when another seed became lost in his pocket, the idea came to him, Why couldn't he put the grain of mustard seed into a plastic ball? He could carry this ball in his pocket or put it on his watch-chain always to remind him that if he had 'faith as a grain of mustard seed, nothing would be impossible unto him'.

He consulted a supposed expert in plastics and asked how to insert a mustard seed in a plastic ball so there would be no bubble. The 'expert' said it could not be done for the reason that it had never been done, which of course was no reason at all.

Flint had enough faith by this time to believe that if he had faith 'even as a grain of mustard seed' he could put a mustard seed in a plastic sphere. He went to work, and kept at it for weeks, and finally succeeded. He made up several pieces of costume jewellery: necklace, bow-pin, key-chain, bracelet, and sent them to me. They were beautiful, and on each gleamed the translucent sphere with the mustard seed within. With each one was a card which bore the title: 'Mustard Seed Remembrancer.' The card also told how this piece of jewellery could be used; how the mustard seed would remind the wearer that 'if he had faith, nothing was impossible'.

He asked me if I thought these articles could be merchandised. I was a bit doubtful, I must admit, and showed them to Grace Oursler, consulting editor of *Guideposts* magazine. She took the jewellery to our mutual friend, Mr. Walter Hoving, president of Bonwit Teller Department Stores, one of the greatest executives in the country. He at once saw the possibilities in this project. Imagine my astonishment and delight when in the New York papers a few days later was a two-column advertisement reading: 'Symbol of faith—a genuine mustard seed enclosed in sparkling glass makes a bracelet with real meaning.' And in the advertisement was the Scripture passage: "If ye have faith as a grain of mustard seed ... nothing shall be impossible unto you." (Matthew xvii. 20.) These articles sold like hot cakes. Now hundreds of great department stores and shops throughout the country find difficulty keeping them in stock.

Mr. and Mrs. Flint have a factory in a Mid-Western city producing Mustard Seed Remembrancers. Curious, isn't it—a failure goes to church and hears a text out of the Bible and creates a great business. Perhaps you had better listen more intently to the reading of the Bible and the sermon the next time you go to church. Perhaps you, too, will get an idea that will rebuild not only your life but your business as well.

Faith in this instance created a business for the manufacturers and distributors of a product that has helped and will help thousands upon thousands of people. So popular and effective is it that others have copied it, but the Flint Mustard Seed Remembrancer is the original. The story of the lives that have been changed by this little device is one of the most romantic spiritual stories of this generation. But the effect on Maurice and Mary Alice Flint—the transformation of their lives, the remaking of their characters, the releasing of their personalities—this is a thrilling demonstration of faith power. No longer are they negative—they are positive. No more are they defeated—they are victorious. They no longer hate. They have overcome resentment and their hearts are filled with love. They are new people with a new outlook and a new sense of power. They are two of the most inspiring people I ever knew.

Ask Maurice and Mary Alice Flint how to get a problem solved right. They will tell you—'Have faith—really have faith.' And believe me, they know.

If as you read this story you have said to yourself negatively (and that is being negative), 'The Flints were never so badly off as I am,' let me tell you that I have scarcely ever seen anybody as badly off as were the Flints. And let me say further that regardless of however desperate your situation may be, if you will use the four techniques, outlined in this chapter, as did the Flints, you, too, can get your problem solved.

In this chapter I have tried to show various methods for solving a problem. Now I wish to give ten simple suggestions as a concrete technique to use generally in solving your problems:

1. Believe that for every problem there is a solution.

2. Keep calm. Tension blocks the flow of thought power. Your brain cannot operate efficiently under stress. Go at your problem easy-like.

3. Don't try to force an answer. Keep your mind relaxed so that the solution will open up and become clear.

4. Assemble all the facts impartially, impersonally, and judicially.

5. List these facts on paper. This clarifies your thinking, bringing the various elements into orderly system. You see as well as think. The problem becomes objective, not subjective.

6. Pray about your problem, affirming that God will flash illumination into your mind.

7. Believe in and seek God's guidance on the promise of the 73rd Psalm: "Thou wilt guide me by thy counsel."

8. Trust in the faculty of insight and intuition.

9. Go to church and let your subconscious work on the problem as you attune to the mood of worship. Creative spiritual thinking has amazing power to give 'right' answers.

10. If you follow these steps faithfully, then the answer that develops in your mind, or comes to pass, is the right answer to your problem.

11 | How to Use Faith in Healing

Is RELIGIOUS FAITH a factor in healing? Important evidence indicates that it is. There was a time in my own experience when I was not convinced of this, but now I am, and that very definitely. I have seen too many evidences to believe otherwise.

We are learning that faith properly understood and applied is a powerful factor in overcoming disease and establishing health.

My conviction regarding this important question is shared by many medical men. Newspapers carried an account of the visit to America of the famous Viennese surgeon, Dr. Hans Finsterer. I quote the newspaper story which was headed 'Honour Surgeon "Guided by God".'

'A Viennese doctor, Dr. Hans Finsterer, who believes "the unseen hand of God" helps make an operation successful, was selected by the International College of Surgeons for its highest honour, "master of surgery". He was cited for his work in abdominal surgery with the use of local anaesthesia only.

'Finsterer, seventy-two-year-old professor at the University of Vienna, has performed more than 20,000 major operations, among them 8,000 gastric resections (removal of part or all of the stomach), using only local anaesthesia. Finsterer said that although considerable progress has been made in medicine and surgery in the past few years, "all advances are not sufficient in themselves to insure a happy outcome in every operation. In many instances," he said, "in what appeared to be simple surgical procedures the patients died, and in some cases where the surgeon despaired of a patient there was recovery.

' "Some of our colleagues attribute these things to unpredictable chance, while others are convinced that in those difficult cases their work has been aided by the unseen hand of God. Of late years, unfortunately, many patients and doctors have lost the conviction that all things depend on the providence of God.

' "When we are once again convinced of the importance of God's help in our activities, and especially in the treatment of our patients, then true progress will have been accomplished in restoring the sick to health." '

So concludes the account of a great surgeon who combines his science with faith.

I spoke at the national convention of an important industry. It was a large gathering of the leaders in an amazingly creative merchandising enterprise that has established this particular industry as a vital factor in American business life.

I was somewhat surprised when one of the leaders of this organisation at the convention luncheon where the discussion centred around taxation, rising costs, and business problems, turned to me and asked: "Do you believe that faith can heal?"

"There are a good many well-authenticated examples on record of people who have been healed by faith," I answered. "Of course, I do not think we should depend on faith alone to heal a physical ailment. I believe in the combination of God and the doctor. This viewpoint takes advantage of medical science and the science of faith, and both are elements in the healing process."

"Let me tell you my story," the man continued. "A number of years ago I had a malady that was diagnosed as osteoma of the jaw, that is, a bone tumour on my jaw. The doctors told me it was practically incurable. You can imagine how that disturbed me. Desperately I sought for help. Although I had attended church with fair regularity, still I was not a particularly religious man. I scarcely ever read the Bible. One day, however, as I lay in my bed it occurred to me that I would like to read the Bible, and I asked my wife to bring one to me. She was very surprised, for I had never before made such a request.

"I began to read, and found consolation and comfort. I also became a bit more hopeful and less discouraged. I continued to read for extended periods every day. But that wasn't the chief result. I began to notice that the condition which had troubled me was growing less noticeable. At first I thought I imagined this, then I became convinced that some change was taking place in me.

"One day while reading the Bible I had a curious inward feeling of warmth and great happiness. It is difficult to describe, and long ago I gave over trying to explain the feeling. From that time on my improvement was more rapid. I went back to the doctors who had first diagnosed my case. They examined me carefully. They were obviously surprised and agreed that my condition had improved, but warned me that this was only a temporary respite. Later, however, upon further examination, it was determined that the symptoms of osteoma had disappeared entirely. Still the doctors told me it would probably start all over again. This did not disturb me, for in my heart I knew that I was healed."

"How long has it been since your healing?" I asked.

"Fourteen years," was the answer.

I studied this man. Strong, sturdy, healthy, he is one of the outstanding men in his industry. The incident was told to me in the factual way that a business man would recount it. There was not the slightest indication of doubt in this man's mind. Indeed how could there be, for whereas he had been condemned to death, here he was alive and vigorous.

What did it? The skilful work of the physician plus! And what was the plus? Obviously the faith that heals.

The healing described by this gentleman is but one of many similar accounts, and so many of them are attested by competent medical evidence that it seems we must encourage people to make greater use of the amazing power of faith in healing. Sadly the healing element in faith has suffered neglect. I am certain that faith can and does work what we call 'miracles', but which are, in truth, the operation of spiritually scientific laws.

There is a growing emphasis in present-day religious practice which is designed to help people find healing from the sickness of mind, heart, soul, and body. This is a return to the original practice of Christianity. Only in recent times have we tended to overlook the fact that for centuries religion carried on healing activities. The very word 'pastor' derives from a word meaning 'the cure of souls'. In modern times, however, man made the false assumption that it is impossible to harmonise the teachings of the Bible with what is called 'science', and so the healing emphasis of religion was abandoned almost entirely to materialistic science. Today, however, the close association of religion and health is increasingly recognised.

It is significant that the word 'holiness' derives from a word meaning 'wholeness' and the word 'meditation', usually used in a religious sense, closely resembles the root meaning of the word 'medication'. The affinity of the two words is startlingly evident when we realise that sincere and practical meditation upon God and His truth acts as a medication for the soul and body.

Present-day medicine emphasises psychosomatic factors in healing, thus recognising the relationship of mental states to bodily health. Modern medical practice realises and takes into consideration the close connection between how a man thinks and how he feels. Since religion deals with thought and feeling and basic attitudes, it is only natural that the science of faith should be important in the healing process.

Harold Sherman, author and playwright, was asked to revise an important radio presentation with the promise that he would be contracted as the permanent writer. After some months of work, he was dismissed and his material used without credit. This resulted in financial difficulty and humiliation. The injustice rankling in his mind developed into a growing bitterness against the radio executive who had broken faith with him. Mr. Sherman declares that this is the one time in his life when he had murder in his heart. His hatred made him subject to a physical affliction in the form of a mycosis, a fungus growth which attacked the membranes of his throat. The best medical attention was secured, but something in addition was required. When he gave up his hate and developed a feeling of forgiveness and understanding, the condition gradually corrected itself. With the aid of medical science and a new mental attitude, he was healed of his affliction.

A sensible and effective pattern for health and happiness is to utilise the skills and methods of medical science to the fullest possible extent and at the same time apply the wisdom, the experience, and the techniques of spiritual science. There is impressive evidence to support the belief that God works through both the practitioner of science, the doctor, and the practitioner of faith, the minister. Many physicians join in this point of view.

At a Rotary Club luncheon I sat at a table with nine other men, one of them a physician who had recently been discharged from military service and had resumed his civilian practice. He said: "Upon my return from the Army, I noticed a change in my patients' troubles. I found that a high percentage do not need medicine but better thought patterns. They are not sick in their bodies so much as they are sick in their thoughts and emotions. They are all mixed up with fear thoughts, inferiority feelings, guilt, and resentment. I found that in treating them I needed to be about as much a psychiatrist as a physician, and then I discovered that not even those therapies helped me fully to do my job. I became aware that in many cases the basic trouble with people was spiritual. So I found myself frequently quoting the Bible to them. Then I fell into the habit of 'prescribing' religious and inspirational books, especially those that gave guidance in how to live."

Directing his statements to me, he said: "It's about time you ministers began to realise that in the healing of many people you, too, have a function to perform. Of course, you are not going to overlap on the work of the physician any more than we shall intrude on your function, but we doctors need the co-operation of ministers in helping people find health and well-being."

I received a letter from a physician in an up-state New York town who said: "Sixty per cent of the people in this town are sick because they are maladjusted in their minds and in their souls. It is hard to realise that the modern soul is sick to such an extent that the physical organs pain. I suppose in time," continues the doctor, "that ministers, priests, and rabbis will understand this relationship."

This physician was kind enough to say that he prescribes my book, *A Guide to Confident Living*, and other similar books to his patients and that noteworthy results have been achieved thereby.

The manageress of a Birmingham, Alabama, bookstore sent me a prescription form made out by a physician of that city to be filled not at a drug-store, but at her book-store. He prescribes specific books for specific troubles.

Dr. Carl R. Ferris, formerly president of the Jackson County Medical Society of Kansas City, Missouri, with whom I had the pleasure of appearing on a joint health-and-happiness radio programme, declared that in treating human ills the physical and spiritual are often so deeply inter-related that there is often no clearly defined dividing line between the two.

Years ago my friend, Dr. Clarence W. Lieb, pointed out to me the effect on health of spiritual and psychiatric problems, and through his wise guidance I began to see that fear and guilt, hate and resentment, problems with which I was dealing, were often closely connected with problems of health and physical well-being. So profoundly does Dr. Lieb believe in this therapy that he, with Dr. Smiley Blanton, inaugurated the religio-psychiatric clinic which for years has ministered to hundreds at the Marble Collegiate Church in New York.

The late Dr. William Seaman Bainbridge and I worked closely together in the relationship of religion and surgery, and we were able to bring health and new life to many.

Two of my medical friends in New York, Dr. Z. Taylor Bercovitz and Dr. Howard Westcott, have been of inestimable help in my pastoral work through their wisely scientific and yet deeply spiritual understanding of the ills of the body, mind, and soul as related to faith.

"We have discovered the psychosomatic cause of high blood pressure as some form of subtle, repressed fear—a fear of things that might happen, not of things that are," says Dr. Rebecca Beard. "They are largely fears of things in the future. In that sense, therefore, they are imaginary, for they may never happen at all. In the case of diabetes, it is grief or disappointment which we found uses up more energy than any other emotion, thereby exhausting the insulin which is manufactured by the pancreas cells until they are worn out.

"Here we find the emotions involved in the past—reliving the past and not being able to go forward into life. The medical world can give relief in disorders like these. They can give something that can lower the blood pressure when it is high, or raise it when it is low, but not permanently. They can give insulin which will burn up more sugar into energy and give the diabetic relief. These are definite aids, but they do not offer complete cure. No drug or vaccine has been discovered to protect us from our own emotional conflicts. A better understanding of our own emotional selves and a return to religious faith seem to form the combination that holds the greatest promise of permanent help to any of us.

"The answer," Dr. Beard concludes, "is in the healing teachings of Jesus."

Another efficient woman physician wrote me of her own development in combining the therapy of medicine and faith. 'I became interested in your straightforward religious philosophy. I had been working at top speed and getting tense, irritable, and at times beset with old fears and guilts, in fact in need of a release from morbid tension. At a low moment early one morning I picked up your book and began to read it. This was the prescription that I needed. Here was God, the great Physician, with faith in Him as an antibiotic to kill the germs of fear and render useless the virus of guilt.

'I began to practise the good Christian principles outlined in your book. Gradually there came a release of tension and I felt relaxed and happier and I slept well. I quit taking vitamin and pep pills. Then,' she adds, and this is what I want to emphasise, 'I began to feel that I wanted to share this new experience with my patients, those who came to me with neuroses. I was surprised to find how many had read your book and others. The patient and I seemed to have a common ground to work on. It has been an enriching experience. To talk about a faith in God has become a natural and easy thing to do.

'As a doctor,' she adds, 'I have seen a number of miraculous recoveries due to Divine aid being given. In the past few weeks I have had an additional experience. My sister had to undergo a serious operation about three weeks ago. Following the operation she developed an intestinal obstruction. On her fifth day she was very critically ill, and as I left the hospital at noon I realised that she must take a turn for the better very soon or her hope of recovery would be slim. I was very worried, so I drove slowly around for about twenty minutes praying for a relief of this obstruction. (Everything that could be done medically was being taken care of.) I had not been home more than ten minutes when the phone rang, and her nurse told me that the obstruction had relieved itself and that she had taken a definite turn for the better, and since that time she has recovered completely. Could I feel otherwise than that God's intervention had saved her life?'

So runs the letter of a successful practising physician.

In the light of this viewpoint, based on a strictly common-sense scientific attitude, we may approach the phenomenon of healing through faith with credibility. If I did not believe sincerely that the faith factor in healing is sound, I would certainly not develop the point of view contained in this chapter.

Over a period of time I have received from many readers and radio listeners as well as from my own parishioners accounts of healings in which the element of faith has been present. I have meticulously investigated many of these to satisfy my own mind as to their truthfulness. Also I wanted to be able to declare to the most cynical that here is a way of health, happiness, and successful living which is so buttressed by evidence that only the person who wants to remain ill because of some subconscious will-to-fail attitude will ignore his possibilities for health implied in these experiences.

The formula which these many incidents together present is briefly stated—the employment of all the resources of medical and psychological science combined with the resources of spiritual science. This is a combination of therapies that can surely bring health and well-being if it is the plan of God for the patient to live. Obviously for each of us there comes a time for this mortal life to end (life itself never ends, only the earthly phase of it).

We in the so-called old-line churches have, in my humble judgment, missed one of our greatest possible contributions by failing to point out with positiveness that there is a sound message of health in Christianity. Failing to find this emphasis in the Church, groups, organisations, and other spiritual bodies have been created to supply this deficiency in Christian teaching. But there is no longer any valid reason why all the churches should not recognise that which is authenticated, namely, that there is healing in faith, and more generally offer sound healing techniques to our people. Fortunately everywhere today throughout our religious organisations thoughtful, scientifically-minded spiritual leaders are taking that extra step of faith based on the facts (and the Scriptures) and are making available to the people as never before the formulas of the marvellous healing grace of Jesus Christ.

In all of the investigations I have made into successful cases of healing, there seems to be certain factors present. First, a complete willingness to surrender oneself into the hands of God. Second, a complete letting go of all error such as sin in any form and a desire to be cleansed in the soul. Third, belief and faith in the combined therapy of medical science in harmony with the healing power of God. Fourth, a sincere willingness to accept God's answer, whatever it may be, and no irritation or bitterness against His will. Fifth, a substantial, unquestioning faith that God can heal.

In all these healings there seems to be an emphasis upon warmth and light and a feeling of assurance that power has passed through. In practically every case that I have examined, in one form or another, the patient talks about a moment when there was warmth, heat, beauty, peace, joy, and a sense of release. Sometimes it has been a sudden experience; other times a more gradual unfolding of the conviction that the healing has occurred.

Always in my investigation of these matters I have waited for elapsed time to prove that the healing is permanent, and those cases which I report are not based on any temporary improvement which might conceivably be the result of a momentary resurgence of strength.

For example, may I relate a healing experience written for me by a woman whose reliability and judgment I profoundly respect. Documentation in this case is thoroughgoing and scientifically impressive. This woman was told that an immediate operation was necessary to remove a growth which had been diagnosed as malignant.

I quote her exact words: 'All precautionary treatments were taken, but the manifestations returned. As may be expected, I was terrified; I knew further hospital treatments were futile. There was no hope, so I turned to God for help. A very consecrated and spiritual child of God helped me by prayer to realise that the right knowledge of God and His healing Christ would help me too. I was most receptive to this kind of thinking, and placed myself in God's hands.

'I had asked for this help one morning, as usual, and

spent the day going about my household duties, which were many at that time. I was preparing the evening meal, all alone in the kitchen. I was aware of an unusually bright light in the room and felt a pressure against my whole left side, as though a person were standing very close beside me. I had heard of healings; I knew prayers were being offered in my behalf, so I decided this must be the healing Christ who was with me.

'I decided to wait until morning, to be sure; if the symptoms of the trouble were gone, then I would know. By morning the improvement was so noticeable, and I was so free in my mind, that I was certain, and reported to my friend that the healing had taken place.

'The memory of that healing and the presence of Christ are as fresh in my mind today as then. That was fifteen years ago, and my health steadily improved until I am in excellent condition now.'

In many heart cases the therapy of faith (a quiet, serene faith in Jesus Christ) undoubtedly stimulates healing. People who experience 'a heart attack' who thereupon thoroughly and completely practise faith in Christ's healing grace, observing at the same time the rules prescribed by their physicians, report remarkable recovery histories. Perhaps such a person may even gain a greater degree of health than previously for having learned his limitations and, realising the excess strains he has been placing upon himself, now conserves his strength.

But more than that he has learned one of the greatest techniques of human well-being, that of surrendering himself to the recuperative power of God. This is done by consciously attaching himself to the creative process through mentally conceiving of re-creative forces as operating within himself. The patient opens his consciousness to the tides of vitality and re-creative energy inherent in the universe which have been barred from his life through tension, high pressure, and other departures from the laws of well-being.

An outstanding man suffered a heart attack about thirty-five years ago. He was told that he would never be able to work again. The orders were that he must spend much of his time in bed. He would likely be an invalid the remainder of his days, which days would be relatively few in number, so he was informed. It is doubtful whether such statements would be made to him in present-day medical practice. At any rate, he listened to these dire prophecies about his future and considered them carefully.

One morning he awakened early and picked up his Bible and by chance (or was it chance?) opened it to the account of one of the healings of Jesus. He also read the statement: "Jesus Christ the same yesterday, and today, and for ever." (Hebrews xiii. 8.) It occurred to him that if Jesus could and did heal people long ago, and that if He is the same as He was then, why couldn't He heal today? 'Why cannot Jesus heal me?' he asked. Then faith welled up within him.

Therefore, with simple confidence, he asked the Lord to heal him. He seemed to hear Jesus say: 'Believest thou that I can do this?' And his answer was: 'Yes, Lord, I believe that You can.'

He closed his eyes and 'seemed to feel the touch of the healing Christ upon his heart'. All that day he had a strange sense of rest. As the days passed he became convinced that there was a rising tide of strength within him. Finally one day he prayed: 'Lord, if it is Your will tomorrow morning I am going to get dressed, go outside, and within a few days I am going back to work. I put myself completely in Your care. If I should die tomorrow as a result of the increased activity, I want to thank You for all the wonderful days I have had. With You to help me, I shall start out tomorrow and You will be with me all day long. I believe I will have sufficient strength, but if I should die as a result of this effort, I will be with You in eternity, and all will be well in either case.'

In this calm faith he increased his activities as the days passed. He followed this formula every day for the entire period of his active career, which numbered thirty years from the date of his heart attack. He retired at seventy-five. Few men I have known have been more vigorous in their undertakings or have made a greater contribution to human welfare. Always, however, he conserved his physical and nervous strength. It was invariably his habit to lie down and rest after lunch, and he never allowed himself to get under stress. He was early to bed and early up, always employing rigorous and disciplinary rules of living.

In all his activities there was an absence of worry, resentment, and tension. He worked hard but easily. The doctors were right. Had he continued according to the debilitating habits of his earlier life he would probably have long since been dead or at least an invalid. The advice of the physicians brought him to the point where the healing work of Christ could be accomplished. Without the heart attack he would not have been mentally or spiritually ready for healing.

Another friend of mine, a prominent business man, suffered a heart attack. For weeks he was confined to his bed, but presently returned to his important responsibilities where he now accomplishes all that he ever did previously, but with much less tension. He seems to possess a new power that he did not enjoy before. His recovery proceeded from a definite and scientific spiritual approach to his health problem. He had competent physicians, and followed their directions explicitly, which is an important factor in such situations.

In addition to the programme of medication and treatment, however, he worked out a spiritual healing formula. He outlined it as follows, writing from the hospital: 'An intimate friend of mine, only twenty-five years old, was brought into the hospital with an attack similar to mine and died within four hours. Two acquaintances of mine have suffered a similar fate in rooms nearby. It must be that I have work yet to do. So I shall return and apply myself to the tasks before me with the expectation of living longer and more abundantly than I might have done without this experience. The doctors were wonderful, the nurses grand, the hospital ideal.'

He then proceeds to outline the technique of spiritual convalescence which he employed. The formula consists of three parts. '(1) During the first stages, when absolute rest was demanded, I heeded the admonition of the Psalmist: "Be still and know that I am God." ' (Psalm xvi. 10.) That is to say, he completely relaxed and rested in the hands of God. '(2) As the days grew brighter, I used the affirmation: "Wait on the Lord: be of good courage, and He shall strengthen thine heart." ' (Psalm xxvii. 14.) The patient put his heart under the care of God and God placed His hand of healing upon his heart and renewed it. '(3) Finally with the return of strength came a new assurance and confidence to which I gave expression in the affirmation: "I can do all things through Christ which strengtheneth me." ' (Philippians iv. 13.) In this he affirmed positively that strength was being conferred upon him and in so doing he received new power.

In this three-point formula this man found healing. The able ministrations of his physicians conserved and stimulated the healing forces of his physical being. The equally wise application of faith completed his recovery by stimulating the spiritual powers within his nature. The two therapies together draw upon the two great renewal forces within our life, one the recuperative power of the human body and the other the restorative forces resident within the mind. One responds to medical treatment, the other to faith treatment, and God presides in both areas. He made both body and mind and He established the processes of health and well-being governing both. ". . . in Him we live and move and have our being." (Acts xvii. 28.)

In the prevention of sickness and in healing mind and body, do not fail to draw upon one of the greatest resources available to you—the faith that heals.

In the light of the principles outlined in this chapter, what can you do of a constructive nature when a loved one or you are ill? Following are eight practical suggestions:

1. Follow the advice of a prominent medical school head who said: "In sickness, send for your minister even as you send for your doctor." In other words, believe that spiritual forces as well as medical technique are important in healing.

2. Pray for the doctor. Realise that God uses trained

human instrumentality to aid His healing powers. As one doctor has put it: 'We treat the patient and God heals him.' Pray, therefore, that the doctor may be an open channel of God's healing grace.

3. Whatever you do, do not become panicky or filled with fear, for if you do, you will send out negative thoughts and therefore destructive thoughts in the direction of your loved one when he requires positive and healing thoughts to assist him.

4. Remember that God does nothing except by law. Also remember that our little materialistic laws are only fragmentary revelations of the great power flowing through the universe. Spiritual law also governs illness. God has arranged two remedies for all illness. One is healing through natural laws applicable by science, and the other brings healing by spiritual law applicable through faith.

5. Completely surrender your loved one into the hands of God. By your faith you can place him in the flow of Divine power. There is healing there, but in order for it to be effective the patient must be completely released to the operation of God's will. This is difficult to understand and equally difficult to perform, but it is a fact that if the great desire for the loved one to live is matched with an equally great willingness to relinquish him to God, healing powers are amazingly set in motion.

6. It is also important that harmony prevail in the family, that is, a spiritual harmony. Remember the emphasis in the scripture, Matthew xviii. 19: "If two of you shall agree on earth as touching any thing that they shall ask, it shall be done for them of my Father which is in heaven." Apparently disharmony and disease are akin.

7. Form a picture in your mind of the loved one as being well. Visualise him in perfect health. Picture him as radiant with the love and goodness of God. The conscious mind may suggest sickness, even death, but nine-tenths of your mind is in the subconscious. Let the picture of health sink into the subconscious, and this powerful part of your mind will send forth radiant health energy. What we believe in the subconscious we usually get. Unless your faith controls the subconscious, you will never get any good thing, for the subconscious gives back only that which your real thought is. If the real thought is negative, the results will also be negative. If the real thought is positive, you will get positive and healing results.

8. Be perfectly natural. Ask God to heal your loved one. That is what you want with all your heart, so ask Him please to do it, but we suggest that you say PLEASE just once. Thereafter in your prayer, thank Him for His goodness. This affirmative being will help to release deep spiritual power and also joy through reassurance of God's loving care. This joy will sustain you, and remember that joy itself possesses healing power.

| # When Vitality Sags, Try this Health Formula

A WOMAN, so I have heard, went into a drug-store and asked for a bottle of psychosomatic medicine.

Such medicine, of course, is not found on drug-store shelves, for it does not come in pills or bottles. But there is a psychosomatic medicine just the same, and many of us need it. It is a prescription compounded of prayer, faith, and dynamic spiritual thinking.

It has been variously computed that from 50 to 75 per cent of present-day people are ill because of the influence of improper mental states on their emotional and physical make-up. Therefore such a medicine is of great importance. Many people who are below par will find that there is a health formula which, in addition to the services of their physician, can be of great value to them.

The manner in which spiritual and emotional treatment can restore declining vitality is illustrated by the sales manager referred to us by the head of a large company. This sales executive, formerly a man of outstanding efficiency and energetic driving power, experienced a serious decline both in ability and energy. He lost his creative skill. Previously his sales ideas had been unique and outstanding. It soon became noticeable to his associates that this sales manager was slipping badly. He was urged to consult a doctor, and the company sent him to Atlantic City for a rest and later to Florida for a second attempt at recovery. Neither of these vacations seemed to be productive of any definite improvement.

His physician, who knew about our religio-psychiatric clinic, recommended to the company president that his sales manager come to us for an interview. The president asked him to come, which he did, but he was rather indignant at being sent to a church.

"This is a pretty pass," he fumed, "when they send a business man to a preacher. I suppose you are going to pray with me and read the Bible," he said irritably.

"I wouldn't be surprised," I answered, "for sometimes our trouble lies in an area where prayer and the therapy of the Bible can have an important effect."

He proved most sullen and unco-operative until finally I was forced to say to him: "I want to tell you bluntly that you had better co-operate with us or you're going to be fired."

"Who told you that?" he demanded.

"Your boss," I replied. "In fact, he says that unless we can straighten you out, as much as he regrets it, you are going to be through."

You never saw such a stunned expression on anybody's face. "What do you think I ought to do?" he stammered.

"Often," I replied, "a person gets into the state in which you find yourself because the mind is filled with fear, anxiety, tension, resentment, guilt, or a combination of all of them. When these emotional impediments accumulate to a certain weight, the personality cannot support them any longer and gives way. Normal sources of emotional, spiritual, and intellectual power become clogged up. So a person becomes bogged down by resentment, by fear, or by guilt. I do not know your trouble, but I would suggest that you think of me as a sympathetic friend with whom you can be absolutely confident, and that you tell me about yourself." I emphasised that it was important he conceal nothing and that he completely empty himself of whatever fears, resentments, or guilt feelings might be in his mind. "I assure you that our interview will be held in strictest confidence. All your company wants is to have you back, the same highly efficient person you were."

In due course the trouble came out. He had committed a series of sins, and these had involved him in a complicated maze of lies. He was living in fear of exposure, and all in all it was a most pathetic mass of inner confusion. It came little short of mental filth.

It was rather difficult to get him to talk, for he was essentially a decent person and had a strong sense of shame. I told him that I understood his reticence, but that this operation had to be performed and that it could not be accomplished without a thorough mind-emptying.

When it was all over, I shall never forget the manner in which he reacted. Standing on his feet he began to stretch. He stood on tiptoes, reaching his fingers towards the ceiling, and then took a deep breath. "My," he said, "I feel good." It was a dramatic expression of release and relief. Then I suggested that he pray and ask God to forgive him and to fill him with peace and cleanness.

"Do you mean for me to pray aloud?" he asked dubiously. "I never did that in my life."

"Yes," I said, "it is a good practice and will strengthen you."

It was a simple prayer, and as best as I can recall it, this is what he said: "Dear Lord, I have been an unclean man and I am sorry for the wrong I have done. I have poured it all out to my friend here. I now ask You to forgive me and to fill me with peace. Also make me strong so that I will never repeat these actions. Help me to be clean again and better—lots better."

He went back to his office that very day. Nothing was ever said to him, and it did not need to be, for soon he got back into stride and is one of the best sales managers in his city today.

Later I met his president, who said: "I don't know what you did to Bill, but he is certainly a ball of fire."

"I did nothing. God did it," I replied.

"Yes," he said, "I understand. Anyway, he is the old-time Bill."

When this man's vitality sagged, he tried a health formula that restored him to normal efficiency. He 'took' some psychosomatic medicine which cured him of an unhealthy spiritual and mental condition.

Dr. Franklin Ebaugh of the University of Colorado Medical School maintains that one-third of all cases of illness in general hospitals are clearly organic in nature and onset, one-third are a combination of emotional and organic, and one-third are clearly emotional.

Dr. Flanders Dunbar, author of *Mind and Body*, says "It is not a question of whether an illness is physical or emotional, but how much of each."

Every thoughtful person who has ever considered the matter realises that the doctors are right when they tell us that resentment, hate, grudge, ill will, jealousy, vindictiveness, are attitudes which produce ill-health. Have a fit of anger and experience for yourself that sinking feeling in the pit of your stomach, that sense of stomach sickness. Chemical reactions in the body are set up by emotional outbursts that result in feelings of ill-health. Should these be continued either violently or in a simmering state over a period of time, the general condition of the body will deteriorate.

In speaking of a certain man whom we both knew, a physician told me that the patient died of 'grudgitis'. The physician actually felt that the deceased passed away because of a long-held hatred. "He did his body such damage that his resistance was lowered," the doctor explained, "so that when a physical malady attacked him he did not possess the stamina or renewing force to overcome it. He had undermined himself physically by the malignancy of his ill will."

Dr. Charles Miner Cooper, San Francisco physician, in an article entitled: 'Heart-to-Heart Advice About Heart Trouble', says: "You must curb your emotional reactions. When I tell you that I have known a patient's blood pressure to jump sixty points almost instantaneously in response to an outburst of anger, you can understand what strain such reactions can throw upon the heart." One who is 'quick on the trigger', he wrote, is likely to blame someone else, impulsively, for a fault or mistake, when it would be wiser simply to avoid being so much disturbed by what is done and is therefore unavoidable. He quoted the great Scottish surgeon, John Hunter. Dr. Hunter had a heart condition himself, and a thorough understanding of the effect of strong emotion on his heart. He said that his life was at the mercy of anyone who could annoy him. And, in fact, his death resulted from a heart attack caused by a fit of anger when he forgot to discipline himself.

Dr. Cooper concludes: "Whenever a business problem starts to vex you or you begin to get angry, let yourself go limp all over. This will dissipate your mounting inner turmoil. Your heart asks that it be permanently housed in a lean, cheerful, placid man who will intelligently curb his physical, mental, and emotional activities."

So if you are under par I suggest that you do a very scrupulous job of self-analysis. Honestly ask yourself if you are harbouring any ill will or resentment or grudges, and if so cast them out. Get rid of them without delay. They do not hurt anybody else. They do no harm to the person against whom you hold these feelings, but every day and every night of your life they are eating at you. Many people suffer poor health not because of what they eat, but from what is eating them. Emotional ills turn in upon yourself, sapping your energy, reducing your efficiency, causing deterioration in your health. And, of course, they siphon off your happiness.

So we realise today the effect of thought patterns upon physical states. We realise that a person can make himself ill by resentment. We know he can develop various kinds of physiological symptoms because of a sense of guilt. Also, one may show definite physical symptoms as a result of fear and anxiety. We know that healing has been accomplished when the thoughts are changed.

Recently a diagnostician told me of a young woman who was admitted to the hospital with a temperature of one hundred and two degrees. She had a definite case of rheumatoid arthritis; her joints were badly swollen.

In order to study the case thoroughly the doctor gave her no medication except a slight sedative to relieve the pain. After two days the young woman asked the doctor: "How long will I be in this condition, and how long must I remain in the hospital?"

"I think I must tell you," replied the physician, "that

you will probably be in the hospital for about six months."

"You mean it will be six months before I can get married?" she demanded.

"I am sorry," he said, "but I cannot promise you anything better than that."

This conversation took place in the evening. The next morning the patient's temperature was normal and the swelling was gone from her joints. Unable to account for the change, the doctor observed her for a few days, then sent her home.

In a month she was back in the hospital in the same condition as before: temperature one hundred and two, joints swollen. Questioning disclosed that her father insisted that she marry a certain man who would be an asset to him in his business connections. The girl loved her father, wanted to do as he wished, but did not want to marry a man whom she did not love. So her subconscious mind came to her assistance and, in effect, gave her rheumatoid arthritis and a temperature.

The doctor explained to the father that if he forced this marriage his daughter could become an invalid. When told that she need not go through with the marriage, the girl's recovery was quick and permanent.

Do not get the idea that if you have arthritis you are married to the wrong person! This incident merely illustrates the profound effect of mental pain on physical conditions.

I was interested to read a statement by a psychologist that infants can 'catch' fear and hatred from people around them more quickly than they can catch measles or other infectious diseases. The virus of fear may burrow deeply into their subconsciousness and remain there for a lifetime. "But," adds the psychologist, "fortunately infants can also catch love and goodness and faith and so grow up to become normal, healthy children and adults."

In an article in the *Ladies' Home Journal*, Constance J. Foster quotes Dr. Edward Weiss of Temple University Medical School in a speech to the American College of Physicians, in which Dr. Weiss stated that chronic victims of pains and aches in the muscles and joints may be suffering from nursing a smouldering grudge against someone close to them. He added that such persons usually are totally unaware that they bear a chronic resentment.

'To clear up any possible misunderstanding,' the author continues, 'it is necessary to state emphatically that emotions and feelings are quite as real as germs and no less respectable. The resultant pain and suffering of diseases caused primarily by the emotions are no more imaginary than those caused by bacteria. In no case is the patient consciously to blame for developing the disease. Such persons are not suffering from any disease of the mind, but rather from a disorder of their feelings, often linked to a marital or parent-child problem.'

In this same magazine article the story is told of a certain Mrs. X who came to the doctor's surgery complaining of a breaking out on her hands, which was diagnosed as eczema. The doctor encouraged Mrs. X to talk about herself. It developed that she was a very rigid person. Her lips were thin and unyielding. She was also rheumatoid. The doctor sent Mrs. X to a psychiatrist, who saw at once that there was some irritating situation in her life which she was translating outwardly in the form of a skin rash, thus taking out on her own person the urge to scratch some thing or person

The doctor finally put it to her bluntly. "What is eating you?" he asked. "You're peeved at something, aren't you?"

"She stiffened up like a ramrod and marched right out of the surgery, so I knew I'd hit the target too closely for comfort. A few days later she came back. Due to the agony of the eczema, she was ready to let me help her, even if it meant she had to give up a hate.

"It turned out to be a family row over a will, with Mrs. X feeling she had been treated unfairly by a younger brother. When she got rid of the hostility, she got well, and when she made up the quarrel with her brother, within twenty-four hours the eczema vanished."

That there is even a relationship between emotional disturbance and the common cold is indicated by Dr. L. J. Saul of the University of Pennsylvania Medical School, who has made a study of this subject.

'Emotional disturbances are believed to affect the blood circulation in the linings of the nose and throat. They also affect glandular secretions. These factors make the mucous membranes more susceptible to attack by cold viruses or germ infection.'

Dr. Edmund P. Fowler, Jr, of Columbia University's College of Physicians and Surgeons, stated: "There are colds which develop in medical students at the time of their examinations and colds which develop in many persons before or after a trip. Colds develop in housewives when they must care for a large family. And one often sees a cold develop in a patient when his mother-in-law comes to live in the house, and it often disappears when she leaves." (Dr. Fowler does not specify the effects on the mother-in-law of a daughter-in-law or son-in-law. Perhaps she has a cold also.)

One of the cases Dr. Fowler reports concerned a twenty-five-year-old sales girl. When she visited the surgery her nose was stuffy, the lining was red and congested, and she suffered from a headache and a mild temperature. These symptoms had persisted for nearly two weeks. Questioning disclosed that they had started a few hours after a violent quarrel with her fiancé.

Local treatments cleared up the cold, but the young woman was back in a few weeks with another attack. This time the trouble had started after an argument with the butcher. Again local treatments brought relief. But the girl continued to have recurring colds, and each time they were traced to a fit of anger. Finally Dr. Fowler was able to persuade the girl that her bad temper was at the root of her chronic cold symptoms. When she learned to lead a calmer existence, her sneezes and sniffles disappeared.

And yet people still think that when the Bible tells you not to hate or to get angry, that it is 'theoretical advice'. The Bible is not theoretical. It is our greatest book of wisdom. It is filled with practical advice on living and on health. Anger, resentment and guilt make you sick, modern physicians tell us, which proves once again that the most up-to-date book on personal well-being is the Holy Bible, neglected by so many or regarded by them as purely a religious book and certainly as one that is not practical. No wonder more copies are read than all other books. That is because in this book we discover not only what is wrong with us but how to correct it as well.

Dr. Fowler calls attention to the 'emotional colds' suffered by children who feel insecure. He reports that many cases of chronic colds occur in children who come from broken homes. An older child often has recurring respiratory infection when a new baby is born because he feels neglected and jealous. A nine-year-old boy had an extremely dictatorial father and an indulgent mother. The conflict between the strictness of one parent and the lenience of the other obviously was disturbing to the child. He particularly feared punishment by his father. This boy suffered for several years from continuous coughs and sniffles. It was noted that the colds disappeared when he went to camp—away from his parents.

Since irritation, anger, hate, and resentment have such a powerful effect in producing ill-health, what is the antidote? Obviously it is to fill the mind with attitudes of goodwill, forgiveness, faith, love, and the spirit of imperturbability. And how is that accomplished? Following are some practical suggestions. They have been used successfully by many in counter-attacking especially the emotion of anger. A consistent application of these suggestions can produce feelings of well-being:

1. Remember that anger is an emotion, and an emotion is always warm, even hot. Therefore, to reduce an emotion, cool it. And how do you cool it? When a person gets angry, the fists tend to clench, the voice rises in stridency, muscles tense, the body becomes rigid. (Psychologically you are poised for fight, adrenalin shoots through the body.) This is the old cave-man hangover in the nervous system. So deliberately oppose the heat of this emotion with coolness—freeze it out. Deliberately, by an act of will, keep your hands from clenching. Hold your fingers out straight. Deliberately reduce your tone; bring it down to a whisper. Remember

that it is difficult to argue in a whisper. Slump in a chair, or even lie down if possible. It is very difficult to get mad lying down.

2. Say aloud to yourself: "Don't be a fool. This won't get me anywhere, so skip it." At that moment it may be a bit hard to pray, but try it, anyway; at least conjure up a picture of Jesus Christ in your mind and try to think of Him mad just as you are. You can't do it, and the effort will serve to puncture your angry emotions.

3. One of the best techniques for cooling off anger was suggested by Mrs. Grace Oursler. She formerly employed the usual 'count to ten' technique, but happened to notice that the first ten words of the Lord's Prayer worked better. "Our Father who art in Heaven, hallowed be Thy name." When angry, say that ten times and your anger will lose its power over you.

4. Anger is a great term expressing the accumulated vehemence of a multitude of minor irritations. These irritations, each rather small in itself, having gathered force by reason of the one being added to the other, finally blaze forth in a fury that often leaves us abashed at ourselves. Therefore, make a list of everything that irritates you. No matter how inconsequential it may be or how silly each is, list it just the same. The purpose in doing this is to dry up the tiny rivulets that feed the great river of anger.

5. Make each separate irritation a special object of prayer. Get a victory over each, one at a time. Instead of attempting to destroy all of your anger, which as we have pointed out is a consolidated force, snip away by prayer each annoyance that feeds your anger. In this way you will weaken your anger to the point where presently you will gain control over it.

6. Train yourself so that every time you feel the surge of anger you say: 'Is this really worth what it is doing to me emotionally? I will make a fool of myself. I will lose friends.' In order to get the full effect of this technique, practise saying to yourself a few times every day: 'It is never worth it to get worked up or mad about anything.' Also affirm: 'It isn't worth it to spend $1,000 worth of emotion on a five-cent irritation.'

7. When a hurt-feeling situation arises, get it straightened out as quickly as possible. Don't brood over it for a minute longer than you can help. Do something about it. Do not allow yourself to sulk or indulge in self-pity. Don't mope around with resentful thoughts. The minute your feelings are hurt, do just as when you hurt your finger. Immediately apply the cure. Unless you do so the situation can become distorted out of all proportion. So put some spiritual iodine on the hurt at once by saying a prayer of love and forgiveness.

8. Apply grievance drainage to your mind. That is, open your mind and let the grievance flow out. Go to someone you trust and pour it out to him until not a vestige of it remains within you. Then forget it.

9. Simply start praying for the person who has hurt your feelings. Continue this until you feel the malice fading away. Sometimes you may have to pray for quite a while to get that result. A man who tried this method told me that he kept account of the number of times he needed to pray until the grievance left and peace came. It was exactly sixty-four times. He literally prayed it out of his system. This is positively guaranteed to work.

10. Say this little prayer: 'May the love of Christ fill my heart.' Then add this line: 'May the love of Christ for ——— (insert the other's name) flood my soul.' Pray

this, mean it (or ask to mean it), and you will get relief.

11. Actually take the advice of Jesus to forgive seventy times seven. To be literal, that means four hundred and ninety times. Before you have forgiven a person that many times you will be free of resentment.

12. Finally, this wild, undisciplined, primitive urge in you which flames to the surface can be tamed only by allowing Jesus Christ to take control. Therefore, complete this lesson by saying to Jesus Christ: 'Even as You can convert a person's morals, so now I ask You to convert my nerves. As You give power over the sins of the flesh, so give me power over the sins of the disposition. Bring my temper under Your control. Give me Thy healing peace in my nervous system as well as in my soul.' If you are beset by temper, repeat the above prayer three times every day. It might be advisable to print it on a card and put it on your desk, or above the kitchen sink, or in your pocket-book.

13 | Inflow of New Thoughts Can Remake You

ONE OF THE most important and powerful facts about you is expressed in the following statement by William James, who was one of the very few wise men America has produced. William James said: "The greatest discovery of my generation *is that human beings can alter their lives by altering their attitudes of mind.*" As you think, so shall you be. So flush out all old, tired, worn-out thoughts. Fill your mind with fresh, new creative thoughts of faith, love, and goodness. By this process you can actually remake your life.

And where do you find such personality-remaking thoughts?

I know a business executive, a modest man, but the type of individual who is never defeated. No problem, no set-back, no opposition ever gets him down. He simply attacks each difficulty with an optimistic attitude and a sure confidence that it will work out right, and, in some strange way, it always does for him. He seems to have a magic touch on life—a touch that never fails.

Because of that impressive characteristic this man always interested me. I knew there was a definite explanation of his being this way and, of course, wanted to hear his story, but in view of his modesty and reticence it was not easy to persuade him to talk about himself.

One day when he was in the mood he told me his secret, an amazingly simple but effective secret. I was visiting his plant, a modern, up-to-date structure, much of it air-conditioned. Latest type machinery and methods of production make it a factory of outstanding efficiency. Labour-management relations seem as nearly perfect as is possible among imperfect human beings. A spirit of goodwill pervades the entire organisation.

His office is ultra-modernistically decorated and furnished with handsome desks, rugs, and panelled with exotic woods. The decorating scheme is five startling colours blended together pleasingly. All in all it is the last word, and then some.

Imagine, then, my surprise to see on his highly polished white mahogany desk an old battered copy of the Bible. It was the only old object in those ultra-modern rooms. I commented upon this seemingly strange inconsistency.

"That book," he replied, pointing to the Bible, "is the most up-to-date thing in this plant. Equipment wears out and furnishing styles change, but that book is so far ahead of us that it never gets out of date.

"When I went to college, my good Christian mother gave me that Bible with the suggestion that if I would read and practise its teachings, I would learn how to get through life successfully. But I thought she was just a nice old lady"—he chuckled—"at my age she seemed old— she wasn't really, and to humour her, I took the Bible, but for years practically never looked at it. I thought I didn't need it. Well," he continued slangily, "I was a dope. I was stupid. And I got my life in a terrific mess.

"Everything went wrong primarily because I was wrong. I was thinking wrong, acting wrong, doing wrong. I succeeded at nothing, failed at everything. Now I realise that my principal trouble was wrong thinking. I was negative, resentful, cocky, opinionated. Nobody could tell me anything. I thought I knew everything. I was filled with gripes at everybody. Little wonder nobody liked me. I certainly was a 'wash-out'.

So ran his dismal story. "One night in going through some papers," he continued, "I came across the long-forgotten Bible. It brought up old memories and I started aimlessly to read it. Do you know it is strange how things happen; how in just a flashing moment of time everything becomes different. Well, as I read, a sentence leaped up at me, a sentence that changed my life—and when I say changed, I mean changed. From the minute I read that sentence everything has been different, tremendously different."

"What is this wonderful sentence?" I wanted to know, and he quoted it slowly: " 'The Lord is the strength of my life . . . in this will I be confident.' (Psalms xxvii. 1, 3.)

"I don't know why that one line affected me so," he went on, "but it did. I know now that I was weak and a failure because I had no faith, no confidence. I was very negative, a defeatist. Something happened inside my mind. I guess I had what they call a spiritual experience. My thought pattern shifted from negative to positive. I decided to put my faith in God and sincerely do my best, trying to follow the principles outlined in the Bible. As I did so I began to get hold of a new set of thoughts. I began to think differently. In time my old failure thoughts were flushed out by this new spiritual experience and an inflow of new thoughts gradually but actually remade me."

So concluded the story of this business man. He

altered his thinking, and the new thoughts which flowed in displaced the old thoughts which had been defeating him and his life was changed.

This incident illustrates an important fact about human nature: you can think your way to failure and unhappiness, but you can also think your way to success and happiness. The world in which you live is not primarily determined by outward conditions and circumstances, but by thoughts that habitually occupy your mind. Remember the wise words of Marcus Aurelius, one of the great thinkers of antiquity, who said: "A man's life is what his thoughts make of it."

It has been said that the wisest man who ever lived in America was Ralph Waldo Emerson, the Sage of Concord. Emerson declared: "A man is what he thinks about all day long."

A famous psychologist says: "There is a deep tendency in human nature to become precisely like that which you habitually imagine yourself to be."

It has been said that thoughts are things, that they actually possess dynamic power. Judged by the power they exercise one can readily accept such an appraisal. You can actually think yourself into or out of situations. You can make yourself ill with your thoughts and by the same token you can make yourself well by the use of a different and healing type of thought. Think one way and you attract the conditions which that type of thinking indicates. Think another way and you can create an entirely different set of conditions. Conditions are created by thoughts far more powerfully than thoughts create conditions.

Think positively, for example, and you set in motion positive forces which bring positive results to pass.

Positive thoughts create around yourself an atmosphere propitious to the development of positive outcomes. On the contrary, think negative thoughts and you create around yourself an atmosphere propitious to the development of negative results.

To change your circumstances, first start thinking differently. Do not passively accept unsatisfactory circumstances, but form a picture in your mind of circumstances as they should be. Hold that picture, develop it firmly in all details, believe in it, pray about it, work at it, and you can actualise it according to that mental image emphasised in your positive thinking.

This is one of the greatest laws in the universe. Fervently do I wish I had discovered it as a very young man. It dawned upon me much later in life and I have found it to be one of the greatest, if not my greatest, discovery, outside of my relationship to God. And in a deep sense this law is a factor in one's relationship with God because it channels God's power into personality.

This great law briefly and simply stated is that if you think in negative terms you will get negative results. If you think in positive terms you will achieve positive results. That is the simple fact which is at the basis of an astonishing law of prosperity and success. In three words: Believe and succeed.

I learned this law in a very interesting manner. Some years ago a group of us consisting of Lowell Thomas, Captain Eddie Rickenbacker, Branch Rickey, Raymond Thornburg, and others established an inspirational self-help magazine called *Guideposts*. This magazine has a double function: first, by relating stories of people who through their faith have overcome difficulties, it teaches techniques of victorious living, victory over fear, over circumstances, over obstacles, over resentment. It teaches faith over all manner of negativism.

Second, as a non-profit, non-sectarian, inter-faith publication it teaches the great fact that God is in the stream of history and that this nation was founded on belief in God and His laws.

The magazine reminds its readers that America is the first great nation in history to be established on a definitely religious premise, and that unless we keep it so our freedoms will deteriorate.

Mr. Raymond Thornburg as publisher and I as editor in starting the magazine had no financial backing to underwrite it. It was begun on faith. In fact, its first offices were in rooms above a grocery store in the little village of Pawling, New York. There was a borrowed typewriter, a few rickety chairs, and that was all; all except a great idea and great faith. Slowly a subscription list of 25,000 developed. The future seemed promising. Suddenly one night fire broke out, and within an hour the publishing house was destroyed and with it the total list of subscribers. Foolishly no duplicate list had been made.

Lowell Thomas, loyal and efficient patron of *Guideposts* from the very start, mentioned this sad circumstance in his radio broadcast and as a result we soon had 30,000 subscribers, practically all the old ones and many new ones.

The subscription list rose to approximately 40,000, but costs increased even more rapidly. The magazine, which has always been sold for less than cost in order widely to disseminate the message, was more expensive than anticipated and we were faced with difficult financial problems. In fact, at one time, it seemed almost impossible to keep it going.

At this juncture we called a meeting, and I'm sure you never attended a more pessimistic, negative, discouraging meeting. It dripped with pessimism. Where were we going to get the money to pay our bills? We figured out ways of robbing Peter to pay Paul. Complete discouragement filled our minds.

A woman had been invited to this meeting whom we all regarded most highly. But one reason she was included in this meeting was because, on a previous occasion, she had contributed $2,000 to help inaugurate *Guideposts* magazine. It was hoped that lightning might strike twice in the same place. But this time she gave us something of more value than money.

As this dismal meeting progressed she remained silent for a long time, but finally said: "I suppose you gentlemen would like me to make another financial contribution. I might as well put you out of your misery. I am not going to give you another cent."

This did not put us out of our misery. On the contrary, it put us deeper into our misery. "But," she continued, "I will give you something far more valuable than money."

This astonished us, for we could not possibly imagine anything of more value than money in the circumstances.

"I am going to give you an idea," she continued, "a creative idea."

'Well,' we thought to ourselves unenthusiastically, 'how can we pay our bills with an idea?'

Ah, but the idea is just what will help you pay bills. Every achievement in this world was first projected as a creative idea. First the idea, then faith in it, then the means of implementing the idea. That is the way success proceeds.

"Now," she said, "here is the idea. What is your

present trouble? It is that you *lack* everything. You *lack* money. You *lack* subscribers. You *lack* equipment. You *lack* ideas. You *lack* courage. Why do you *lack* all these requirements? Simply because you are thinking *lack*. If you think *lack* you create the conditions that produce a state of *lack*. By this constant mental emphasis upon what you *lack* you have frustrated the creative forces that can give impetus to the development of *Guideposts*. You have been working hard from the standpoint of doing many things, but you have failed to do the one all-important thing that will lend power to all your other efforts: you have not employed positive thinking. Instead, you have thought in terms of *lack*.

"To correct that situation—reverse the mental process and begin to think prosperity, achievement, success. This will require practice, but it can be done quickly if you will demonstrate faith. The process is to visualise; that is, to see *Guideposts* in terms of successful achievement. Create a mental picture of *Guideposts* as a great magazine, sweeping the country. Visualise large numbers of subscribers, all eagerly reading this inspirational material and profiting thereby. Create a mental image of lives being changed by the philosophy of achievement which *Guideposts* teaches monthly in its issues.

"Do not hold mental pictures of difficulties and failures, but lift your mind above them and visualise powers and achievements. When you elevate your thoughts into the area of visualised attainments you look down on your problems rather than from below up at them and thus you get a much more encouraging view of them. Always come up over your problems. Never approach a problem from below.

"Now let me continue further," she said. "How many subscribers do you need at the moment to keep going?"

We thought quickly and said: "100,000." We had 40,000.

"All right," she said confidently, "that is not hard. That is easy. Visualise 100,000 people being creatively helped by this magazine and you will have them. In fact, the minute you can see them in your mind, you already have them."

She turned to me and said: "Norman, can you see 100,000 subscribers at this minute? Look out there, look ahead of you. In your mind's eye can you see them?"

I wasn't convinced as yet, and I said rather doubtfully: "Well, maybe so, but they seem pretty dim to me."

She was a little disappointed in me. I thought, as she asked: "Can't you imaginatively visualise 100,000 subscribers?"

I guess my imagination wasn't working very well because all I could see was the insufficient but actual 40,000.

Then she turned to my old friend Raymond Thornburg, who has been blessed with a gloriously victorious personality, and she said, calling him by his nickname: "Pinky, can you visualise 100,000 subscribers?"

I rather doubted that Pinky would see them. He is a rubber manufacturer who gives his time freely from his own business to help advance this inspirational, non-profit magazine, and you would not ordinarily think that a rubber manufacturer would respond to this type of thinking. But he has the faculty of creative imagination. I noticed by the fascinated look on his face that she had him. He was gazing straight ahead with rather a look of wonder when she asked: "Do you see the 100,000 subscribers?"

"Yes," he cried with eagerness, "yes, I do see them."

Electrified I demanded: "Where? Point them out to me?"

Then I, too, began to visualise them.

"Now," continued our friend, "let us bow our heads and together thank God for giving us 100,000 subscribers."

Frankly I thought that was pushing the Lord rather hard, but it was justified by a verse in the Scriptures where it says: "And all things, whatsoever ye shall ask in prayer, believing, ye shall receive them." (Matthew xxi. 22.) That means when you pray for something, at the same time visualise what you pray for. Believe that if it is God's will and is worth while, not selfishly sought after, but for human good, that it is at that moment given you.

If you have difficulty in following this reasoning, let me tell you that from that moment until the present writing *Guideposts* never lacked for anything. It has found wonderful friends and has had fine support. It has been able always to meet its bills, purchase needed equipment, finance itself, and as I write these words *Guideposts* is nearing the half-million mark and more subscriptions are coming in regularly, sometimes as many as three or four thousand per day.

I recite this instance not for the purpose of advertising *Guideposts*, although I strongly recommend this magazine to all my readers, and if you would like to be a subscriber, write to *Guideposts*, Pawling, New York, for information. But I tell the story because I was awed by this experience, realising that I had stumbled upon a law, a tremendous law of personal victory. I decided to apply it thereafter to my own problems and wherever I have done so can report a marvellous result. Wherever I have failed to do so, I have missed great results.

It is as simple as this—put your problem in God's hands. In your thoughts rise above the problem so that you look down upon it, not up at it. Test it according to God's will. That is, do not try to get success from something that is wrong. Be sure it is right morally, spiritually, and ethically. You can never get a right result from an error. If your thinking is wrong, it is wrong and not right and can never be right so long as it is wrong. If it is wrong in the essence it is bound to be wrong in the result.

Therefore be sure it is right, then hold it up to God's name and visualise a great result. Keep the idea of prosperity, of achievement, and of attainment firmly fixed in your mind. Never entertain a failure thought. Should a negative thought of defeat come into your mind, expel it by increasing the positive affirmation. Affirm aloud, 'God is now giving me success. He is now giving me attainment.' The mental vision which you create and firmly hold in consciousness will be actualised if you continually affirm it in your thoughts and if you work diligently and effectively. This creative process simply stated is: visualise, prayerise, and finally actualise.

People in all walks of life who accomplish notable achievements know the value of this law in their experience.

Henry J. Kaiser told me that at one time he was building a levee along a river-bank, and there came a great storm and flood which buried all his earth-moving machinery and destroyed the work that had been done. Upon going out to observe the damage after the water receded, he found his workers standing around glumly looking at the mud and the buried machinery.

He came among them and said with a smile: "Why are you so glum?"

"Don't you see what has happened?" they asked. "Our machinery is covered with mud."

"What mud?" he asked brightly.

"What mud?" they repeated in astonishment. "Look around you. It is a sea of mud."

"Oh," he laughed, "I don't see any mud."

"But how can you say that?" they asked him.

"Because," said Mr. Kaiser, "I am looking up at a clear blue sky, and there is no mud up there. There is only sunshine, and I never saw any mud that could stand against sunshine. Soon it will be dried up, and then you will be able to move your machinery and start all over again."

How right he is. If your eyes are looking down in the mud and you feel a sense of failure, you will create defeat for yourself. Optimistic visualisation combined with prayer and faith will inevitably actualise achievement.

Another friend of mine who started from the lowliest beginnings has performed some outstanding achieve‐ ments. I remember him in his school-days as an awk‐ ward, unprepossessing, very shy country boy. But he had character and one of the keenest brains I have ever encountered. Today he is an outstanding man in his line. I asked him: "What is the secret of your success?"

"The people who have worked with me across the years and the unlimited opportunity given any boy in the United States of America," he replied.

"Yes, I know that is true, but I am sure you must have some personal technique, and I would be interested in having it," I said.

"It all lies in how you think about problems," he replied. "I attack a problem and shake it to pieces with my mind. I put all the mental power I have upon it. Second, I pray about it most sincerely. Third, I paint a mental picture of success. Fourth, I always ask myself: 'What is the right thing to do?' for," he said, "nothing will be right if it is wrong. Nothing that is wrong will ever come out right. Fifth, I give it all I've got. But let me emphasise again," he concluded, "if you're thinking defeat, change your thoughts at once. Get new and positive thoughts. That is primary and basic in overcoming difficulties and in achieving."

At this very minute, as you read this book, potential ideas are in your mind. By releasing and developing these ideas you can solve your financial problem, your business situation, you can care for yourself and your family, and attain success in your ventures. A steady inflow and practical use of these creative thoughts can remake your life and you along with it.

There was a time when I acquiesced in the silly idea that there is no relationship between faith and prosperity; that when one talked about religion one should never relate it to achievement, that it dealt only with ethics and morals or social values. But now I realise that such a viewpoint limits the power of God and the development of the individual. Religion teaches that there is a tremendous power in the universe and that this power can dwell in personality. It is a power that can blast out all defeat and lift a person above all difficult situations.

We have seen the demonstration of atomic energy. We know that astonishing and enormous energy exists in the universe. This same force of energy is resident in the human mind. Nothing on earth is greater than the human mind in potential power. The average individual is capable of much greater achievement than he has ever realised.

This is true regardless of who is reading this statement. When you actually learn to release yourself you will discover that your mind contains ideas of such creative value that you need not lack anything. By the full and proper use of your power stimulated by God power, you can make your life successful.

You can make just about anything of your life—anything you will believe or will visualise, anything you will pray for and work for. Look deeply into your mind. Amazing wonders are there.

Whatever your situation may be, you can improve it. First, quiet your mind so that inspirations may rise from its depths. Believe that God is now helping you. Visualise achievement. Organise your life on a spiritual basis so that God's principles work within you. Hold firmly in your mind a picture not of failure but of success. Do these things and creative thoughts will flow freely from your mind. This is an amazing law, one that can change anybody's life, including your own. An inflow of new thoughts can remake you regardless of every difficulty you may now face, and I repeat—*every difficulty*.

In the last analysis the basic reason a person fails to live a creative and successful life is because of error within himself. He thinks wrong. He needs to correct the error in his thoughts. He needs to practise right thinking. When the 23rd Psalm says: "He leadeth me in the paths of righteousness," it not only means the paths of goodness, but the paths of right-mindedness as well. When Isaiah says: "Let the wicked forsake his way and the un-righteous man his thoughts" (Isaiah lv. 7), it not only means that a person is to depart from evil and do good, but that he is to change his thinking from wrong to right, from error to truth. The great secret of successful living is to reduce the amount of error in oneself and increase the amount of truth. An inflow of new, right, health-laden thoughts through the mind creatively affects the circumstances of life, for truth always pro-duces right procedures and therefore right results.

Years ago I knew a young man who for a while was one of the most complete failures in my entire experience. He had a potentially delightful personality, but he failed at everything. A person would employ him and be enthusiastic about him, but soon his enthusiasm would cool and it was not long until he was out of that position. This failure pattern was repeated many times. He was a failure as a person as well as an employee. He missed connections with everything. He just couldn't do any-thing right, and he used to ask me: "What is wrong with me that everything goes wrong?"

Still he had a lot of conceit. He was cocky and smug, and had the irritating habit of blaming everybody but himself. Something was wrong with every office with which he was connected or every organisation that employed him. He blamed everybody else for his failures —never himself. He would never look inside himself. It never occurred to him that anything could be wrong with him.

One night, however, he wanted to talk with me, and as I had to make a drive of about a hundred miles to deliver a speech he drove there and back with me. On our return we stopped along about midnight at a road-side stall for a hamburger and a cup of coffee. I don't know what was in that hamburger sandwich, but since this incident I have had a new respect for hamburgers, for of a sudden he shouted: "I've got it! I've got it!"

"You've got what?" I asked in astonishment.

"I've got the answer. Now I know what's the trouble with me. It's that everything goes wrong with me because I myself am wrong."

I clapped my hand on his back and said: "Boy, at last you are on your way."

"Why, it's as clear as a crystal," he said. "I have been thinking wrong, and as a result I have created wrong outcomes."

By this time we were out in the moonlight standing alongside my car, and I said to him: "Harry, you must go one step further and ask God to make you right inwardly." I quoted this passage from the Bible: " 'Ye shall know the truth, and the truth shall make you free.' " (John viii. 32.) Get the truth into your mind and you will be free of your failures.

He became an enthusiastic practising follower of Jesus Christ. Through real faith and a complete change of thoughts and personal habits, wrong thinking and wrong acting were removed from his nature. He straightened out by developing a right (or righteousness) pattern instead of an error pattern. When he was made right, then everything began to go right for him.

Following are seven practical steps for changing your mental attitudes from negative to positive, for releasing creative new thoughts, and for shifting from error

235

patterns to truth patterns. Try them—keep on trying them. They will work.

1. For the next twenty-four hours, deliberately speak hopefully about everything, about your job, about your health, about your future. Go out of your way to talk optimistically about everything. This will be difficult, for possibly it is your habit to talk pessimistically. From this negative habit you must restrain yourself even if it requires an act of will.

2. After speaking hopefully for twenty-four hours, continue the practice for one week, then you can be permitted to be 'realistic' for a day or two. You will discover that what you meant by 'realistic' a week ago was actually pessimistic, but what you now mean by 'realistic' is something entirely different; it is the dawning of the positive outlook. When most people say they are being 'realistic' they delude themselves: they are simply being negative.

3. You must feed your mind even as you feed your body, and to make your mind healthy you must feed it nourishing, wholesome thoughts. Therefore, today start to shift your mind from negative to positive thinking. Start at the beginning of the New Testament and underscore every sentence about *Faith*. Continue doing this until you have marked every such passage in the four books, Matthew, Mark, Luke, and John. Particularly note Mark xi., verses 22, 23, 24. They will serve as samples of the verses you are to underscore and fix deeply in your consciousness.

4. Then commit the underscored passages to memory. Commit one each day until you can recite the entire list from memory. This will take time, but remember you have consumed much more time becoming a

negative thinker than this will require. Effort and time will be needed to unlearn your negative pattern.

5. Make a list of your friends to determine who is the most positive thinker among them and deliberately cultivate his society. Do not abandon your negative friends, but get closer to those with a positive point of view for a while, until you have absorbed their spirit, then you can go back among your negative friends and give them your newly acquired thought pattern without taking on their negativisim.

6. Avoid argument, but whenever a negative attitude is expressed, counter with a positive and optimistic opinion.

7. Pray a great deal and always let your prayer take the form of thanksgiving on the assumption that God is giving you great and wonderful things; for if you think He is, He surely is. God will not give you any greater blessing than you can believe in. He wants to give you great things, but even He cannot make you take anything greater than you are equipped by faith to receive. "According to your faith (that is, in proportion to) be it unto you." (Matthew ix. 29.)

The secret of a better and more successful life is to cast out those old dead, unhealthy thoughts. Substitute for them new vital, dynamic faith thoughts. You can depend upon it—an inflow of new thoughts will remake you and your life.

14 | Relax for Easy Power

"Every night in the United States more than six million sleeping tablets are required to put the American people to sleep."

This startling statement was made to me several years ago by a drug manufacturer at a convention of that industry where I was giving a speech. Though his assertion seemed incredible, I have been told by others who are in a position to know that the above estimate is now an understatement.

In fact, I heard another good authority assert that the American people are using about twelve million doses of sleeping tablets per day. That is enough to put every twelfth American to sleep tonight. Statistics show that the use of sleeping tablets has risen 1,000 per cent in recent years. But a more recent statement is even more startling. According to the vice-president of a large drug manufacturing concern approximately seven billion one-half-grain tablets are consumed yearly, which works out at about nineteen million tablets per night.

What a pathetic situation. Sleep is a natural restorative process. One would think that any person after a day's work would be able to sleep peacefully, but apparently Americans have even lost the art of sleeping. In fact, so keyed up are they that I, a minister with ample opportunity to test the matter, must report that the American people are so nervous and highly-strung that now it is almost next to impossible to put them to sleep with a sermon. It has been years since I have seen anyone asleep in church. And that is a sad situation.

A Washington official who loves to juggle figures, especially astronomical figures, told me that last year in the United States there was a total of seven and a half billion headaches. This works itself out at approximately fifty headaches per head per annum. Have you had your quota yet this year? Just how this official arrived at these figures he did not say, but shortly after our conversation I noticed a report that in a recent year the drug industry sold eleven million pounds of aspirin. Perhaps this era might appropriately be termed 'The Aspirin Age', as one author called it.

An authoritative source declares that every other hospital bed in the United States is occupied by a patient who was put there not because he encountered a germ or had an accident or developed an organic malady, but because of his inability to organise and discipline his emotions.

In a clinic 500 patients were carefully examined and 386, or 77 per cent, were found to be ill of psychosomatic difficulties—physical illness caused largely by unhealthy mental states. Another clinic made a study of a large number of ulcer cases and reported that nearly half were made ill, not as the result of physical troubles, but because the patients worried too much or hated too much, had too much guilt, or were tension victims.

A doctor from still another clinic made the observation that in his opinion medical men, despite all extraordinary scientific developments, are now able to heal by

239

the means of science alone less than half the maladies brought them. He declares that in many cases patients are sending back into their bodies the diseased thoughts of their minds. Prominent among these diseased thoughts are anxiety and tension.

This unhappy situation has become so serious that in our own Marble Collegiate Church, Fifth Avenue at 29th Street, New York City, we now have twelve psychiatrists on the staff under the supervision of Dr. Smiley Blanton. Why psychiatrists on the staff of a church? The answer is that psychiatry is a science. Its function is the analysis, diagnosis, and treatment of human nature according to certain well-authenticated laws and procedures.

Christianity may also be thought of as a science. It is a philosophy, a system of theology, a system of metaphysics, and a system of worship. It also works itself out in moral and ethical codes. But Christianity also has the characteristics of a science in that it is based upon a book which contains a system of techniques and formulas designed for the understanding and treatment of human nature. The laws are so precise and have been so often demonstrated when proper conditions of understanding, belief and practice are applied, that religion may be said to form an exact science.

When a person comes to our clinic the first counsellor is perhaps a psychiatrist who in a kindly and careful manner studies the problem and tells the patient 'why he does what he does'. This is a most important fact to learn. Why, for example, have you had an inferiority complex all your life long, or why have you been haunted by fear, or, again, why do you nurse resentment? Why have you always been shy and reticent, or why do you do stupid things or make inept statements? These phenomena of your human nature do not just happen. There is a reason why you do what you do and it is an important day in your life experience when at last you discover the reason. Self-knowledge is the beginning of self-correction.

Following the self-knowledge process the psychiatrist turns the patient over to the pastor who tells him how to do what he ought to do. The pastor applies to the case, in scientific and systematic form, the therapies of prayer, faith, and love. The psychiatrist and the minister pool their knowledge and combine their therapies with the result that many people have found new life and happiness. The minister does not attempt to be a psychiatrist nor the psychiatrist a pastor. Each performs his own function, but always in co-operation.

The Christianity utilised in this procedure is the undiluted teachings of Jesus Christ, Lord and Saviour of man's life. We believe in the practical, absolute workability of the teachings of Jesus. We believe that we can indeed "do all things through Christ." (Philippians iv. 13.) The Gospel as we work with it proves to be a literal fulfilment of the astonishing promise: "Eye hath not seen, nor ear heard, neither have entered into the heart of man, the things which God hath prepared for them that love Him." (I Corinthians ii. 9.) Believe (in Christ); believe in His system of thought and practice; believe and you will overcome all fear, hate, inferiority, guilt, and every form and manner of defeat. In other words, no good thing is too good to be true. You have never seen, never heard, never even imagined the things God will give to those who love Him.

In the work of the clinic one frequent problem is that

of tension. This, to a very large degree, may be called the prevailing malady of the American people. But not only the American people seem to suffer from tension. The Royal Bank of Canada some time ago devoted its monthly letter to this problem under the title: 'Let's Slow Down', and says in part: 'This monthly letter does not set itself up as a counsellor of mental and physical health, but it is attempting to break down a problem that bedevils every adult person in Canada,' and, I might add, in the United States as well.

The bank letter goes on to say: 'We are victims of a mounting tension; we have difficulty in relaxing. Our high-strung nervous systems are on a perpetual binge. Caught up as we are in the rush all day, every day, and far into the night, we are not living fully. We must remember what Carlyle called "the calm supremacy of the spirit over its circumstances".'

When a prominent banking institution calls to the attention of its customers the fact that they are failing to derive from life what they really want from it because they have become victims of tension, it is certainly time something was done about the situation.

In St. Petersburg, Florida, I actually saw a machine on the street equipped with a sign: 'What is your blood-pressure?' You could put a coin in a slot and get the bad news. When you can buy a reading on blood-pressure like you buy gum out of a slot-machine, it indicates that many people have this problem.

One of the simplest methods for reducing tension is to practise the easy-does-it attitude. Do everything more slowly, less hectically, and without pressure. My friend Branch Rickey, famous baseball man, told me that he would not use a player no matter how well he hits, fields, or runs if he is guilty of 'overpressing'. To be a success-ful big-league baseball player there must be a flow of easy power through every action and of course through the mind. The most effective way to hit a ball is by the easy method, where all the muscles are flexible and operating in correlated power. Try to kill the ball and you will slice it or maybe miss it altogether. This is true in golf, in baseball, in every sport.

In a world series game many years ago Ty Cobb, one of the greatest heroes in baseball, hit four home runs, a record so far as I know that has never been surpassed. Ty Cobb presented the bat with which he performed this extraordinary feat to a friend of mine. I was per-mitted to take this bat in my hand, which I did with considerable awe. In the spirit of the game I struck a pose, as if to bat. Doubtless my batting stance was not in any sense reminiscent of the immortal slugger. In fact, my friend, who was himself at one time a minor-league baseball player, chuckled and said: "Ty Cobb would never do it that way. You are too rigid, too tense. You are obviously over-trying. You would probably strike out."

It was beautiful to watch Ty Cobb. The man and the bat were one. It was a study in rhythm, and one marvelled at the ease with which he got into the swing. He was a master of easy power. It is the same in all success. Analyse people who are really efficient and they always seem to do things easily, with a minimum of effort. In so doing they release maximum power.

One of my friends, a famous business man who handles important affairs and varied interests, always seems to be at ease. He does everything efficiently and quickly but is never in a dither. He never has that anxious, frazzled look on his face which marks people who cannot handle either their time or their work. I inquired the secret of his obviously easy power.

He smiled and replied: "Oh, it isn't much of a secret. I just try to keep myself in tune with God. That's all. Every morning after breakfast," he explained, "my wife and I go into the living-room for a period of quietness. One of us reads aloud some inspirational piece to get us into the mood of meditation. It may be a poem or a few paragraphs of a book. Following that we sit quietly, each praying or meditating according to his own mood and manner, then together we affirm the thought that God is filling us with strength and quiet energy. This is a definite fifteen-minute ritual and we never miss it. We couldn't get along without it. We would crack up. As a result I always seem to feel that I have more energy than I need and more power than is required." So said this efficient man who demonstrates easy power.

I know a number of men and women who practise this or similar techniques for reducing tension. It is becoming a quite general and popular procedure nowadays.

One February morning I was rushing down the long veranda of a Florida hotel with a handful of mail just in from my office in New York. I had come to Florida for a mid-winter vacation, but hadn't seemed to get out of the routine of dealing with my mail the first thing in the morning. As I hurried by, headed for a couple of hours' work with that mail, a friend from Georgia who was sitting in a rocking-chair with his hat partially over his eyes stopped me in my headlong rush and said in his slow and pleasant Southern drawl: "Where are you rushing to, Doctor? That's no way to do down here in the Florida sunshine. Come over here and 'set' in one of these rocking-chairs and help me practise one of the greatest of the arts."

Mystified, I said: "Help you practise one of the greatest of the arts!"

"Yes," he replied, "an art that is passing out. Not many people know how to do it any more."

"Well," I asked, "please tell me what it is. I don't see you practising any art."

"Oh, yes, I am," he said. "I am practising the art of just sittin' in the sun. Sit here and let the sun fall on your face. It is warm-like and it smells good. It makes you feel peaceful inside. Did you ever think about the sun?" he asked. "It never hurries, never gets excited, it just works slowly and makes no noise—doesn't push any buzzers, doesn't answer any telephones, doesn't ring any bells, just goes on a-shining, and the sun does more work in the fraction of an instant than you and I could ever do in a lifetime. Think of what it does. It causes the flowers to bloom, keeps the trees growing, warms the earth, causes the fruit and vegetables to grow and the crops to ripen, lifts water to send back on the earth, and it makes you feel 'peaceful-like'.

"I find that when I sit in the sun and let the sun work on me it puts some rays into me that give me energy; that is, when I take time to sit in the sun.

"So throw that mail over in the corner," he said, "and sit down here with me."

I did so, and when finally I went to my room and got at my mail I finished it in no time at all. And there was a good part of the day left for vacation activities and for more 'sittin' in the sun'.

Of course I know a lot of lazy people who have been sittin' in the sun all their lives and never amounted to anything. There is a difference between sittin' and relaxing, and just sittin'. But if you sit and relax and think about God and get yourself in tune with Him and open yourself to the flow of His power, then sittin' is not laziness; in fact it is about the best way to renew power. It produces driving energy, the kind of energy *you* drive, not the kind that drives you.

The secret is to keep the mind quiet, avoiding all hectic reactions of haste, and to practise peaceful thinking. The essence of the art is to keep the tempo down; to perform your responsibilities on the basis of the most efficient conservation of energy. It is advisable to adopt one or two workable plans through the use of which you can become expert in the practice of relaxed and easy power

One of the best such plans was suggested to me by Captain Eddie Rickenbacker. A very busy man, he manages to handle his responsibilities in a manner indicating reserves of power. I found one element of his secret quite by accident.

I was filming a programme for television with him. We had been assured that the work could be done quickly, leaving him free to go to the many other matters on his daily agenda.

However, the filming was delayed long beyond the time anticipated. I noted, however, that the captain showed no signs of agitation. He did not become nervous or anxious. He did not pace up and down, putting in frantic calls to his office. Instead, he accepted the situation gracefully. There were a couple of old rocking-chairs at the studio, apparently intended for use in a set other than ours. He sat in one rocker in a very relaxed manner.

I have always been a great admirer of Eddie Ricken-backer and I commented on his lack of tension. "I know how busy you are," I said, "and I marvel at the way you sit quiet, composed, and peaceful-like."

For myself, I was a bit disturbed largely because I regretted to take so much of Captain Rickenbacker's time. "How can you be so imperturbable?" I asked.

He laughingly replied: "Oh, I just practise what you preach. Come on, easy does it. Sit down here beside me."

I pulled up the other rocking-chair and did a little relaxing on my own. Then I said: "Eddie, I know you have some technique to attain this impressive serenity. Tell me about it, please."

He is a modest man, but because of my persistence he gave me a formula which he says he uses frequently. I now use it myself and it is very effective. It may be described as follows:

First, collapse physically. Practise this several times a day. Let go every muscle in the body. Conceive of yourself as a jellyfish, getting your body into complete looseness. Form a mental picture of a huge burlap bag of potatoes. Then mentally cut the bag, allowing the potatoes to roll out. Think of yourself as the bag.

What is more relaxed than an empty burlap bag?

The second element in the formula is to 'drain the mind'. Several times each day drain the mind of all irritation, all resentment, disappointment, frustration, and annoyance. Unless you drain the mind frequently and regularly, these unhappy thoughts will accumulate until a major blasting-out process will be necessary. Keep the mind drained of all factors which would impede the flow of relaxed power.

Third, think spiritually. To think spiritually means to turn the mind at regular intervals to God. At least three times a day 'lift up your eyes unto the hills'. This keeps you in tune with God's harmony. It refills you with peace.

This three-point programme greatly impressed me, and I have been practising it for some months. It is an excellent method for relaxing and living on the basis of easy does it.

From my friend Dr. Z. Taylor Bercovitz, of New York City, I have learned much of the art of working relaxed. Often when under pressure, with an office full of patients and telephone calls coming in, he will suddenly stop, lean against his desk, and talk to the Lord in a manner both natural and respectful. I like the style of his prayer. He tells me that it runs something like this: "Look, Lord, I am pushing myself too hard. I am getting jittery. Here I am counselling people to practise quietness, now I must practise it. Touch me with your healing peace. Give me composure, quietness, strength, and conserve my nervous energy so that I can help these people who come to me."

He stands quietly for a minute or two. Then he thanks the Lord and proceeds with full but easy power to do his work.

Often in making sick calls about the city he finds himself in a traffic jam. He has a most interesting method of using these potentially irritating delays as opportunities to relax. Shutting off his engine, he slumps in his seat, putting his head back, closing his eyes, and has even been known to go to sleep. He says there is no reason to be concerned about going to sleep because the strident honking of horns will awaken him when traffic begins to move.

These interludes of complete relaxation in the midst of traffic last for only a minute or two, but they have energy-renewal value. It is surprising how many minutes or fractions of minutes during the day you can use to rest where you are. If even in such fractional periods you deliberately draw on God's power, you can maintain adequate relaxation. It isn't length of relaxation time that produces power; it is the quality of the experience.

I am told that Roger Babson, the famous statistician, frequently goes into an empty church and sits quietly. Perhaps he reads one or two hymns and in so doing finds rest and renewal. Dale Carnegie, under tension, used to go to a church near his New York office to spend a quarter-hour in prayerful meditation. He said he left his office for this purpose when busiest. This demonstrates control of time rather than being controlled by it. It also indicates watchfulness lest tension develop beyond a controllable degree.

I encountered a friend on a train from Washington to New York one night. This man is a member of Congress and he explained that he was on his way to his district to speak at a meeting of his constituents. The particular group he was about to address was hostile to him, he said, and would probably try to make things very difficult for him. Although they represented a minority in his district, he was going to face them just the same.

"They are American citizens and I am their representative. They have a right to meet me if they want to."

"You do not seem to be much worried about it," I commented.

"No," he answered, "if I get worried about it, then I will be upset and will not handle the situation well."

"Do you have any particular method for handling such a tense situation?" I asked.

"Oh yes," he replied, "they will be a noisy crowd. But I have my own way of meeting such situations without tension. I will breathe deeply, talk quietly, speak sincerely, be friendly and respectful, hold my temper, and trust in God to see me through.

"I have learned one important fact," the Congressman continued, "and that is in any situation be relaxed, keep calm, take a friendly attitude, have faith, do your best. Do this, and usually you can make things come out all right."

I have no doubt about the ability of this Congressman to live and work without tension, and, what is more, successfully to attain his objectives.

When we were doing some construction work at my farm in Pawling, New York, I watched a workman swinging a shovel. He was shovelling a pile of sand. It was a beautiful sight. Stripped to the waist, his lean and muscular body worked with precision and correlation. The shovel rose and fell in perfect rhythm. He would push the shovel into the pile, lean his body against it, and drive it deep into the sand. Then, in a clear, free swing it came up and the sand was deposited without a break in the motion. Again the shovel went back into the sand, again his body leaned against it, again the shovel lifted easily in a perfect arc. One almost had a feeling that one could sing in rhythm to the motion of this workman. Indeed the man did sing as he worked.

I was not surprised when the foreman told me that he is considered one of his best workmen. The foreman also spoke of him as good-humoured, happy, and a pleasant person with whom to work. Here was a relaxed man who lived with joyous power, master of the art of 'easy does it'.

Relaxation results from re-creation, and the process of re-creation should be continuous. The human being is meant to be attached to a continual flow of force that proceeds from God through the individual and back to God for renewal. When one lives in tune with this constantly re-creative process he learns the indispensable quality to relax and work on the basis of easy does it.

Now, how to master this skill. Here are ten rules for taking the hard way out of your job. Try these proven methods for working hard easily. They will help you to relax and have easy power.

1. Don't get the idea that you are Atlas carrying the world on your shoulders. Don't strain so hard. Don't take yourself so seriously.

2. Determine to like your work. Then it will become a pleasure, not drudgery. Perhaps you do not need to change your job. Change yourself and your work will seem different.

3. Plan your work—work your plan. Lack of system produces that 'I'm swamped' feeling.

4. Don't try to do everything at once. That is why time is spread out. Heed that wise advice from the Bible: "This one thing I do."

5. Get a correct mental attitude, remembering that ease or difficulty in your work depends upon how you think about it. Think it's hard and you make it hard. Think it's easy and it tends to become easy.

6. Become efficient in your work. 'Knowledge is power' (over your job). It is always easier to do a thing right.

7. Practise being relaxed. Easy always does it. Don't press or tug. Take it in your stride.

8. Discipline yourself not to put off until tomorrow what you can do today. Accumulation of undone jobs makes your work harder. Keep your work up to schedule.

9. Pray about your work. You will get relaxed efficiency by so doing.

10. Take on the 'unseen partner'. It is surprising the load He will take off you. God is as much at home in offices, factories, stores, kitchens, as in churches. He knows more about your job than you do. His help will make your work easy.

15 | How to Get People to Like You

WE MIGHT as well admit it, we want people to like us.

You may hear someone say: "I don't care whether people like me or not." But whenever you hear anyone say that, just put it down as a fact that he is not really telling the truth.

The psychologist, William James, said: "One of the deepest drives of human nature is the desire to be appreciated." The longing to be liked, to be held in esteem, to be a sought-after person, is fundamental in us.

A poll was taken among some high-school students on the question: 'What do you most desire?' By overwhelming majority the students voted that they wanted to be popular. The same urge is in older people as well. Indeed it is doubtful if anybody ever outlives the desire to be well thought of, to be highly regarded, or to have the affection of his associates.

To be master of the art of popularity, be artless. Strive deliberately after popularity and the chances are you will never attain it. But become one of those rare personalities about whom people say: "He certainly has something," and you can be certain you are on the way to having people like you.

I must warn you, however, that despite your attainments in popularity you will never get everybody to like you. There is a curious quirk in human nature whereby some people just naturally won't like you. A quatrain inscribed on a wall at Oxford says:

> 'I do not love thee, Dr. Fell,
> The reason why I cannot tell;
> But this alone I know full well,
> I do not love thee, Dr. Fell.'

That verse is very subtle. The author did not like Dr. Fell. He didn't know why but he just knew he didn't like him. It was most likely an unreasonable dislike, for undoubtedly Dr. Fell was a very nice person. Perhaps if the author had known him better he would have liked him, but poor Dr. Fell never did become popular with the author of those lines. It may have been due simply to a lack of *rapprochement*, that baffling mechanism by which we either do or do not 'click' with certain people.

Even the Bible recognises this unhappy fact about human nature, for it says: "If it be possible, as much as lieth in you, live peaceably with all men." (Romans xii. 18.) The Bible is a very realistic book and it knows people, their infinite possibilities as well as their imperfections. The Bible advised the disciples that if they went into a village and after trying their best to get along with people still couldn't do so, they were to shake off the very dust of the village from their feet—"And whosoever will not receive you, when ye go out of that city, shake off the very dust from your feet for a testimony against them." (Luke ix. 5.) This is all by way of saying that you will be wise if you do not let it too seriously affect you if you do not achieve perfect popularity with everyone.

However, there are certain formulas and procedures which, if followed faithfully, can make you a person whom other people like. You can enjoy satisfactory personal relationships even if you are a 'difficult' person or by nature shy and retiring, even unsocial. You can make of yourself one who enjoys easy, normal, natural, and pleasing relationships with others.

I cannot urge you too strongly to consider the importance of this subject and to give time and attention to its mastery, for you will never be fully happy or successful until you do. Failure in this capacity will adversely affect you psychologically. To be liked is of profounder importance than mere ego satisfaction. As necessary as that is to your success in life, normal and satisfactory personal relations are even more important.

The feeling of not being wanted or needed is one of the most devastating of all human reactions. To the degree to which you are sought after or needed by other people will you become a fully-released person. The 'lone wolf', the isolated personality, the retiring individual these people suffer a misery which is difficult to describe. In self-defence they retire even farther within themselves. Their ingrowing, introverted nature is denied the normal development which the outgoing, self-giving person experiences. Unless the personality is drawn out of itself and can be of value to someone, it may sicken and die. The feeling of not being wanted or needed produces frustration, ageing, illness. If you have a feeling of uselessness, if nobody needs or wants you, you really ought to do something about it. It is not only a pathetic way to live but is serious psychologically. Those who deal with the problems of human nature constantly encounter this problem and its unfortunate results.

For example, at a Rotary Club luncheon in a certain city two physicians were at my table: one an elderly man who had been retired for several years, the other the most popular young doctor in town. The young doctor, looking frazzled, dashed in late and slumped down with a weary sigh. "If only the telephone would stop ringing," he complained. "I can't get anywhere because people call me all the time. I wish I could put a silencer on that telephone."

The old doctor spoke up quietly: "I know how you feel, Jim," he said. "I used to feel that way myself, but be thankful the telephone does ring. Be glad people want and need you." Then he added pathetically: "Nobody ever calls me any more. I would like to hear the telephone ring again. Nobody wants me and nobody needs me. I'm a has-been."

All of us at the table who sometimes feel a bit worn by numerous activities did a lot of thinking as we listened to the old doctor.

A middle-aged woman complained to me that she didn't feel well. She was dissatisfied and unhappy. "My husband is dead, the children are grown, and there is no place for me any more. People treat me kindly, but they are indifferent. Everyone has his own interest and nobody needs me—nobody wants me. I wonder, could that be a reason I do not feel well?" she asked. Indeed that could very likely be an important reason.

In a business office the founder of the firm just past seventy was walking restlessly and aimlessly around. He talked with me while his son, present head of the business, whom I had come to see, was on the telephone. The older man said gloomily: "Why don't you write a book on how to retire? That is what I need to know. I thought it was going to be wonderful to give up the burdens of the job," he continued, "but now I find that nobody is interested in anything I say. I used to think I was a popular fellow, but now when I come down here and sit around the office everyone says 'hello', then they forget me. I might as well stay away altogether for all they care. My son is running the business and he is doing a good job of it, but," he concluded pathetically, "I'd like to think they needed me a little bit."

These people are suffering one of the most pathetic and unhappy experiences in this life. Their basic desire is to be sought after and this desire is not being satisfied. They want people to appreciate them. The personality longs for esteem. But it isn't only in retirement that this situation develops.

A girl of twenty-one told me that she had been unwanted ever since birth. Someone had given her the notion she was an unwanted child. This serious idea had sunk into her subconscious, giving her a profound sense of inferiority and self-depreciation. It made her shy and backward, causing her to retreat into herself. She became lonely and unhappy and was, in fact, an underdeveloped personality. The cure for her condition was to revamp her life spiritually, especially her thinking, which process in time made her a well-liked person by setting her personality free of herself.

Countless other people, not particularly victims of deep, unconscious psychological conflicts, have never mastered the knack of being popular. They try hard enough. They even go to extremes, often acting in a manner they do not really enjoy, but which they employ only because of their intense desire to have people like them. Everywhere today we see people putting on an act because of their inordinate desire for popularity in the superficial sense in which the word is often used in modern society.

The fact is that popularity can be attained by a few simple, natural, normal, and easily mastered techniques. Practise them diligently and you can become a well-liked person.

First, become a comfortable person, that is, one with whom people can associate without a sense of strain. Of some persons it is said: 'You can never quite get next to him.' There is always a barrier that you can't get over. A comfortable person is easy-going and natural. He has a pleasant, kindly, genial way about him. Being with him is not unlike wearing an old hat or an old pair of shoes, or an easy old coat. A stiff, reserved, unresponsive individual never meshes into the group. He is always just a bit out of it. You never quite know how to take him or how he will react. You just aren't easy-like with him.

Some young people were talking about a seventeen-year-old boy whom they liked very much. Of him they said: "He is good company. He is a good sport. He is easy to be with." It is very important to cultivate the quality of being natural. Usually that sort of individual is large-souled. Little people who are much concerned about how you treat them, who are jealous of their place or position, who meticulously stand on their prerogatives, are stiff and easily offended.

A man who is an outstanding example of these truths is James A. Farley, former Postmaster General of the United States.

I met Mr. Farley for the first time a number of years ago. Months later I met him in a large crowd of people and he called me by name. Being human, I never forgot that, and it is one reason I have always liked Mr. Farley.

An interesting incident illustrates the secret of this man who is an expert in how to get people to like him. I was to speak in Philadelphia at a book-and-author luncheon along with Mr. Farley and two other authors. I did not actually witness the scene I am about to describe, as I was late in arriving, but my publisher did. The speakers at this luncheon were walking along the hotel corridor together when they passed a coloured maid standing by a cart loaded with sheets, towels, and other equipment with which she was servicing the rooms. She was paying no attention to this group of people as they turned aside to avoid her cart. Mr. Farley walked up to her, put out his hand, and said, "Hello, there. How are you? I'm Jim Farley. What's your name? Glad to see you."

My publisher looked back at her as the group passed down the hall. The girl's mouth was wide with astonishment and her face broke into a beautiful smile. It was an excellent example of how an unegotistical, comfortable, outgoing person is successful in personal relationships.

A university psychology department conducted an analysis of the personality traits by which people are liked or disliked. One hundred traits were scientifically analysed and it was reported that one must have forty-six favourable traits in order to be liked. It is rather discouraging to realise that you must have so large a number of characteristics to be popular.

Christianity, however, teaches that one basic trait will go far toward getting people to like you. That trait is a sincere and forthright interest in and love for people.

Perhaps if you cultivate this basic trait, other traits will naturally develop.

If you are not the comfortable type of person, I suggest that you make a study of your personality with a view toward eliminating conscious and unconscious elements of strain which may exist. Do not assume that the reason other people do not like you is because of something wrong with them. Assume, instead, that the trouble is within yourself and determine to find and eliminate it. This will require scrupulous honesty and it may also involve the assistance of personality experts. The so-called 'scratchy' elements in your personality may be qualities which you have taken on through the years. Perhaps they have been assumed defensively, or they may be the results of attitudes developed in your younger days. Regardless of origin they can be eliminated by a scientific study of yourself and by your recognition of the necessity for change followed by a process of personality rehabilitation.

A man came to our clinic at the church seeking help in the problem of personal relationships. About thirty-five years of age, he was the type of person whom you would certainly look at twice if not three times. He was splendidly proportioned and impressive. Superficially regarding him it was surprising that people should not like him. But he proceeded to outline an unhappy and continuous set of circumstances and instances to illustrate his dismal failure in human relations.

"I do my best," he explained. "I have tried to put into practice the rules I have been taught about getting along with people, but get nowhere with the effort. People just don't like me and what is more I am aware of it."

After talking with him it was not difficult to understand the trouble. There was in his manner of speech a persistently critical attitude thinly veiled but nonetheless apparent. He had an unattractive manner of pursing his lips which indicated a kind of primness or reproof for everybody, as if he felt just a bit superior and disdainful towards other people. In fact there was about him a noticeable attitude of superiority. He was very rigid, with no flexibility of personality.

"Isn't there some way to change myself so that people will like me?" he demanded. "Isn't there some way I can stop unconsciously rubbing people the wrong way?"

The young man was decidedly self-centred and egotistical. The person he really liked was himself. Every statement, every attitude was unconsciously measured in terms of how it reacted on himself. We had to teach him to love other people and to forget himself, which was of course a complete reversal of his development. It was vital, however, to the solution of his problem. I found that this young man was irritable with people and he picked on them in his own mind, though no outward conflicts with other persons developed. Inwardly he was trying to make everybody over to suit himself. Unconsciously people realised this, though perhaps they did not define the trouble. Barriers were erected in their minds towards him.

Since he was being unpleasant to people in his thoughts, it followed that he was less than warm in his personal attitudes. He was polite enough and managed not to be boorish and unpleasant, but people unconsciously felt coolness in him, so gave him the 'brush-off' of which he complained. The reason they did so was because in his mind he had 'brushed them off'. He liked himself too well, and to build up his self-esteem he disliked others. He was suffering from self-love, a chief cure for which is the practice of love for others.

He was bewildered and baffled when we outlined his difficulty. But he was sincere and meant business. He practised the suggested techniques for developing love of others in place of self-love. It required some fundamental changes to accomplish this, but he succeeded in doing so.

One method suggested was that at night before retiring he make a list of persons he had met during the day, as, for example, the bus driver or the newsboy. He was to picture mentally each person whose name appeared on the list, and as he brought each face up before him he was to think a kindly thought about that person. Then he was to pray for each one. He was to pray around his little world. Each of us has his own world, people with whom we do business or are associated in one way or another.

For example, the first person outside the family whom this young man saw in the morning was the elevator man in his apartment house. He had not been in the habit of saying anything to him beyond a perfunctory and growled 'good morning'. Now he took the time to have a little chat with the elevator man. He asked him about his family and about his interests. He found that the elevator operator had an interesting point of view and some experiences which were quite fascinating. He began to see new values in a person whom to him previously had been a mechanical robot, who ran the elevator up and down to his floor. He actually began to like the elevator operator and in turn the elevator man, who had formed a pretty accurate opinion of the young man, began to revise his views. They established a friendly relationship. So the process went from person to person.

One day the young man said to me, "I have found that the world is filled with interesting people and I never realised it before."

When he made that observation he proved that he was losing himself, and when he did that, as the Bible so wisely tells us, he found himself. In losing himself he found himself and lots of new friends besides. People learned to like him.

Learning to pray for people was important in his rehabilitation, for when you pray for anyone you tend to modify your personal attitude towards him. You lift the relationship thereby to a higher level. The best in the other person begins to flow out towards you as your best flows towards him. In the meeting of the best in each a higher quality of understanding is established.

Essentially, getting people to like you is merely the other side of liking them. One of the most popular men who lived in the United States within the lifetime of most of us was the late Will Rogers. One of the most characteristic statements he ever made was, "I never met a man I didn't like." That may have been a slight exaggeration, but I am sure Will Rogers did not regard it as such. That is the way he felt about people, and as a result people opened up to him like flowers to the sun.

Sometimes the weak objection is offered that it is difficult to like some people. Granted, some people are by nature more likeable than others, nevertheless a serious attempt to know any individual will reveal qualities within him that are admirable, even lovable.

A man had the problem of conquering feelings of irritation towards persons with whom he was associated. For some people he had a very profound dislike. They irritated him intensely, but he conquered these feelings simply by making an exhaustive list of everything he could possibly admire about each person who annoyed him. Daily he attempted to add to this list. He was surprised to discover that people whom he thought he did not like at all proved to have many pleasing qualities. In fact, he was at a loss to understand how he ever disliked them after becoming conscious of their attractive qualities. Of course, while he was making these discoveries about them, they, in turn, were finding new and likeable qualities in him.

If you have gone through life up to this point without having established satisfactory human relationships, do not assume that you cannot change, but it will be necessary to take very definite steps towards solving the problem. You can change and become a popular person, well liked and esteemed, if you are willing to make the effort. May I remind you as I remind myself that one of the greatest tragedies of the average person is the tendency to spend our whole lives perfecting our faults? We develop a fault and we nurse it and cultivate it, and never change it. Like a needle caught in the groove of a defective record on a gramophone, it plays the same old tune over and over again. You must lift the needle out of the groove, then you will have disharmony no longer, but harmony. Don't spend more of your life perfecting faults in human relations. Spend the rest of your life perfecting your great capacities for friendliness, for personal relations are vitally important to successful living.

Still another important factor in getting people to like you is to practise building up the ego of other persons. The ego, being the essence of our personalities, is sacred to us. There is in every person a normal desire for a feeling of self-importance. If I deflate your ego and therefore your self-importance, though you may laugh it off, I have deeply wounded you. In fact, I have shown disrespect for you, and while you may exercise charity towards me, even so, unless you are finely developed spiritually, you are not going to like me very well.

On the other hand, if I elevate your self-respect and contribute to your feeling of personal worth, I am showing high esteem for your ego. I have helped you to be your best self and therefore you appreciate what I have done. You are grateful to me. You like me for it.

The deflation of another person's ego may be mildly done perhaps, but one can never evaluate how deep the depreciation goes from even a remark or an attitude that is not meant to be unkind. Here is the way in which ego is often deflated.

The next time you are in a group and someone tells a joke and everybody laughs with appreciation and pleasure except yourself, when the laughter has died down say patronisingly, "Well, that is a pretty good joke all right. I saw it in a magazine last month."

Of course it will make you feel quite important to let others know of your superior knowledge, but how does it make the man feel who told the joke? You have robbed him of the satisfaction of having told a good story. You have crowded him out of his brief moment in the limelight and usurped attention to yourself. In fact you have taken the wind out of his sails and left him flat and deflated. He enjoyed his momentary little prominence, but you took it away from him. Nobody in that group is going to like you for what you did, and certainly not the man whose story you spoiled. Whether you like the joke or not, let the storyteller and the others enjoy it. Remember he may be a little embarrassed and shy. It would have done him good to have received a response. Don't deflate people. Build them up and they will love you for it.

While writing this chapter I enjoyed a visit with an old and dear friend. Dr. John W. Hoffman, one-time president of Ohio Wesleyan University. As I sat with him in Pasadena, I realised once again how much this great personality has always meant to me. Many years ago, on the night before my graduation from college, we had a banquet at our fraternity house at which he was present and made a speech. After dinner he asked me to walk with him to the president's house.

It was a beautiful moonlight night in June. All the way up the hill he talked to me about life and its opportunities and told me what a thrill awaited me as I entered the outside world. As we stood in front of his house he put his hand on my shoulder and said, "Norman, I have always liked you. I believe in you. You have great possibilities. I shall always be proud of you. You have got it in you." Of course he over-estimated me, but that is infinitely better than to depreciate a person.

It being June and the night before graduation and excitement being in my heart, my sentiments were pretty close to the surface, and I said good night to him through a mist of tears which I tried to conceal. It has been many years since then, but I never forget what he said nor how he said it on that June night long ago. I have loved him all across the years.

I discovered that he made similar statements to many other boys and girls long since become men and women and they, too, love him because he respected their personalities and was constantly building them up. Through the years he would write to me and to others congratulating us on some little thing that we had done, and a word of approval from him meant much. Little wonder this honoured guide of youth has the affection and devotion of thousands of people whose lives he touched.

Whomever you help to build up to become a better, stronger, finer person will give you his undying devotion. Build up as many people as you can. Do it unselfishly. Do it because you like them and because you see possibilities in them. Do this and you will never lack for friends. You will always be well thought of. Build people up and love them genuinely. Do them good and their esteem and affection will flow back towards you.

The basic principles of getting people to like you need no prolonged and laboured emphasis, for they are very simple and easily illustrate their own truth. However, I list ten practical rules for getting the esteem of others. The soundness of these principles has been demonstrated innumerable times. Practise them until you become expert at them and people will like you.

1. Learn to remember names. Inefficiency at this point may indicate that your interest is not sufficiently outgoing. A man's name is very important to him.

2. Be a comfortable person so there is no strain in being with you—be an old-shoe, old-hat kind of individual.

3. Acquire the quality of relaxed easy-goingness so that things do not ruffle you.

4. Don't be egotistical. Guard against giving the impression that you know it all. Be natural and normally humble.

5. Cultivate the quality of being interesting so that people will want to be with you and get something of stimulating value from their association with you.

6. Study to get the 'scratchy' elements out of your personality, even those of which you may be unconscious.

7. Sincerely attempt to heal, on an honest Christian basis, every misunderstanding you have had or now have. Drain off your grievances.

8. Practise liking people until you learn to do so genuinely. Remember what Will Rogers said, "I never met a man I didn't like." Try to be that way.

9. Never miss an opportunity to say a word of congratulation upon anyone's achievement, or express sympathy in sorrow or disappointment.

10. Get a deep spiritual experience so that you have something to give people that will help them to be stronger and meet life more effectively. Give strength to people and they will give affection to you.

16 | Prescription for Heartache

"PLEASE GIVE ME a prescription for heartache."

This curious and rather pathetic request was made by a man who had been informed by his doctor that the feelings of disability of which he complained were not of a physical nature. His trouble lay in an inability to rise above sorrow. He was suffering from 'an ache in his personality' as a result of grief.

His doctor advised him to secure spiritual consultation and treatment. So continuing to use the terminology of medicine, he repeated his question, "Is there a spiritual prescription which will reduce my constant inner suffering? I realise that sorrow comes to everyone and I should be able to meet it the same as others. I have tried my best but find no peace." Again he asked with a sad, slow smile, "Give me a prescription for heartache."

There is indeed a 'prescription' for heartache. One element in the prescription is physical activity. The sufferer must avoid the temptation to sit and brood. A sensible programme which substitutes physical activity for such fruitless brooding reduces the strain on the area of the mind where we reflect, philosophise, and suffer mental pain. Muscular activity utilises another part of the brain and therefore shifts the strain and gives relief.

An old country lawyer who had a sound philosophy and much wisdom told a sorrowing woman that the best medicine for a broken heart is "to take a scrubbing brush and get down on your knees and go to work. The best medicine for a man," he declared, "is to get an axe and chop wood until physically tired." While this is not guaranteed to be a complete cure for heartache, yet it does tend to mitigate such suffering.

Whatever the character of your heartache, one of the first steps is to resolve to escape from any defeatist situation which may have been created around yourself, even though it is difficult to do so, and return once again to the normal courses of your life. Get back into the main stream of life's activities. Take up your old associations. Form new ones. Get busy walking, riding, swimming, playing—get the blood to coursing through your system. Lose yourself in some worth-while project. Fill your days with creative activity and emphasise the physical aspect of activity. Employ healthy mind-relieving busyness, but be sure that it is of a worth-while and constructive nature. Superficial escapism through feverish activity merely deadens pain temporarily and does not heal, as, for example, parties and drinking.

An excellent and normal release from heartache is to give way to grief. There is a foolish point of view current today that one should not show grief, that it is not proper to cry or express oneself through the natural mechanism of tears and sobbing. This is a denial of the law of nature. It is natural to cry when pain or sorrow comes. It is a relief mechanism provided in the body by Almighty God and should be used.

To restrain grief, to inhibit it, to bottle it up, is to fail to use one of God's means for eliminating the pressure of sorrow. Like every other function of the human body and nervous system, this must be controlled, but it should not be denied altogether. A good cry by either man or woman is a release from heartache. I should warn, however, that this mechanism should not be used unduly nor allowed to become a habitual process. Should that happen, it partakes of the nature of abnormal grief and could become a psychosis. Unrestraint of any kind should not be allowed.

I receive many letters from people whose loved ones have died. They tell me that it is very difficult for them to go to the same places they were in the habit of frequenting together or to be with the same people with whom they associated as a couple or as a family. Therefore they avoided the old-time places and friends.

I regard this as a serious mistake. A secret of curing heartache is to be as normal and natural as possible. This does not imply disloyalty or indifference. This policy is important in avoiding a state of abnormal grief. Normal sorrow is a natural process and its normality is evidenced by the ability of the individual to return to his usual pursuits and responsibilities and continue therein as formerly.

The deeper remedy for heartache, of course, is the curative comfort supplied by trust in God. Inevitably the basic prescription for heartache is to turn to God in an attitude of faith and empty the mind and heart to Him. Perseverance in the act of spiritual self-emptying will finally bring healing to the broken heart. This generation, which has suffered fully as much if not more heartache than people in preceding eras, needs to relearn that which the wisest men of all time have known, namely, that there is no healing of the pain suffered by humanity except through the benign ministrations of faith.

One of the greatest souls of the ages was Brother Lawrence, who said, "If in this life we would know the serene peace of Paradise, we must school ourselves in familiar, humble, and loving converse with God." It is not advisable to attempt to carry the burden of sorrow and mental pain without Divine help, for its weight is more than the personality can bear. The simplest and most effective of all prescriptions for heartache then is to practise the presence of God. This will soothe the ache in your heart and ultimately heal the wound. Men and women who have experienced great tragedy tell us that this prescription is effective.

Another profoundly curative element in the prescription for heartache is to gain a sound and satisfying philosophy of life and death and deathlessness. For my part, when I gained the unshakable belief that there is no death, that all life is indivisible, that the here and hereafter are one, that time and eternity are inseparable, that this is one unobstructed universe, then I found the most satisfying and convincing philosophy of my entire life.

These convictions are based upon sound foundations, the Bible for one. I believe that the Bible gives us a very subtle and, as will be proved ultimately, a scientific series of insights into the great question. 'What happens when a man leaves this world?' Also the Bible very wisely tells us that we know these truths by faith. Henri Bergson, the philosopher, says that the surest way into truth is by perception, by intuition, by reasoning to a certain point, then by taking a 'mortal leap', and by intuition attaining the truth. You come to some glorious moment where you simply 'know'. That is the way it happened to me.

I am absolutely, wholeheartedly, and thoroughly convinced of the truth of which I write and have no doubt of it, even to an infinitesimal degree. I arrived at this positive faith gradually, yet there came one moment when I knew.

This philosophy will not ward off the sorrow which comes when a loved one dies and physical, earthly separation ensues. But it will lift and dissipate grief. It will fill your mind with a deep understanding of the meaning of this inevitable circumstance. And it will give you a deep assurance that you have not lost your loved one. Live on this faith and you will be at peace and the ache will leave your heart.

Take into your mind and heart one of the most marvellous texts in the Holy Bible—"Eye has not seen, nor ear heard, neither have entered into the heart of man, the things which God hath prepared for them that love Him." (I Corinthians ii. 9.)

This means that you have never seen, no matter what you have seen, however wonderful it is, you have never seen anything to compare with the marvellous things that God has prepared for those who love Him and who put their trust in Him. Moreover, it says that you have never heard anything to compare with the astonishing marvels that God has laid up for those who follow His teaching and live according to His spirit. Not only have you never seen nor ever heard, but you have never even dimly imagined what He is going to do for you. This sentence goes all out in promising comfort and immortality and reunion and every good thing to those who centre their lives in God.

After many years of reading the Bible and being intimately connected with all the phases of the lives of hundreds of people, I wish to state unequivocally that I have found this Biblical promise to be absolutely true. It applies even to this world. People who really practise living on a Christlike basis have the most incredible things happen to them.

This passage also relates to the state of existence of those now living on the other side and our relationship, while we live, to those who have preceded us across that barrier which we call death. I use the word 'barrier' somewhat apologetically. We have always thought of death as a barrier with a concept of a separatist nature.

Scientists working today in the field of parapsychology and extra-sensory perception and experimenting in precognition, telepathy, clairvoyance (all of which were formerly considered paraphernalia of the cranks, but which are now of sound, scientific usage in the laboratories), are expressing themselves as believing that the soul survives the barrier of time and space. In effect, we are on the edge of one of the greatest scientific discoveries in history which will substantiate, on a laboratory-exploratory basis, the existence of the soul and its deathlessness.

For many years I have been accumulating a series of incidents, the validity of which I accept and which bear out the conviction that we live in a dynamic universe where life, not death, is the basic principle. I have confidence in the people who have described the following experiences and am convinced that they indicate a world impinged upon or intertwined with our own through the meshes of which human spirits, on both sides of death, live in unbroken fellowship. The conditions of life on the other side, as we know them in mortality, are modified. Undoubtedly those who have crossed to the other side dwell in a higher medium than we do and their understanding is amplified beyond ours, yet all the facts point to the continued existence of our loved ones and the further fact that they are not far away, and still another fact implied, but no less real, that we shall be reunited with them. Meanwhile, we continue in fellowship with those who dwell in the spirit world.

William James, one of America's greatest scholars, after a lifetime of study, said he was satisfied that the human brain is only a medium for the soul's existence and that the mind as now constituted will be exchanged at last for a brain that will allow the owner to reach out into untapped areas of understanding. As our spiritual being is amplified here on earth and as we grow in age and experience we become more conscious of this vaster world all around us, and when we die it is only to enter into an enlarged capacity.

Euripides, one of the greatest thinkers of antiquity, was convinced that the next life would be one of infinitely greater magnitude. Socrates shared the same concept. One of the most comforting statements ever made was his remark: "No evil can befall a good man in this life or in the next."

Natalia Kalmus, scientific expert in technicolour, tells about the death of her sister. The following account given by this scientifically trained woman appeared in the inspirational magazine *Guideposts*.

Natalie Kalmus quotes her dying sister as saying: " 'Natalie, promise me that you won't let them give me any drugs. I realise that they are trying to help relieve my pain, but I want to be fully aware of every sensation. I am convinced that death will be a beautiful experience.'

"I promised. Alone, later, I wept, thinking of her courage. Then as I tossed in bed on through the night, I realised that what I thought to be a calamity my sister intended to be triumph.

"Ten days later the final hour drew near. I had been at her bedside for hours. We had talked about many things, and always I marvelled at her quiet, sincere confidence in eternal life. Not once did the physical torture overcome her spiritual strength. This was something that the doctors simply hadn't taken into account.

" 'Dear kind God, keep my mind clear and give me peace,' she had murmured over and over again during those last days.

"We had talked so long that I noticed she was drifting off to sleep. I left her quietly with the nurse and retired to get some rest. A few minutes later I heard my sister's voice calling for me. Quickly I returned to her room. She was dying.

"I sat on her bed and took her hand. It was on fire. Then she seemed to rise up in bed almost to a sitting position.

" 'Natalie,' she said, 'there are so many of them. There's Fred ... and Ruth ... what's she doing here? Oh, I know!'

"An electric shock went through me. She had said Ruth. Ruth was her cousin who had died suddenly the week before. But Eleanor had not been told of Ruth's sudden death.

"Chill after chill shot up and down my spine. I felt on the verge of some powerful, almost frightening knowledge. She had murmured Ruth's name.

"Her voice was surprisingly clear. 'It's so confusing. So many of them!' Suddenly her arms stretched out as

276

happily as when she had welcomed me! 'I'm going up,' she said.

"Then she dropped her arms around my neck—and relaxed in my arms. The will of her spirit had turned final agony into rapture.

"As I laid her head back on the pillow, there was a warm, peaceful smile on her face. Her golden-brown hair lay carelessly on the pillow. I took a white flower from the vase and placed it in her hair. With her petite, trim figure, her wavy hair, the white flower, and the soft smile, she looked once more—and permanently—just like a schoolgirl."

The mention of her cousin Ruth by the dying girl and the evident fact that she saw her clearly is a phenomenon that recurs again and again in the incidents which have come to my attention. So repetitive is this phenomenon and so similar are the characteristics of this experience as described by many that it amounts to a substantial evidence that the people whose names are called, whose faces are seen, are actually present.

Where are they? What is their condition? What sort of body have they? These are questions that are difficult. The idea of a different dimension is probably the most tenable, or it may be more accurate to believe that they live in a different frequency cycle.

It is impossible to see through the blades of an electric fan when it is in a stationary position. At high speed, however, the blades appear to be transparent. In the higher frequency or the state in which our loved ones dwell, the impenetrable qualities of the universe may open to the gaze of one passing into the mysteries. In deep moments of our own lives it is entirely possible that we enter to a degree at least into that higher frequency.

In one of the most beautiful lines in English literature, Robert Ingersoll suggests this great truth: 'In the night of death, hopes sees a star and listening love can hear the rustle of a wing.'

A famous neurologist tells of a man who was at death's door. The dying man looked up at the physician sitting beside his bed and began to call off names which the physician wrote down. The doctor was personally unfamiliar with any name mentioned. Later the physician asked the man's daughter: "Who are these people? Your father spoke of them as if he saw them."

"They are all relatives," she said, "who have been dead a long time."

The physician said he believes his patient did see them.

Friends of mine, Mr. and Mrs. William Sage, lived in New Jersey and I was often in their home. Mr. Sage, whom his wife called Will, died first. A few years later, when Mrs. Sage was on her deathbed, the most surprised look passed across her face, and it lighted up in a wonderful smile as she said: "Why, it is Will." That she saw him those about her had no doubt whatsoever.

Arthur Godfrey, famous radio personality, tells of being asleep in his bunk on a destroyer in World War I. Suddenly his father stood beside him. He put out his hand, smiled, and said: "So long, son," and Godfrey answered: "So long, Dad."

Later he was awakened and given a cablegram telling him of the death of his father. The time of his passing was given, and it was the precise period during which Godfrey in his sleep 'saw' his father.

Mary Margaret McBride, also a famous radio personality, was overwhelmed with grief upon the death of her mother. They had been very close to each other. She awakened one night and sat on the edge of her bed. Suddenly she had the feeling, to use her own words, that "Mama was with me." She did not see her mother nor hear her speak, but from that time on, "I knew that my mother isn't dead—that she is nearby."

The late Rufus Jones, one of the most famous spiritual leaders of our time, tells about his son Lowell who died at twelve years of age. He was the apple of his father's eye. The boy was taken ill when Dr. Jones was on the ocean bound for Europe. The night before entering Liverpool, while lying in his bunk, he experienced an indefinable, inexplainable feeling of sadness. Then he said that he seemed to be enveloped in the arms of God. A great feeling of peace and a sense of a profound possession of his son came to him.

Upon landing in Liverpool he was advised that his son had died, his death occurring at the precise hour when Dr. Jones had felt a sense of God's presence and the everlasting nearness of his son.

A member of my church, Mrs. Bryson Kalt, tells of an aunt whose husband and three children were burned to death when their house was destroyed by fire. The aunt was badly burned but lived for three years. When finally she lay dying a radiance suddenly came over her face. "It is all so beautiful," she said. "They are coming to meet me. Fluff up my pillows and let me go to sleep."

Mr. H. B. Clarke, an old friend of mine, was for many years a construction engineer, his work taking him into all parts of the world. He was of a scientific turn of mind, a quiet, restrained, factual, unemotional type of man. I was called one night by his physician, who said that he did not expect him to live but a few hours. His heart action was slow and the blood pressure was extra-ordinarily low. There was no reflex action at all. The doctor gave no hope.

I began to pray for him, as did others. The next day his eyes opened and after a few days he recovered his speech. His heart action and blood pressure returned to normal. After he recovered strength he said: "At some-time during my illness something very peculiar happened to me. I cannot explain it. It seemed that I was a long distance away. I was in the most beautiful and attractive place I have ever seen. There were lights all about me, beautiful lights. I saw faces dimly revealed, kind faces they were, and I felt very peaceful and happy. In fact, I have never felt happier in my life.

"Then the thought came to me: 'I must be dying.' Then it occurred to me: 'Perhaps I have died.' Then I almost laughed out loud, and asked myself: 'Why have I been afraid of death all my life? There is nothing to be afraid of in this.' "

"How did you feel about it?" I asked. "Did you want to come back to life? Did you want to live, for you were not dead, although the doctor felt that you were very close to death. Did you want to live?"

He smiled and said: "It did not make the slightest difference. If anything, I think I would have preferred to stay in that beautiful place."

Hallucination, a dream, a vision—I do not believe so. I have spent too many years talking to people who have come to the edge of 'something' and had a look across, who unanimously have reported beauty, light, and peace, to have any doubt in my own mind.

The New Testament teaches the indestructibility of life in a most interesting and simple manner. It describes

Jesus after His crucifixion in a series of appearances, disappearances, and reappearances. Some saw Him and then He vanished out of their sight. Then others saw Him and again He vanished. It is as if to say: 'You see me and then you do not see me.' This indicates that He is trying to tell us that when we do not see Him, it does not mean He is not there. Out of sight does not mean out of life. Occasional mystical appearances which some experience indicate the same truth, that He is nearby. Did He not say: ". . . because I live, ye shall live also." (John xiv. 19.) In other words, our loved ones who have died in his faith are also nearby and occasionally draw near to comfort us.

A boy serving in Korea wrote to his mother, saying: "The strangest things happen to me. Once in a while at night, when I am afraid, Daddy seems to be with me." Daddy had been dead for ten years. Then the boy wistfully asks his mother: "Do you think that Daddy can actually be with me here on these Korean battlefields?" The answer is: 'Why not?' How can we be citizens of a scientific generation and not believe that this could be true? Again and again proofs are offered that this is a dynamic universe, surcharged with mystic, electric electronic, atomic forces, and all are so wonderful that we have never yet comprehended them. This universe is a great spiritual sounding-house, alive and vital.

Albert E. Cliff, well-known Canadian writer, tells of the death of his father. The dying man had sunk into a coma and it was thought he was gone. Then a momentary resurgence of life occurred. His eyes flickered open. On the wall was one of those old-time mottoes which said: 'I know That My Redeemer Liveth.' The dying man opened his eyes, looked at that motto, and said: "I *do know* that my Redeemer liveth, for they are all here around me—mother, father, brothers, and sisters." Long gone from this earth were they all, but evidently he saw them. Who is to gainsay?

The late Mrs. Thomas A. Edison told me that when her famous husband was dying he whispered to his physician: "It is very beautiful over there." Edison was the world's greatest scientist. All his life he had worked with phenomena. He was of a factual cast of mind. He never reported anything as a fact until he saw it work. He would never have reported: 'It is very beautiful over there' unless, having seen, he knew it to be true.

Many years ago a missionary went to the South Sea Islands to work among a cannibal tribe. After many months he converted the chief to Christianity. One day this old chief said to the missionary: "Remember the time you first came among us?"

"Indeed I do," replied the missionary. "As I went through the forest I became aware of hostile forces all around me."

"They did indeed surround you," said the chief, "for we were following you to kill you, but something prevented us from doing it."

"And what was that?" asked the missionary.

"Now that we are friends, tell me," coaxed the chief, "who were those two shining ones walking on either side of you?"

My friend, Geoffrey O'Hara, famous song-writer, author of the popular World War I song, 'Katy', also 'There Is No Death', 'Give a Man a Horse He can Ride', and other songs, tells of a colonel in World War I whose regiment was wiped out in a bloody engagement. As he paced up and down the trench he says he could feel their hands and sense their presence. He said to Geoffrey O'Hara: "I tell you, there is no death." Mr. O'Hara wrote one of his greatest songs using that title, 'there is no death'.

Of these deep and tender matters I personally have no doubt whatsoever. I firmly believe in the continuation of life after that which we call death takes place. I believe there are two sides to the phenomenon known as death—this side where we now live and the other side where we shall continue to live. Eternity does not start with death. We are in eternity now. We are citizens of eternity. We merely change the form of the experience called life, and that change, I am persuaded, is for the better.

My mother was a great soul, and her influence on me will ever stand out in my life as an experience that cannot be surpassed. She was a wonderful conversationalist. Her mind was keen and alert. She travelled the world over and enjoyed wide contacts as a Christian leader in missionary causes. Her life was full and rich. She had a marvellous sense of humour. She was good company, and I always loved to be with her. She was considered, by all who knew her, an unusually fascinating and stimulating personality.

During my adult years whenever I had the opportunity I would go home to see her. I always anticipated the arrival at the family home, for it was an exciting experience in which everyone talked at once as we sat around the breakfast table. What happy reunions— what glorious meetings. Then came her death, and we tenderly laid her body in the beautiful little cemetery at Lynchburg in southern Ohio, a town where she had lived as a girl. I was very sad the day we left her there, and went away heavy-hearted. It was in the fullness of summer-time when we took her home to her last resting-place.

It came autumn, and I felt that I wanted to be with my mother again. I was lonely without her, therefore I decided to go to Lynchburg. All night long on the train I thought sadly of the happy days now gone and how things were utterly changed and would never be the same again.

So I came to the little town. The weather was cold and the sky overcast as I walked to the cemetery. I pushed through the old iron gates and my feet rustled in the leaves as I walked to her grave where I sat sad and lonely. Of a sudden the clouds parted and the sun came through. It lighted up the Ohio hills in gorgeous autumn colours, the hills where I grew up as a boy, which I have always loved so well, where she herself had played as a girl in the long ago.

Then all of a sudden I seemed to hear her voice. Now I didn't actually hear the voice, but I seemed to. I am sure I heard it by the inward ear. The message was clear and distinct. It was stated in her beloved old-time tone, and this is what she said: "Why seek ye the living among the dead? I am not here. Do you think that I would stay in this dark and dismal place? I am with you and my loved ones always." In a burst of inner light I became wondrously happy. I knew that what I had heard was the truth. The message came to me with all the force of actuality. I could have shouted, and I stood up and put my hand on the tombstone and saw it for what it is, only a place where mortal remains lay. The body was there, to be sure, but it was only a coat that had been laid off because the wearer needed it no longer.

But she, that gloriously lovely spirit, she was not there.

I walked out of that place and only rarely since have I returned. I like to go back there and think of her and the old days of my youth, but no longer is it a place of gloom. It is merely a symbol, for she is not there. She is with us her loved ones. "Why seek ye the living among the dead?" (Luke xxiv. 5.)

Read and believe the Bible as it tells about the goodness of God and the immortality of the soul. Pray sincerely and with faith. Make prayer and faith the habit of your life. Learn to have real fellowship with God and with Jesus Christ. As you do this you will find a deep conviction welling up in your mind that these wonderful things are true indeed.

". . . if it were not so, I would have told you." (John xiv. 2.) You can depend upon the reliability of Christ. He would not let you believe and hold convictions so sacred in nature unless they are absolutely true.

So in this faith, which is a sound, substantial, and rational view of life and eternity, you have the prescription for heartache.

17 | How to Draw Upon that Higher Power

FOUR MEN WERE sitting in the locker-room of a country club after a game. Talk about golf scores drifted into a discussion of personal difficulties and problems. One man was especially despondent. The others, his friends, realising his unhappy state of mind, had arranged this game to get his mind off his difficult situation. They hoped a few hours on the golf course might afford him some relief.

Now, as they sat around after the game, various suggestions were offered him. Finally one of the men rose to go. He knew about difficulties, for he'd had plenty himself, but he had found some vital answers to *his* problems. He stood hesitantly, then laid his hand on his friend's shoulder. "George," he said, "I hope you won't think I am preaching at you. Really, I'm not, but I would like to suggest something. It's the way I got through my difficulties. It really works if you work it, and it's this. 'Why not draw upon that Higher Power?'"

He slapped his friend affectionately on the back and left the group. The other men sat mulling this over. Finally the discouraged man said slowly: "I know what he means and I know where the Higher Power is. I only wish I knew how to draw upon it. It's what I need all right."

Well, in due course he discovered how to draw upon that Higher Power, and it changed everything for him. Now he is a healthy, happy man.

The advice given at the golf club is really very wise. There are many people today who are unhappy and depressed and just not getting anywhere with themselves or with conditions. And they do not need to be that way. Really they don't. The secret is to draw upon that Higher Power. And how is that done?

Let me tell you about a personal experience. When quite young I was called to a large church in a university community and many of my congregation were professors in the university as well as leading citizens of the city. I wanted to justify the confidence of those who gave me such an outstanding opportunity and accordingly worked very hard. As a result I began to experience over-strain. Everyone should work hard, but there is no virtue in over-trying or over-pressing to such an extent that you do not work efficiently. It is somewhat like making a golf shot. Try to 'kill' the ball and you execute the shot poorly. You can do likewise in your job. I began to get rather tired and nervous and had no feeling of normal power.

One day I decided to call on one of the professors, the late Hugh M. Tilroe, a great friend of mine. He was a wonderful teacher, and he was also a great fisherman and hunter. He was a man's man, an outdoor personality. I knew that if I did not find him at the university he would be out on the lake fishing, and sure enough there he was. He came ashore at my hail. "The fish are biting—come on," he said. I climbed in his boat and we fished awhile.

"What's the matter, son?" he asked with understanding.

I told him how hard I was trying and that it was getting me down nervously. "I have no feeling of lift or power," I said.

He chuckled. "Maybe you're trying too hard."

As the boat scraped the shore he said: "Come in the house with me." As we entered his cabin he ordered: "Lie down there on that couch. I want to read you something. Shut your eyes and relax while I find the quotation."

I did as directed, and thought he was going to read me some philosophical or perhaps diverting piece, but instead he said: "Here it is. Listen quietly while I read it to you. And let these words sink in. 'Hast thou not known? Hast thou not heard, that the everlasting God, the Lord, the Creator of the ends of the earth, fainteth not, neither is weary? There is no searching of his understanding. He giveth power to the faint; and to them that have no might he increaseth strength. Even the youths shall faint and be weary, and the young men shall utterly fall. But they that wait upon the Lord shall renew their strength; they shall mount up with wings as eagles; they shall run, and not be weary; and they shall walk, and not faint.' " (Isaiah xl. 28–31.) Then he asked: "Do you know from what I am reading?"

"Yes, the fortieth chapter of Isaiah," I answered.

"I'm glad you know your Bible," he commented. "Why don't you practise it? Now relax. Take three deep breaths—in and out slowly. Practise resting yourself in God. Practise depending upon Him for His support and power. Believe He is giving it to you now and don't get out of touch with that power. Yield yourself to it—let it flow through you.

"Give your job all you've got. Of course you must do

that. But do it in a relaxed and easy manner like a batter in a big-league ball game. He swings the bat easy-like, and doesn't try to knock the ball out of the park. He just does the best he can and believes in himself because he knows that he has lots of reserve power." Then he repeated the passage again. " 'They that wait upon the Lord shall renew their strength.' "

That was a long time ago, but I never forgot that lesson. He taught me how to draw upon that Higher Power, and believe me, his suggestions worked. I continue to follow my friend's advice, and it has never failed me in the more than twenty years that have passed since then. My life is crowded with activity but that power formula gives me all the strength I need.

A second method for drawing upon that Higher Power is to learn to take a positive, optimistic attitude towards every problem. In direct proportion to the intensity of the faith which you muster will you receive power to meet your situations. "According to your faith be it unto you" (Matthew ix. 29), is a basic law of successful living.

There is a Higher Power, and that Power can do everything for you. Draw upon it and experience its great helpfulness. Why be defeated when you are free to draw upon that Higher Power? State your problem. Ask for a specific answer. Believe that you are getting that answer. Believe that now, through God's help, you are gaining power over your difficulty.

A man and his wife who were in real trouble came to see me. This gentleman, a former magazine editor, was a distinguished figure in music and artistic circles. Everyone liked him for his geniality and friendliness. His wife was held in similar high regard. She was in poor health and as a result they had retired to the country where they were living in semi-seclusion.

This man told me he had experienced two heart attacks, one quite severe. His wife was in a steady decline and he was deeply concerned about her. The question he put was this: "Can I get hold of some power that can help us recover ourselves physically and give us new hope and courage and strength?" The situation as he described it was a series of discouragements and defeats.

Frankly I felt that he was a bit too sophisticated to permit himself to adopt and utilise the simple trust that would be necessary if faith were to rehabilitate him. I told him I rather doubted he had the capacity to practise simple faith enough to open the sources of power according to the techniques of Christianity.

But he assured me he was in earnest and was open-minded and would follow any directions given. I saw his honesty and the real quality of his soul and have had a great affection for him ever since. I gave him a simple prescription. He was to read the New Testament and the Psalms until his mind was saturated with them. I gave him the usual suggestion of committing passages to memory. Principally I urged him to utilise the formula of putting his life in the hands of God, at the same time believing that God was filling him with power, and his wife also, and that the two of them were to believe unfalteringly that they were being guided in even the most commonplace details of their lives.

They were also to believe that in co-operation with their physician, whom I happened to know and admire, that the healing grace of Jesus Christ was being given them. I suggested that they picturise the healing power of the Great Physician as already working within them.

Seldom have I seen two people who became more gloriously childlike in their faith and whose trust was more complete. They became enthusiastic about the Bible and would often telephone me about 'some wonderful passage' they had just found. They gave me fresh insights into the truths of the Bible. It was a truly creative process working with this man and his wife.

The next spring Helen (that is the wife's name) said: "I have never experienced a more wonderful springtime, The flowers this year are the loveliest I have ever seen. and have you noticed the sky with its extraordinary cloud formations and the delicate colours at dawn and sunset? The leaves seem greener this year, and I have never heard the birds sing with such ecstasy and melody." When she said this there was an ecstatic light on her face and I knew she had been reborn in the spirit. And she began to improve physically, regaining a large share of her old-time strength. Her native creative power began to flow forth once again and life took on new meaning.

As for Horace, there has been no more heart trouble, and physical, mental, and spiritual vigour mark him as extraordinarily vital. They have moved into a new community and have become a centre of its life. Wherever they go they touch people with a strange uplifting force.

What is the secret which they discovered? Simply that they learned to draw upon that Higher Power.

This Higher Power is one of the most amazing facts in human existence. I am awe-struck, no matter how many times I have seen the phenomenon, by the thoroughgoing, tremendous, overwhelming changes for good that it accomplishes in the lives of people. Personally, I am so enthusiastic about all that the Higher

Power can do for people that I am loath to bring this book to a close. I could recite story after story, incident after incident of those who by laying hold of this power have had a new birth of life.

This power is constantly available. If you open to it, it will rush in like a mighty tide. It is there for anybody under any circumstances or in any condition. This tremendous inflow of power is of such force that in its inrush it drives everything before it, casting out fear, hate, sickness, weakness, moral defeat, scattering them as though they had never touched you, refreshing and re-strengthening your life with health, happiness, and goodness.

For many years I have been interested in the problem of the alcoholic and in the organisation known as Alcoholics Anonymous. One of their basic principles is that before a person can be helped he must recognise that he is an alcoholic and that of himself he can do nothing; that he has no power within himself; that he is defeated. When he accepts this point of view he is in a position to receive help from other alcoholics and from the Higher Power—God.

Another principle is the willingness to depend upon the Higher Power from whom he derives a strength which he does not himself possess. The working of this power in men's lives is the most moving and thrilling fact in this world. No other manifestation of power of any kind is equal to it. Materialistic power achievement is a romantic story. Men discover laws and formulas and harness power to do remarkable things. Spiritual power also follows laws. Mastery of these laws works wonders in an area more complicated than any form of mechanics, namely, human nature. It is one thing to make a machine work right. To make human nature work right is something else. It requires greater skill, but it can be done.

I sat one day under swaying palm trees in Florida listening to the story of a demonstration of Higher Power activity in the life of a man who narrowly escaped tragedy. He told me that he started drinking at the age of sixteen. "As it was the so-called smart thing to do." After twenty-three years, beginning as a social drinker, he "came to the end of the road on April 24, 1947." A growing hatred and bitterness towards his wife who had deserted him and towards his mother-in-law and sister-in-law culminated in his decision to kill these three women. I relate the story as he told it to me, in his own language.

"To strengthen myself for this gory task I went into a bar. A few more drinks would give me the courage to commit this triple murder. As I entered the bar I saw a young man by the name of Carl drinking coffee. Although I had hated Carl from boyhood I was utterly astounded to note his immaculate appearance, and I was also astonished to see him drinking coffee in a bar where he had spent on an average of $400 a month for drinks alone. Also I was mystified by what seemed a strange light on his face. Being fascinated by his appearance, I approached Carl and asked: 'What happened to you that you are drinking coffee?'

" 'I have not had a drink for a year,' Carl replied.

"I was utterly amazed, because Carl and I had been on many drinking bouts together. A strange incident in this affair is that even though I hated Carl I was strangely moved. I could not help but listen when he asked: 'Ed, did you ever want to quit drinking?'

" 'Yes, I have quit a thousand times,' I replied.

"Carl smiled and said: 'If you really want to do something about your problem, get sober and attend a meeting at the Presbyterian Church at nine on Saturday. It is a meeting of Alcoholics Anonymous.'

"I told him I had no interest in religion, but that maybe I would come. I was unimpressed, but still I could not get that light in his eyes out of my mind.

"Carl did not insist that I attend the meeting, but repeated that if I wanted to do something for myself he and his associates had an answer to my problem. After making that statement Carl left and I stood up to the bar to order a drink, but somehow it had lost its appeal. So, instead, I went home, the only home I had remaining, my mother's home.

"May I explain that I had been married for seventeen years to a very fine girl, but being an impatient person and having no faith in me due to my drinking, she finally decided upon getting a divorce, so not only my job and all my material assets but my home also were completely lost.

"Upon getting to my mother's home I wrestled with a bottle until 6 a.m. but still could not take the drink. I kept thinking of Carl's appearance. So on Saturday morning I went to Carl and asked him what I could do to keep from taking a drink until nine o'clock that night when the meeting would be held.

"Carl said: 'Every time you come to a bar or whisky sign or beer garden, just say one little prayer—"Please God, get me past this place," ' and then he added: 'Run like hell. That will be co-operating with God. He will hear your prayer and the running will be your part.'

"I did exactly as Carl told me to do. For many hours,

anxious and shaky, accompanied by my sister, I walked around the streets of the town. Finally at eight o'clock my sister said: 'Ed, there are seven drinking joints between here and the place where you are to attend the meeting. You go by yourself, and if you don't make it and come home drunk we will still love you and hope for the best, but somehow I feel that this meeting will be different from any you have ever attended.' With God's help I got by those seven places.

"At the church entrance I happened to look around and the sign over one of my favourite drinking places glared me straight in the eyes. The battle to decide whether to go into that bar or into the Alcoholics Anonymous meeting is one I shall never forget, but a Power greater than myself pulled me to the meeting.

"Upon entering the meeting-room I was utterly astounded to receive the firm handshake of my ex-hated friend, Carl. My resentment towards him was disappearing. A round of introductions began to many men in all walks of life—doctors, lawyers, bricklayers, millwrights, coal miners, construction workers, plasterers, labourers—all types were there. I had been drinking with some of these men for the last ten to twenty-five years and here they were all sober on a Saturday night, and above all, they were happy.

"What happened at that meeting is rather vague. All I know is that a rebirth had taken place. I felt different deep within.

"Happily leaving the meeting-room at midnight, I went home with a glorious air-lifting feeling and slept peaceably for the first time in more than five years. Upon awakening the next morning, I recall something clearly saying to me: 'There is a Power greater than yourself. If you will turn your will and your life over to the care of God as you understand Him, He will give you strength.'

"It was Sunday morning, and I decided to go to church. I attended a service where the preacher was a man whom I had hated from childhood. (The author wishes to comment at this point how inevitably hate is associated with emotional and spiritual sickness. When the mind is emptied of hate, a long step has been taken towards recovery. Love is a tremendous curative force.) This preacher was one of those sedate, swallow-tailed-coat-wearing Presbyterian ministers. I had no use for him, but that was my fault. He was all right really. I sat nervously through the singing and the collection taking. Then the preacher read his Scripture, and his sermon was based upon the theme: 'Never belittle anyone's experience—he had it.' I shall never forget that sermon as long as I live. It taught me a valuable lesson—never to belittle an experience because someone had it, for he and God know the depth and sincerity of that experience.

"Later I came to love this minister as one of the greatest, most sincere men I have ever known.

"Just where my new life began is a matter that is difficult to determine. Whether it was when I met Carl in the bar, or wrestling past the drinking places, or at the Alcoholics Anonymous meeting, or at the church, I do not know. But I, who had been a hopeless alcoholic for twenty-five years, suddenly became a sober man. I could never have done this alone, for I had tried it a thousand times and failed. But I drew upon a Higher Power and the Higher Power, which is God, did it."

I have known the narrator of the foregoing story for several years. Since becoming 'dry' he has had to face some difficult financial and other problems. But never once has he weakened. In talking with him I find myself strangely moved. It isn't what he says or even the way he says it, but one is conscious of a power emanating from this man. He is not a famous person. He is an everyday, hard-working salesman, but the Higher Power is in him, flowing through him, operating within his experience, and it transmits itself to others. It transmitted itself to me.

This chapter is not intended as a dissertation on alcoholism, although I will use still another reference in connection with this problem. I cite these experiences to show conclusively that if there is a Power able to deliver a person from alcoholism, the same Power can help any other person to overcome any other form of defeat he may face. There is nothing more difficult to overcome than the problem of alcoholism. The Power that can accomplish that difficult feat can, I assure you, help you to overcome your difficulties whatever they may be.

Let me give still another experience. I narrate this incident for the same purpose, namely, to emphasise that there is a Power which can be applied, drawn upon, and used, that mysteriously but surely gives to people who demonstrate faith the most remarkable victories.

In the Hotel Roanoke at Roanoke, Virginia, one night a man who has since become a good friend told me the following story. Two years before he had read my book, *A Guide to Confident Living*. At that time he was considered by himself and by others to be an utterly hopeless alcoholic. He is a business man in a Virginia town and is of such ability that despite his drinking problem he was able to keep going with fair success. He had absolutely no control over his drinking, however, and evident deterioration was taking place.

Upon reading the book above mentioned, the idea was lodged in his mind that if he could only get to New York he could be cured of his difficulty. He came to New York but was dead drunk when he arrived. A friend took him to a hotel and left him. He recovered sufficient consciousness to call a bell-boy and told him that he wanted to go to the Townes Hospital, a famous institution for alcoholics, presided over by the late Dr. Silkworth, one of the greatest men in the field of alcoholism—now deceased but never to be forgotten.

After robbing him of one hundred or more dollars which he had in his pocket, the bell-boy delivered him to the hospital. After several days of treatment, Dr. Silkworth came in to see him and said: "Charles, I think we have done for you all that we can do. I have a feeling that you are well."

This was not Dr. Silkworth's usual practice, and the fact that he handled this case in this manner causes one to sense the guiding hand of a Higher Power.

Still somewhat shaky, Charles made his way downtown until he found himself outside the office door of the Marble Collegiate Church, 1 West 29th Street, New York City. It happened to be a legal holiday and the church was closed. (Other than such holidays the church is always open.) He stood there hesitantly. He had hoped that he might go into the church and pray. Not being able to gain entrance, he did a strange thing. He took from his wallet one of his business cards and dropped it through the mail slot in the door.

The instant he did that a tremendous wave of peace came over him. He had an amazing sense of release. He put his head against the door and sobbed like a baby, but he knew that he was free, that some tremendous change had happened to him, the validity of which is attested by the fact that from that minute on there has been no turning back. He has lived in complete sobriety from that moment.

There are several features about this incident which mark it as impressive. For one, Dr. Silkworth seemed to have released him from the hospital at the proper psychological, spiritual, and shall we say supernatural moment, indicating that the doctor himself was the subject of Divine guidance.

When Charles told me this story in the Hotel Roanoke two years after it happened, I had a feeling as he related it that I had heard it before in precise detail. But he had never told me this story. In fact, I had never previously talked to him. It occurred to me that perhaps he had written the story to me and I had read it, but he said he had never written me. I then asked him if he had told the story to one of my secretaries, associates, or any other person who could have related it to me, but he said he had never told the story to any other individual save his wife and I had not met her until that night. Apparently this incident had been transmitted to my subconscious at the time it happened for now I 'remembered' it.

Why did he drop the card in the mail-slot? Perhaps he was symbolically reporting to his spiritual home, reporting to God. It was a dramatic and symbolic separation of himself from his defeat and the turning to a Higher Power which immediately took him out of himself and healed him.

The incident indicates that if there is deep desire, intensity of longing, and a sincere reaching out after the Power, it will be given.

In this chapter I have related victory stories out of

human experience, each in its own way indicating the continual presence and availability of a life-renewing Power, beyond but resident within ourselves. Your problem may not be alcoholism, but the fact that the Higher Power can heal a person of this most difficult malady emphasises the tremendous truth related in this chapter and throughout the entire book and that there is no problem, difficulty, or defeat that you cannot solve or overcome by faith, positive thinking, and prayer to God. The techniques are simple and workable. And God will help you always, just as the writer of the following letter was helped.

Dear Dr. Peale: When we think of all the wonderful things that have happened to us since we first met you and started coming to the Marble Church, it seems nothing short of a miracle. When you realise that just six years ago this month I was totally broke—in fact thousands of dollars in debt—a complete physical wash-out—and had hardly a friend in the world because of my excess drinking—you can see why we have to pinch ourselves every now and then to realise that our good fortune isn't all a dream.

As you well know, alcohol wasn't the only problem I had six years ago. It has been said that I was one of the most negative people you ever saw. That's only a half-truth. For I was filled with gripes, all sorts of irritation, and was one of the most super-critical, impatient, cocky individuals that you could have possibly met even in all your travels.

Now, please don't think I feel I have overcome all these obsessions. I haven't. I am one of those people that have to do a day-to-day job on myself. But gradually, by trying to follow your teachings, I am learning to control myself and be less critical of my fellow man. And it is like being released from a prison. I just never dreamed that life could be so full and wonderful. Sincerely (Signed) Dick.

Why not draw upon that Higher Power?

Epilogue

You have finished this book. What have you read?

Simply a series of practical and workable techniques for living a successful life. You have read a formula of belief and practice which should help you win victory over every defeat.

Examples have been given of people who have believed and who have applied the suggested techniques. These stories have been told to demonstrate that through the same methods you can obtain the same results as they did. But reading is not enough. Now please go back and persistently practise each technique in this book. Keep at it until you obtain the desired results.

I wrote this book out of a sincere desire to help you. It will give me great happiness to know that the book has helped you. I have absolute confidence and belief in the principles and methods outlined in this volume. They have been tested in the laboratory of spiritual experience and practical demonstration. They work when worked.

We may never meet in person, but in this book we have met. We are spiritual friends. I pray for you. God will help you—so believe and live successfully.

Norman Vincent Peale

Some details of
books by Dr. Peale
and other authors
which will be of interest
to readers of

THE POWER OF
POSITIVE THINKING

———

Send for
a complete free list
of Cedar Books
to the publishers

WORLD'S WORK LTD

THE PRESS AT KINGSWOOD
TADWORTH · SURREY

The latest book by
Dr. Norman Vincent Peale

ENTHUSIASM MAKES THE DIFFERENCE

How can enthusiasm help you to a better life?

Positive thinking is how you think about a problem. Enthusiasm is how you feel about a problem. And the two together determine what you do about a problem. Enthusiasm develops and maintains the quality of determination which is vitally important in overcoming barriers to a better life.

Within this framework, Dr. Peale brings the problems of today into focus and provides hard-hitting, practical advice on how to cope with them. He shares with you the essence of true experiences and a lifetime of counselling men and women from all walks of life.

Dr. Peale writes about the proven magic formula for success: *how enthusiasm develops and maintains the quality of determination which helps you overcome fear and builds self-confidence; how enthusiasm kindles the powerful motivation that makes things happen.* This new book is filled with gripping stories about amazing people whose enthusiasm acted as a catalyst to bring about amazing events in their lives.

In a special chapter devoted to salesmen, Dr. Peale outlines and illustrates with case histories an eleven-point salesmanship course which comprises the important elements in effective selling. Still another important chapter tells how to use enthusiasm in your job, how it can be used as a stepping-stone to greater success and advancement. Every page of this book offers encouragement and common sense ideas for improving every activity of your life.

Cloth-bound 21s   £1·05 *net*

An important and topical book by
Norman Vincent Peale

MAN
MORALS
AND MATURITY

Morality in sex among teenagers and among adults is on the decline and at the same time the divorce and crime rates are increasing. Racial antagonism is in the news every day. Parental authority is less in evidence than a generation ago. Even basic honesty is no longer a firm rule. Officially and unofficially restraints of all kinds have been removed. Off-colour films and pornographic literature are issued freely. Excessive drinking is commonplace. Pre-marital sex is a fact of life among students at many colleges. The old rules of behaviour seem hopelessly out of date in the modern world.

Dr. Peale urges the reader to take stock—"survey yourself with discontent"—and do something about it. Take a moral inventory. There is a new freedom, but if you simply follow the crowd, you are not free. Determine instead that you will make your own decisions and be in control of yourself and your own destiny.

This is Norman Vincent Peale's finest book since *The Power of Positive Thinking*.

Previously published in cloth-bound edition
under the title *Sin, Sex and Self-Control*.

Cedar Book (paperback) No. 148   8s   40p net

Other books by
Dr. Norman Vincent Peale

════════

STAY ALIVE ALL YOUR LIFE

Stay Alive All Your Life, successor to Dr. Peale's world-renowned *The Power of Positive Thinking*, carries further this great and popular minister's philosophy of successful and happy living.

The emphasis in this book is on faith, and Dr. Peale shows in example after example, drawn from life, how the magic of this attitude can perform miracles in your daily experience.

Paper-bound Cedar Book No. 98   10s   50p *net*

THE TOUGH-MINDED OPTIMIST

In his most recent book, Dr. Peale answers some of his critics, gives what he thinks are the reasons for the decline of religious influence in modern life, and as in his other books considers the personal problems of men and women in the 1960s and suggests to his readers ways of getting more out of life than ever before.

Cedar Book (paperback) No. 125   7s 6d   37½p *net*   *Cloth-bound* 18s *net*

THE AMAZING RESULTS OF
POSITIVE THINKING

Dr. Peale shows how the philosophy of confidence changed the lives of countless readers.

Cedar Book (paperback) No. 108   6s   30p *net*   *Cloth-bound* 18s *net*

THE POWER OF POSITIVE THINKING
FOR YOUNG PEOPLE

The author has re-written this, the most successful of his books, so that it may be of the greatest help to boys and girls in their teens.

Cedar Book (paperback) No. 110   8s   40p *net*   *Cloth-bound* 12s 6d *net*

Edited by Dr. Peale

UNLOCK YOUR FAITH-POWER

Personal messages of inspiration and faith from men and women in all walks of life, taken from the pages of *Guideposts Magazine*.

Cedar Book (paperback) No. 69   7s 6d   37½p *net*

INSPIRING MESSAGES FOR DAILY LIVING

Here Dr. Peale points the way towards a more rewarding and satisfying life.

Cedar Book (paperback) No. 61   6s   30p *net*

A GUIDE TO CONFIDENT LIVING

Here are prescriptions for dealing with chronic worry, a sense of inferiority, and frustration.

Cedar Book (paperback) No. 29   6s   30p

JESUS OF NAZARETH
by Norman Vincent Peale

This is the moving and inspiring story of Joshua, nephew of the apostle Peter, as he recounts the life of Christ from Bethlehem to Calvary.

Through the eyes of this young man, you will see many of the major events of Christ's ministry and talk with those who were closest to Him. This profoundly moving narrative offers fresh, new insights into the Gospel stories.

Cloth-bound 5s   25p *net*